T0244208

WIND, FIRE, AND ICE

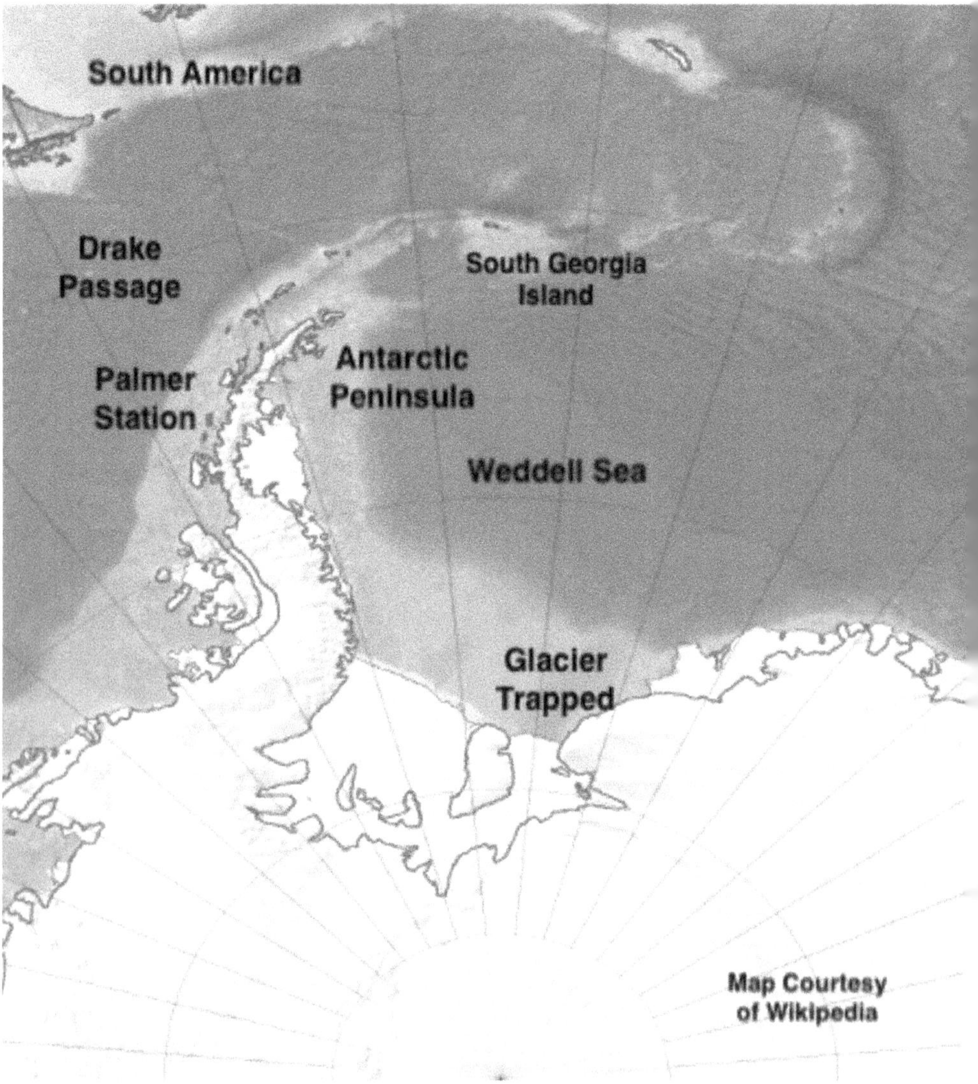

South America

Drake
Passage

South Georgia
Island

Palmer
Station

Antarctic
Peninsula

Weddell Sea

Glacier
Trapped

Map Courtesy
of Wikipedia

WIND, FIRE, AND ICE

The Perils of a Coast Guard Icebreaker in Antarctica

ROBERT M. BUNES, MD

Guilford, Connecticut

An imprint of Globe Pequot, the trade division of
The Rowman & Littlefield Publishing Group, Inc.
4501 Forbes Boulevard, Suite 200, Lanham, Maryland 20706
rowman.com

Distributed by NATIONAL BOOK NETWORK

British Library Cataloguing in Publication Information available

Library of Congress Cataloging-in-Publication Data
Names: Bunes, Robert M., 1943– author.
Title: Wind, fire, and ice : the perils of a coast guard icebreaker in Antarctica / Robert M. Bunes.
Description: Guilford, Connecticut : Lyons Press, 2021. | Includes bibliographical references.
Identifiers: LCCN 2021016540 (print) | LCCN 2021016541 (ebook) | ISBN 9781493060344
  (cloth) | ISBN 9781493063734 (epub)
Subjects: LCSH: Glaciers—Antarctica—History—20th century. | Icebreakers (Ships)—Arctic
  Regions—History—20th century. | Survival at sea—Arctic Regions—History—20th century. |
  Medical personnel—Arctic Regions. | United States. Coast Guard.
Classification: LCC GC461 .B86 2021 (print) | LCC GC461 (ebook) | DDC 910.9167—dc23
LC record available at https://lccn.loc.gov/2021016540
LC ebook record available at https://lccn.loc.gov/2021016541

∞™ The paper used in this publication meets the minimum requirements of American National
Standard for Information Sciences—Permanence of Paper for Printed Library Materials, ANSI/
NISO Z39.48-1992.

To Chief Warrant Officer (CWO4) Warren J. Toussaint (in memoriam), and to the crew of the USCGC Glacier

CONTENTS

CONTENTS

Introduction

IN 1969, I VOLUNTEERED TO SERVE AS A DOCTOR ABOARD A UNITED States Coast Guard icebreaker bound for Antarctica. At the time, I was twenty-six years old, naive, and poorly informed. I was going to be on the *Glacier*, the largest, toughest, and most powerful icebreaker in the free world. I had specifically asked to be assigned to this ship because it reportedly received the most exotic assignments—an enticing induce-ment for a guy from the Midwest. The main reason I had volunteered for any Antarctic deployment was because of all the fun and interesting ports normally a part of such a voyage.

The *Glacier* was under the command of Captain Eugene McCrory, a knowledgeable and experienced captain, who had successfully skippered the ship in Antarctica the previous year. I was blissfully ignorant of all the dangers that lay ahead. What I expected when I volunteered and what I later experienced were shockingly different.

Having grown up in Minnesota, I thought I knew a thing or two about cold, storms, and ice, but I had no idea how severe these conditions could be in the southernmost part of our planet. Comparing Minnesota's version of natural forces to those in Antarctica seemed akin to comparing a slingshot to a machine gun. Both could hurt you, but the latter was far more likely to be lethal.

I knew little about the sea—very little. Other than a half-day in a small sailboat in the sheltered waters of San Francisco Bay, I had never been sailing. The only times I had been on the open ocean had been on my surfboard. In other words, I was about as clueless a mariner as had ever cruised the seven seas.

There are numerous perils a ship faces in Antarctica and the surround-ing seas: hitting an iceberg, becoming trapped in a crushing ice pack, bat-tling mountainous waves. We did not face just one of these perils—we faced them all. Other shipboard dangers can occur anywhere, such as a fire aboard a ship. Most fires on a ship are extinguished in a few minutes. We had an inferno that lasted three hours.

This book is primarily about my experiences confronting a number of significant challenges as a ship's doctor and as a human being during a remarkable era and transformative time of my life. It is not just my story, but also that of my shipmates, as well as some of the brave sailors and explorers who preceded us, such as Sir Ernest Shackleton. Like Shackleton, we faced total destruction of our ship while held powerless in a crushing ice pack.

My story necessarily touches on my cultural background, the prevailing culture during the sixties, the culture of the military, and the general issue of leadership. My deployment was during the time of the Vietnam War—an era exemplified by such sayings as "Don't trust anyone over thirty" and "Question authority." As the ship's doctor, my major responsibility was for the health and welfare of the crew. There were times that Captain McCrory—an authoritative, arrogant, hard-core military type—had a different agenda. Conflict was inevitable.

Of the many problems the crew and I faced aboard the *Glacier*, I did not know which difficulties were due to bad luck and which were due to "pilot error," or something similar. Nor did I know if the answers I had been given back when the ship was in trouble were the whole truth. As the ship's doctor, I was not part of the operational command of the ship. In the process of doing extensive research for this book, I ventured to better understand the seriousness of the situations we faced and why they occurred. Mysteries I wanted to solve.

Many of the things the crew and I experienced aboard the *Glacier* are relevant for people traveling to Antarctica today. Most will travel there by ship and will potentially be exposed to some of the same dangers. For example, on December 24, 2013, a Russian icebreaker, the MV *Akademik Shokalskiy*, carrying passengers and research scientists, was trapped in ice pack adjacent to the Antarctic continent south of Australia. The nearest icebreaker, a Chinese ship, the *Xue Long* (aka, the *Snow Dragon*), sailed 600 miles to rescue them, only to become icebound within sight of the Russian ship.

The plight of these two ships became international news. Climate change skeptics claimed that the high level of sea ice trapping the vessels was evidence of the lack of global warming. These uninformed few did not realize that it is the disappearance of land ice—not changes in sea ice—that causes our sea levels to rise.

The only available ship powerful enough to break them free was the US Coast Guard Cutter icebreaker, the USCGC *Polar Star*, which even though eight to nine days away, sped to their rescue. How did the Russian ship get trapped in the first place? Were the two ships in much danger? Would the *Polar Star* be able to rescue them? How much was their situation like the one we had faced aboard the *Glacier*? All questions which I will endeavor to answer.

Antarctica can be a very dangerous place to visit, particularly aboard a ship. Although this book is partly a cautionary tale, it is also an ode to an exceptionally beautiful and exciting part of the world. In words, pictures, and curated videos, I hope to share some of that beauty and excitement.

In Shackleton's Wake

ALTHOUGH THE SHIP VIBRATED FROM THE THRUST OF ITS MASSIVE DIE-
sel engines, it barely moved. I dreaded to think what that might mean.

I stood alone on the cheerless fantail, aimlessly looking at broken
chunks of ice pack rocking back and forth in the prop wash. Most of the
fractured pieces of ice were about the size of a flattened pickup truck. A
small group of penguins stood off to the side, squawking and staring, as
if they had never seen a human being or a ship before. Maybe that was
true. We were deep in the Weddell Sea, off the coast of Antarctica. It had
been over fifty years since another ship had traversed this particular patch
of ocean: Sir Ernest Shackleton's ill-fated ship, the *Endurance*. Shackleton
was the leader of the Imperial Trans-Antarctic Expedition (1914–1916),
the most heroic and epic in Antarctica's history.

I knew too much about what Shackleton and his men had suffered.

A serpentine trail of fractured ice extended off our stern for about 200
yards. It had taken most of the day to travel this short distance. On either
side of our wake lay a blinding white expanse of sea ice. Jagged ridges
of tented and buckled ice crisscrossed this expanse. Massive icebergs in
the distance dwarfed the compressed ridges. Some of the bergs were 100
feet high and 20 miles square. Yet even those huge icebergs looked small
compared to the nearby continental ice shelf, which soared 150 feet into
the crystalline blue sky. And it stretched from east to west as far as the
eye could see.

The face of this ice cliff was vertical, multifaceted, and angular. It
was a mixture of intensely reflected light, distinct shadows, and shades of
blue-gray. It looked as if some giant with a hammer, chisel, and icepick

had roughly fashioned a towering wall. I thought it was the edge of the continent, but it wasn't. It was the toe of a monstrous glacier floating on the surface of the sea. About 100 miles to the south, the glacier rested on the solid rock of the continent. This glacial mass—the Filchner Ice Shelf—was named after the leader of a German expedition in 1912. Filchner's expedition, which had preceded Shackleton's by several years, had been a colossal failure.

Our ship was the US Coast Guard Cutter (USCGC) *Glacier*. The year was 1970. At the time, the *Glacier* was the largest and most powerful icebreaker in the free world. It had the power to break through sea ice up to 20 feet thick. But there was one major problem: There was no place for the ice to go. There was too much pressure on all sides. The nearest open water was 100 miles away. We were trapped. Hemmed in. Or to use the nautical term, *beset*.

Brutal storms frequent this part of the world. For three days a gale blowing in from the northeast had crammed the ice pack against our ship. The storm pushed us toward the continental ice shelf and held us in its icy grip. The pressure of the ice pack against the ship showed no signs of letting up.

We all knew that the Weddell Sea ice pack had crushed Shackleton's stout ship. Everyone aboard had to wonder if that was going to be our fate as well.

Our two helicopters diligently searched for open leads in the ice. We needed an escape route. If there were leads, they had to be close, or we would never be able to reach them. But there wasn't a lead in sight.

Unlike the *Endurance*, which was a wooden ship, ours was made of welded steel. And it was specifically built for icebreaking. It was not the kind of ship that could be easily crushed. However, the *Endurance* hadn't exactly been built out of balsa wood. It too was a tough, stoutly built, heavily reinforced ship. A special type of hardwood covered its hull— wood so dense that normal tools could not cut it. Furthermore, when the *Endurance* was trapped in the ice, her hull was intact. Our outer hull was already torn and leaking. A 20-foot section of it had buckled inward.

Thanks to the *Glacier*'s double-hull construction, we had been able to remain afloat, in spite of the damage. Although our thinner inner hull had buckled, it had remained mostly intact. Whether or not it would remain that way under the mounting pressure was an unknown. Sections of the structural frame had been damaged. The bilge pumps, which had been operating continuously for over a month, were controlling the leak. We were focused now on whether the bilge pumps would be able to keep up, as we knew that a small leak in a damaged hull can easily become a big one.

Alfred Lansing's book *Endurance* (which I highly recommend) is based on firsthand accounts from Shackleton and his twenty-seven crewmembers. It describes in detail what eventually happened to the *Endurance* after drifting for ten months in the ice pack. Ice floes on the starboard side, both fore and aft, held the ship like a vise. Pressure from the ice pack partially caved in the center of the ship, where the sides were an impressive 1.5 to 2 feet thick. A heavier mass of ice slowly ground away at the stern, splitting it open. The deck planking separated and water poured in. One of Shackleton's crew described the sensation of the crushing pressure as being "something colossal . . . something in nature too big to grasp."

Finally, the pressure became so great that the decks of *Endurance* buckled. The heavily reinforced beams broke and the stern vaulted 20 feet into the air. Frigid seawater poured into the bow. It quickly turned into ice. The heavily weighted bow started to sink. There was nothing else they could do to save her. Their only option was to off-load their longboats, along with as much of their essential supplies as possible. They had to hope they could survive, living on the pack ice, then somehow make it safely back to civilization.

Shackleton's expedition was privately funded, its goal, to be the first to traverse the Antarctic continent. Although called the "Imperial Trans-Antarctic Expedition," neither the British government nor the Crown officially supported it. The expedition was "Imperial" in name only, the impressive label helpful when it came time to market it to private investors. There was no rescue ship coming after them if they got into trouble. Even if there had been a rescue ship, they would not have known where to look for them. They were in a frozen wilderness—beyond vast. And they did not have a functioning radio. If they were going to survive, they would have to rely upon their bravery, wits, and skills.

The final sinking of *Endurance*. (Courtesy of Royal Geographical Society and Wikimedia)

Although our situation aboard the *Glacier* was grave, it was not as horrific as the one Shackleton had faced. Unlike him, we had good radios. Although there were some fluctuations due to atmospheric conditions, we were in touch with the world most of the time. However, the world knowing of our plight was one thing; actually providing help was another. Our chances of an eventual rescue or even escaping under our own power were certainly better than Shackleton's, but there was the risk of any rescue or escape attempt being too little, too late.

We faced a number of real and immediate problems. The Antarctica summer season was almost over. The current was taking us closer and closer to the continent. The ice was freezing an inch thicker each day. Temperatures were dropping. The farther south we drifted, the colder it would get. The extent of the ice pack surrounding the continent would soon double—increasing by 40,000 square miles *each day*. By the end of winter, the ice pack in the Weddell Sea—a million square miles—would more than quadruple. Further storms could increase the pressure ridges to 20 to 30 feet thick—too thick for the *Glacier* to break, even with backing and ramming. Then there were those massive icebergs—floating glacial ice with a tensile strength greater than steel.

During the preceding couple of days we had burned over 100,000 gallons of fuel trying to escape. Despite our valiant efforts, we had traveled about as far as a good tee shot by Tiger Woods. At this rate, it was clear we would exhaust our fuel reserves long before reaching navigable waters. It was senseless to try to fight the forces of nature any longer, and we couldn't count on having another icebreaker come to our rescue.

The other two Coast Guard icebreakers in Antarctica at the time were Wind-class icebreakers. They were slightly smaller and had only about half the horsepower. The *Glacier* was known as "The Mighty G" or "The Big G." To some, we were known as "The Big Elephant." Our motto was "Follow Me." We were the ship meant to rescue others, but right now we were the 800-pound gorilla in an 8,000-ton dilemma.

If our two Wind-class icebreakers had been able to reach us, they might have been able to help; they had done it before. But they were too far away. By the time they could get anywhere near, we would be fully in the grip of the dreaded Antarctic winter, when icebreaking, particularly deep in the Weddell Sea, becomes impossible.

We had to accept the bitter reality of our situation. Our voyage, which was part of what was called Operation Deep Freeze, had come to a standstill. Our deployment was supposed to last through the Antarctic summer season and end up in sunny California, where the trip had begun. That wasn't going to happen. We were trapped. *Beset.*

Given the rapidly deteriorating conditions, our only reasonable hope for escape seemed to rest with an early spring thaw. It was apparent to everyone that we would be spending the winter in Antarctica. Were we prepared for such a situation? Good question. Maybe we wouldn't be crushed by the ice pack. Maybe the ice wouldn't catch in the jagged hull and tear us apart.

Maybe.

Largely because of his magnificent leadership and his vast polar experience, Shackleton was able to keep his crew alive, despite extreme hardships, until they were finally rescued two years later. Our captain was an experienced and competent sailor, with good and bad points. But he was no Shackleton.

Our exact location was latitude 77.28° S, longitude 38.09° W. We were just north of the Filchner Ice Shelf and Vahsel Bay. In Shackleton's case, the *Endurance*'s position was latitude 76.27° S, longitude 28.46° W when he became trapped. In other words, out of the million square miles encompassing the Weddell Sea, our positions differed by about 70 miles. One had to think, as Winston Churchill once said, "Those who fail to learn from history are doomed to repeat it."

Although our relative positions were almost identical, the seasonal timing was different. We became trapped in the ice pack on February 23, whereas the *Endurance* was beset on January 18. Thus, we were over a month closer to the brutal winter weather of the Southern Hemisphere.

Given that the prevailing currents had not changed much between 1915 and 1970, it was likely that the ice pack and the *Glacier* would soon be heading in the same direction the *Endurance* had taken. Initially, we would be going south, but later we would be heading north. The main problem was that the current would also push us west—to an area where

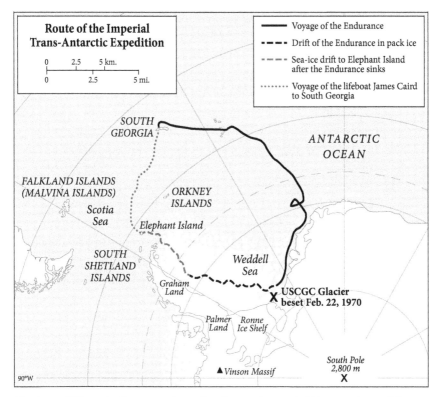

Route of the Imperial Trans-Antarctic Expedition

0   2.5   5 km.

0   2.5   5 mi.

—— Voyage of the Endurance

- - - - Drift of the Endurance in pack ice

- - - - Sea-ice drift to Elephant Island after the Endurance sinks

········ Voyage of the lifeboat James Caird to South Georgia

SOUTH GEORGIA

ANTARCTIC OCEAN

FALKLAND ISLANDS (MALVINA ISLANDS)

Scotia Sea

ORKNEY ISLANDS

Elephant Island

SOUTH SHETLAND ISLANDS

Graham Land

Weddell Sea

USCGC Glacier beset Feb. 22, 1970

Palmer Land

Ronne Ice Shelf

▲ Vinson Massif

South Pole 2,800 m

90°W

The large "X" marks the area where *Glacier* was trapped. (Map courtesy of Bourrichon and Wikimedia Commons)

the ice becomes even denser as it packs up alongside the edge of the Antarctic Peninsula. An area too hazardous for any icebreaker. At any time of the year.

In Shackleton's case, he and his crew were attempting to complete a first-ever, truly historic expedition. Shackleton, who had already survived two legendary Antarctic expeditions, handpicked his crew. He knew the kind of men he would need. He had the good fortune of being able to choose from thousands of volunteers, many of whom had responded to his advertisement in the *Times* of London: *Men wanted for hazardous journey. Small wages, bitter cold, long months of complete darkness, constant danger, safe return doubtful. Honor and recognition in case of success.*

About five thousand people applied for the position. The crew signing up for Shackleton's Imperial Trans-Antarctic Expedition knew they would be heroes if they survived. His well-publicized expedition was truly for the glory of the British Empire. And it occurred during the time commonly known as the "Heroic Age" of Antarctic exploration. It was an era when polar explorers such as Scott, Amundsen, and Shackleton were akin to modern-day rock stars. The King of England had knighted Shackleton because he had previously come close to being the first person to reach the South Pole.

The *Glacier* crew didn't sign up for some glorious expedition to enhance the prestige of an American Empire. We weren't going to become famous celebrities or heroes just because we survived a winter in Antarctica, no matter what befell us. We were supposedly on a simple and modest mission. Part of our task was to open a channel for supply ships going to the US Navy base on the Antarctic Peninsula. We also were going to provide logistical support for research scientists, including some that stayed on the ship. Nothing incredible. Nothing "Imperial." Nothing heroic.

While the Coast Guard did not consider our mission particularly dangerous for a large icebreaker, no deployment deep into the Weddell Sea should ever be considered "routine." The crew understood that our assignment would expose us to certain inevitable and unavoidable risks, such as sailing in iceberg-filled, uncharted waters. "Hazardous duty pay" for some of the officers and a double-food ration for the enlisted men partially compensated for the difficulties we would endure.

One thing was certain: Our orders did not include wintering over in the cold, dark, Antarctic night.

━━

Imprisoned in the ice pack off the Filchner Ice Shelf, we had no choice but to accept our fate. At first blush, the general attitude of the men seemed to be positive and constructive—a "Let's make the best of a bad situation" kind of outlook—but not everyone felt that way. And those with a positive attitude might not be able to maintain that perspective for long. Behind the macho "Let's take the bull by the horns" spirit, there was

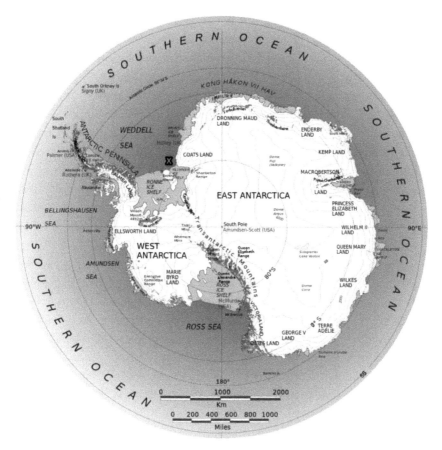

The "X" marks the area where *Glacier* was trapped. (Map courtesy of the US Geological Survey)

an unspoken deeper feeling, a mixture of fear, worry, and dread. There was tremendous uncertainty and many unanswered questions.

One unresolved question was "Why?" Why did the free world's largest and most powerful icebreaker—one capable of breaking ice 20 feet thick—end up in such a horrendous, Shackleton-like situation? It was a mystery to me. Were we trapped merely because of bad luck? Or had our situation been reasonably avoidable? Maybe there were no answers to these questions. Or maybe there were.

Our commanding officer (CO), Captain Eugene McCrory, probably could have answered the "Why" question, but he wasn't talking. Certainly not to me. If he had deigned to answer any of my questions, I expected at best half-truths. I was not part of Command and Control.

Even so, I wanted to get the whole story. What were our rescue options, and who would be rescued? I was told that ferrying all the men on the *Glacier* to the continent by helicopter was one option. In theory, fixed-wing planes could land and take off from the adjacent ice shelf. A large-scale evacuation. A crew could come back in the spring to rescue the ship after the ice had broken up. But evacuating everyone, as far as the crew knew, was never seriously considered. I never learned whether that idea was rejected because it was the consensus opinion of the senior command officers, or the overriding opinion of the captain.

We soon learned that the decision about who would be rescued had been made. A minimal crew would remain aboard the ship. If possible, everyone else would be evacuated. Out of two hundred crewmembers, only forty people were selected to remain. Those forty would stay with the ship through the dark, frigid, polar winter. They were the ones deemed "essential for the operation of the ship."

I was not surprised that I was one of the "essentials." They didn't need me to operate the ship. They needed me for the crew. I was the ship's doctor.

Freakishly good luck would change everything. It was nothing the crew or I expected. If anyone aboard did expect a reversal of our bad fortune, they weren't talking about it. It was not a time anyone chose to project false hopes. We would end up escaping the Weddell Sea prior to the quadrupling of the ice pack that occurs every winter.

But I will tell the story as I experienced it, describing in detail what likely would have happened aboard the *Glacier* had we remained in our Shackleton-like trap, partly based on what happened to those in similar icebound situations who were less fortunate than ourselves.

Although we eventually escaped the Weddell Sea, our good luck would not hold out. We avoided one perilous situation only to face dangers far more acute—the kind where one minute or one gust of wind makes all the difference.

2

The Year Before

THE COOL CLEAR WATER IN THE SWIMMING POOL FELT REFRESHING after a long day's work. My tight muscles eased as I stretched out in rhythmic strokes.

I needed the swim, as I had a lot on my mind in the spring of 1969. Being on a ship in Antarctica was not one of those things. That possibility, if someone had suggested it to me, would have seemed ludicrous. I would have thought being struck by a meteor more plausible.

Interning at Highland General Hospital, the county hospital for Oakland, California, was a tough job. I had little time for recreation, much less for a regular aerobic workout. The swimming pool was not one of the perks of the job. A pool table provided the only recreational outlet in the interns' dorm, where I had lived for the previous nine months. Playing pool was somewhat entertaining, but not nearly as refreshing as a good swim. I had always loved water sports. Moving out of the interns' dorm and into an apartment complex with a pool had been a big improvement.

I tried to swim laps two days out of three. The third day I was always on call and had to work late—oftentimes, most of the night. My semi-regular swims gave rise to one small problem. My eyes were becoming bloodshot from the chlorine in the pool. If I had had any spare change or extra time, I would have bought a pair of swimming goggles, but I didn't have much of either. Opening my eyes underwater allowed me to see well enough.

In order to minimize my exposure to chlorine, I decided to close my eyes for the majority of each lap. I would count my strokes and then open my eyes a couple of strokes before I reached the opposite side. This technique worked well for a couple of weeks, until one day when my strokes must have been unusually strong. Just as I opened my eyes at the appropriate stroke count, I felt an excruciating pain in my left hand. I had jammed it into the side of the pool. When I looked at my hand, my knuckles no longer lined up. I had broken the bone attached to the base of my fifth finger, my fifth metacarpal.

It was the first time I had ever broken a bone. To add insult to injury, I had suffered what is commonly known as a "boxer's fracture." The most common cause is punching someone or something. My fellow interns couldn't resist giving me a hard time about it. Their most frequent question was, "Who did you punch?" They were not about to accept my swimming accident story (or admit they believed it).

In retrospect, I was fortunate to have suffered this fracture. It later turned out to be a blessing when I was deep in Antarctica.

I shared the hilltop apartment with two of my intern buddies. It was small, but it had a view of both the Bay Bridge and the Golden Gate. I was only making $300 a month as an intern, but, back in 1969, that was enough to pay for basic living expenses as well as my share of the rent. I had borrowed some money from my uncle to buy a 1965 Austin-Healey 3000 sports car. My 1956, rusted-out, baling-wire-reinforced Chevy had finally died while valiantly trying to ascend one of San Francisco's steeper hills. The Mark 3000 was a vibrant red, with a white, rolled-leather interior and a burled walnut dashboard. I loved its classic lines, curve-hugging traction, mellow-sounding pipes, and powerful engine. After living hand to mouth through college and medical school, I was feeling like one lucky guy.

Growing up in the flatlands of Minnesota—the suburbs of Minneapolis, to be precise—I had never lived in a home with a good view. The first place I remember living had a view of a busy street. The last place I lived with my family was in Richfield, a middle-class suburb adjacent to Minneapolis, where I viewed small, single-story tract homes much like my own. I had a typical, middle-class upbringing. Midwestern. Nothing fancy. Low-key. Modest. Religious. Down-to-earth. Solid values.

I was the second of three children. The only boy. In some ways, I felt like a firstborn—the one meant to succeed. My parents owned a small paint and wallpaper store. It had been a good business for a while, but then the building boom ebbed. By the time I started high school, we were just making ends meet. Somehow, my parents scraped together enough money to send me to a good Catholic high school. Education was important, particularly to my mother. To me, too.

My mother had been valedictorian of her high school class. She had grown up on a farm during the Depression. There were times when the only food she had was cranberries—they grow wild in northern Minnesota. As an adult, come Thanksgiving, there were no cranberries on her plate.

By the end of high school, my parents' business had declined considerably and they struggled to avoid bankruptcy. They were not the kind to pressure me into following any particular career path. They simply advised me, "Don't go into the paint and wallpaper business," and "Go to college." In general, they supported my independent decisions. When I later told them I was going to be a physician on an icebreaker going to Antarctica, they were only mildly shocked, and they did not try to dissuade me.

If I went to college, I knew I was going to have to do it without their help. I became quite self-sufficient, perhaps to a fault, as I later learned when I started my deployment on the *Glacier*. Fortunately, hard work and I were not strangers. My first job was as a caddie when I was ten years old, carrying golf bags that seemed to weigh as much as I did. In high school, I landed a night job as a dishwasher. The worst part about the job was scrubbing dirty pots and pans, attempting to remove layers of burnt-on grease, while watching the cook add more industrial-sized pots to my pile. The job included free dinner—usually the cheapest meal on the menu. It was an "authentic German restaurant." Alan Wong was the head chef.

During the summers, I continued to work as a caddie, often doing "doubles." With a heavy golf bag on each shoulder, I had to pray not to get paired up with a "hooker" and a "slicer," or I would be spending a good part of the round zigzagging across the fairway. Some days I could make extra money doing doubles for thirty-six holes.

The golf course was a pleasant place to work. Most of the country club golfers were nice people, but I could never imagine being like them—rich. They were a different class of people than my friends or relatives.

In the late spring of 1961, when I was a senior in high school, the "caddie master" at Minnesota Valley Country Club, the golf course where I worked, told me about the Evans Scholarship—an academic scholarship for caddies. To qualify, one needed to be poor, have good grades, and have worked as a caddie for at least two years. Although I fit those criteria, I couldn't see myself as being such an exemplary person that I deserved a full scholarship. However, no caddie from that country club had ever won an Evans Scholarship, so the caddie master insisted that I at least try, and my mother heavily supported the idea.

At some point, I began to think I might even have a chance to win the scholarship, which was a critical step for me. When I get it in my head that something is doable and I am motivated to do it, then I am not easily dissuaded. Some people call me a stubborn Norwegian. (It's true. I am.)

I applied for the scholarship with a singular focus. If I didn't win the scholarship, I realized I would have a very tough time putting myself through school. I knew I would do whatever I had to do to get through school, even if I didn't win the scholarship, but I dreaded that possibility.

Several weeks after completing the arduous application and interview process, I was beginning to think my chances of winning were about as good as lighting a match on a wet cake of soap. Then the letter came. I was shaking as I picked up the envelope. It was heavy. It was thick. I didn't even open it up; I just started shouting and jumping for joy. I knew it couldn't be a rejection letter—it was too fat. The letter, when I finally opened it, started with "We are pleased to inform you . . ."—which was about as far as I got before I started running around again like a giddy fool.

Receiving the Evans Scholarship was like finding a treasure map—and realizing the treasure was buried in my backyard. It changed my life. With the help of this scholarship, I knew I could pursue my dreams. One of them was to become a doctor. Another was to see the world.

In June of 1968, after completing pre-med and medical school at the University of Minnesota, I started my internship at Highland General

Hospital in Oakland, California. It was a rotating internship, including psychiatry, emergency room medicine, internal medicine, pediatrics, and surgery. Going into the internship, I was leaning toward later specializing in either internal medicine or psychiatry. Other specialties, like emergency room medicine or surgery, were scarier to consider, because the risks of an immediate death of a patient were greater. Nonetheless, I didn't want to rule out any specialty because I was afraid of it or because I had almost no experience in that field.

Since I was still uncertain about a specialty, and because I wanted the most experience I could get, during each rotation I told the head of that service that I was seriously considering entering their specialty. It made a big difference. Instead of regarding me as someone marking time, I was treated like a peer-in-training. The residents and attending staff would go out of their way to show me special cases or let me scrub in on more-complicated surgeries. This strategy and experience would prove to be invaluable when I was assigned to the *Glacier*.

About halfway through my internship, one of the oral surgeons at Highland General told me, "If you ever get into the Coast Guard, try to get assigned to an icebreaker going to Antarctica. They always go to Hawaii, Tahiti, New Zealand, Australia, and South America. And if you're lucky, you'll get to travel around the world."

He also said, "Try to get assigned to the *Glacier*. It's the biggest icebreaker and gets the most exotic duty."

I had no idea why he told me this, but it was such an odd piece of advice that I remembered it. I had no plans to go into any military service. I planned to serve my country—and satisfy the mandatory draft requirements at that time—by going into the United States Public Health Service (USPHS).

I had applied to three different divisions of the USPHS: Chronic Disease Services, Mental Health, and Indian Health (the federal health program for Native Americans and Alaska Natives). While my USPHS applications were pending, I received three calls from the US Navy asking me to report for my pre-induction physical. It was the peak year of the doctor draft for the Vietnam War (the military draft was the "law of the land" until 1973, when military service became voluntary). From what everyone had told me, a navy assignment for a doctor in 1969 typically meant the marines, and Vietnam.

On each occasion when the navy called, I replied that there was no need to bother with a pre-induction physical, as I was going into the Public Health Service. They politely accepted my explanation. In the meantime, I had heard that a pre-induction physical for a physician was little more than a farce. One physician I knew suffered from gout, which can be diagnosed by a simple urine test and normally would qualify one for a medical deferment. When this physician had his physical, he gladly provided a urine sample, telling the lab technician, "If you test my urine, you'll see that I have gout."

The lab tech replied, "Oh, that doesn't matter. You're a doctor."

The doctor then watched in horror as the lab tech grinned—and poured his urine sample down the drain.

It really didn't matter to me whether the physical was a farce or not. I was physically fit, except for being bespectacled and flat-footed—but then I wasn't going to be an aviator or in the infantry.

I applied to three different divisions of the Public Health Service. One division turned me down because they were short on funds. A second turned me down because I did not have enough clinical experience. I wasn't worried, though, because I was positive of gaining a position with the Indian Health Service. The director of my internship program had been the boss of the physician who, at that time, was the head of Indian Health.

I was in the internship director's office when he called the head of the Indian Health Division. He sang my praises and gave me an unequivocal recommendation. I smiled. My immediate future was secure.

The head of Indian Health said he would certainly accept me, except for one thing. They had no record of my ever having applied for a position. They had lost my application.

I immediately sent in another application. By the time it arrived, it was too late. All the positions had been filled. My heart sank. I was facing the marines and Vietnam. I was in a state of shock.

Shortly after learning that my last hope had been dashed, I received another call from the navy. The naval staff person spoke in an entirely different tone. He did not ask me to report for a pre-induction physical. He basically said, "You *will* report for your pre-induction physical." He scheduled my appointment for the following week, and suggested that if I did not go willingly, the navy would send an "escort" to pick me up.

In order to better understand my situation in the spring of 1969, as well as the era in which this story takes place, a little background information is in order. People who weren't alive during the Vietnam War may have difficulty fully understanding what it was like then. Millions of people were actively demonstrating against the war. I was not one of those active demonstrators, but I did not believe in the Vietnam War. A military dictator ran South Vietnam. I saw no reason to risk my life to support a dictatorship in a war not reinforced by the political will of the people, a war of essentially no strategic importance to the United States.

In my bones, I knew there was something rotten about the war. I suspected our government was not telling us the whole story. For example, we were led to believe that the North Vietnamese precipitated the war by firing on our naval ships in the Gulf of Tonkin. According to historians, we provoked the attack by firing on them. In addition, we were repeatedly told that we were winning the war, which was probably never true. At best, we won some battles. The leader of the North Vietnamese Army, General Vo Nguyen Giap, told the Americans, as he had the French, "You can kill ten of my men for every one I kill of yours, but even at those odds, you will lose and I will win." He was right. There was no way the American people were willing to suffer extreme casualties for such an unpopular war—one that would eventually cost us $100 billion and fifty-eight thousand lives.

Given my thoughts and feelings about the Vietnam War, I did not know what to do. I loved my country, my family, my home. I did not want to be labeled a "draft dodger" or a "coward." My father had served in the US Navy during World War II. He was thirty-three years old and the father of two children when he was drafted. I knew he deeply resented one of my uncles who had somehow avoided the draft. I did not think he would understand my feelings about the Vietnam War. I don't know. We never talked about it. In fact, we rarely talked much about anything. He didn't talk much when he was sober. And I certainly wasn't going to try to talk to him when he was drunk.

I was more than willing to dedicate two years to serving my country and even risk my life in a military service. If it had been World War II, I would have volunteered. After the Japanese bombed Pearl Harbor, it would have been an easy decision. If someone attacks your country, you fight to defend it. But I was not going to volunteer for a cause in which I did not believe. I was not going to lie to the draft board and say I was a conscientious objector. And I wasn't going to try to come up with some bogus medical excuse for a deferment, like many people I knew. My nightmarish options seemed to boil down to, "Serve in Vietnam or move to Canada." It was tearing me apart. I could not make a decision one way or the other.

Then I got a call from the US Public Health Service. I did not know who made the call. I never asked. All I can remember was some woman saying, "How would you like to be a Public Health Service doctor . . . assigned to the Coast Guard?"

Those were the sweetest words I had ever heard.

I could serve my country.

I would not have to go to Vietnam.

I could not believe my good fortune.

They were offering me a position for which I had never applied and one I never knew even existed.

I responded to her with a resounding, "*Yes.*"

The next words out of my mouth were, "And could I be assigned to an icebreaker going to Antarctica?"

There was a pause at the other end. I assume my request took her a bit by surprise. I was, after all, going against the military service maxim, "Never volunteer for anything."

After a short pause, she responded simply, "Okay."

"And can I be assigned to the *Glacier*?"

There was an even longer pause, after which she said something like, "That can be arranged."

I will always wonder whether those pauses had any meaning other than mere surprise. The woman I was talking to, I later learned, was

Dottie Step, the secretary for the doctor in charge of all Public Health Service physicians, Admiral Fishburne. Dottie was a powerful, influential, and knowledgeable person. Doctors, in her experience, did not volunteer for an icebreaker assignment; they were ordered to take it. In addition, she likely knew about icebreaker life as well as the *Glacier's* mission plan. If she did, then she had all the more reason to be taken aback by my requests.

If she had spoken her mind, she would have said something like, "Are you sure you know what you're doing?"

Or, more to the point, "Are you crazy?"

3

Introduction to Military Life

THE COAST GUARD HAD TWO BASIC TRAINING CENTERS IN 1969. ONE WAS in Cape May, New Jersey, located on the southern tip of the state. The other was in Alameda, California, about 10 miles from where I was living in Oakland. Prior to my icebreaker duty, I was going to be assigned to one of these boot camps as a GMO (general medical officer). I would be responsible for providing my own housing, but the Coast Guard would be covering all of my moving expenses. Obviously, it would have been far cheaper to let me stay in Oakland, where there would have been no moving expenses at all. I loved the Bay Area and would have been delighted to remain there. That is not what happened, however. I was assigned to Cape May. Everything I owned was shipped there at government expense—your tax dollars at work.

I never expected the Coast Guard to give my personal happiness a high priority, but I did expect it to be reasonable, logical, and economical. Apparently, one of the reasons it was going to pay my shipping expenses to the East Coast was because of a policy aimed at young men enlisting who were just out of high school. The worry was that these kids would become homesick and run back home, particularly if home was nearby. Thus, no one was allowed to go to a boot camp within 50 miles of their home. I considered that a reasonable policy, but I did not see how it related to me. I had lived away from home for eight years. And my home was in Minnesota.

At the end of my internship, I sold my beloved sports car. It wasn't practical, and I knew I couldn't afford to keep up with the repair bills.

I flew to New York, where my first stop was the Brooklyn Navy Yard. I went there to purchase a set of uniforms, essentially like the ones worn by naval officers: basic khaki, dress blues, and white uniforms. (Unlike the enlisted men, officers had to buy their uniforms.)

Wearing my new khaki uniform, I took time for a sightseeing tour of New York City. It wasn't long before a few people started shouting expletives at me and making obscene gestures. One person even tried to spit on me. They were all expressing their disapproval toward the military during the Vietnam War. I was more shocked than angry. I explained that I was in the Public Health Service, hoping that this might elicit an apology, but all I got were dirty looks. It left me feeling unsettled, like I was being branded part of some evil empire, regardless of my actual role or personal beliefs. I could understand someone disagreeing with governmental policies and demonstrating against them, but taking it out on individual soldiers seemed grossly unjust.

The US Coast Guard is different from other military services. During peacetime, it operates under the Department of Homeland Security (previously, it had been assigned to the Department of Transportation). In wartime, it operates as part of the US Navy. It is our nation's oldest maritime service dating back to August 4, 1790, when it was called the Revenue Cutter Service and assigned to the Department of the Treasury. Between 1790 and 1798, it was the only armed service protecting our coasts. Part of its duties involved capturing smugglers, including about five hundred slave ships from Africa. In 1915, it merged with the US Lifesaving Service and became the US Coast Guard.

The Coast Guard is a small branch of the armed services. There were only about thirty-five thousand active members when I became part of it in 1969—smaller than the New York City Police Department. As of 2016, there were about forty-two thousand on active duty, providing a huge range of important services, including marine safety, drug interdiction, environmental protection, navigation aids, combat missions, lifesaving missions, and guarding against terrorism. The Coast Guard is active not only along America's coasts, but also from the Far East to the Mediterranean and from one polar region to the other. In short, it's a relatively small service doing a great deal of good, over a wide area, for a lot of people.

Public Health Service doctors serving with the Coast Guard in 1969 did not receive any introductory military training. I expected something like boot camp, but wasn't disappointed when I learned it was not a requirement. However, I would have appreciated some sort of "cultural boot camp" training. It would have been helpful.

I arrived at Cape May in late June of 1969 in my new car—a faded-black, used Volkswagen convertible with a sagging top. I drove onto the base dressed in my khaki uniform, except for my hat. I parked by the medical clinic and started walking toward the base PX two blocks away. I needed to purchase a hat that consisted of a frame and two different covers.

Purchases in hand, I walked back toward the clinic, holding the hat frame in one hand while trying to get the cover on with the other. Halfway there I realized the covers were the wrong size. I returned to the PX for another set. As I strolled back toward the clinic, I continued to fiddle with the cover. Just before reaching the clinic, I finally got it to fit. I put on my new hat and walked up the steps.

The door flung open, and there stood Captain John Brennan, the doctor in charge of the clinic.

"What the hell are you doing walking around the base without your hat on? I've been getting calls from all over the base!" he yelled.

In retrospect, his first words were particularly telling. I was in a different world—a world where military protocol was a very big deal. Who knew it was a military requirement to wear a hat at all times when outdoors? Based on the intensity of the reaction I'd generated, one would think I had been walking around wearing rows of dynamite taped to my chest, a detonator switch in my hand. I was going to be in the military for the next two years—two *long* years, I thought.

Although I was in the military, it was not like I was "regular" military. There were different expectations of USPHS doctors in the Coast Guard. On the one hand, I had to follow certain rules and forms of military protocol. On the other, as a doctor, particularly one doing a two-year stint, I wasn't expected to behave like a regular officer. If that had been the expectation, the Coast Guard would have given me and my fellow doctors some type of basic military training. It quickly became clear that we were there because we were highly trained medical professionals. First and foremost, the Coast Guard wanted us to be doctors—but we were definitely not civilians.

Although doctors entered the Coast Guard as full lieutenants, the rank did not mean much, other than a higher pay grade. We were not about to go around ordering some chief petty officer or junior grade lieutenant, just because we outranked them. On the other hand, if a captain came to us for a medical problem, we expected him to follow our medical "orders." While standards for us were clearly different, we were still expected to follow military customs, like wearing our hats whenever we were outside a building. And we were expected to look like military officers. The long hair and beards many of us had during the 1960s had to go.

Ideally, the Coast Guard would have liked us to be spit-and-polish military types, but that wasn't going to happen. Nor did the Coast Guard really expect it. Apparently, the military services had decided long ago that if they wanted to get the most out of their doctors, they had to cut them some slack and judge them by a different standard. For example, as a unit, the medical and dental officers at Cape May flunked every military inspection we ever had. We went out of our way to flaunt our independent status. We failed inspections because of such things as wearing alligator shoes or stethoscopes around our necks. Unzipped flies were also common. We took a kind of perverse pride in our perfect failure rate.

Fortunately, we worked under Captain Brennan. He was a salt-of-the-earth, old-country-doctor type. He told the rest of the base, "If you have any problems with any of my people, you come to me. I'll handle it." He had our backs, and he let us slide a bit on matters regarding military protocol. But he damn well expected us to be good doctors. He led by example, and I really respected him.

One of the things he told me that I never forgot was, "If a mother calls about a sick child, it is always a medical emergency." I learned a lot from him.

It was particularly good for me to work under someone like Captain Brennan, as I didn't have the best attitude toward authority figures.

The medical crew at Cape May, 1969. Front row (from left to right): Jerry Pitman, MD; John Ehrhart, MD; Captain Brennan, MD; and myself. Back row (from left to right): an unidentified officer; the chief nurse; Tom Taylor, MD; and the lieutenant in charge of the corpsmen. (Courtesy of US Coast Guard Archives)

My father had something to do with that. When he was drunk, he was often verbally abusive. When sober, my father was not overtly abusive, but he treated me in a passive and distant manner. Even if he had been an ideal father, I suspect I still would have had a strong independent streak, although I probably would have fit more easily into a military culture.

Given my background, it felt good to both like and respect Captain Brennan as an authority figure. It was easy to follow his commands. He was not only a good doctor, but also someone of excellent moral character. And you could tell he truly cared, not only for his patients, but also for the people working under him. I know I would have had problems dealing with a military leader with less-admirable qualities.

As doctors, our general attitude was much like that depicted by our counterparts in the Korean War movie *M*A*S*H* (an acronym for Mobile Army Surgical Hospital). This antiwar film released in 1970 spawned the long-running and eminently successful *M*A*S*H* TV series. As depicted in both the movie and the series, our goal was always to be good doctors while often thumbing our noses at military protocol. One episode of the TV series dealt with General Douglas MacArthur coming to inspect the M*A*S*H unit. The two lead doctors in the series, Hawkeye and Trapper, appeared at this auspicious inspection wearing, respectively, a bathrobe and a Hawaiian shirt. We medical officers were not that radical, but we certainly could identify with the spirit of the movie and the series.

We doctors tried to do what we thought was best from a medical point of view, in spite of the military. If we could get away with bending a military rule in order to help a patient, then that is what we did. From my perspective, it was not a matter of being *against* the military—I had, and still have, tremendous respect for our men in uniform—but I saw myself as a doctor first and an officer second.

The general medical officers at Cape May took care of all military personnel and their dependents, but our main duty was caring for the newly enlisted sailors receiving their basic training. After all, Cape May was primarily a boot camp. When we would see these new enlistees as patients, they would notice our lieutenant or lieutenant commander bars, snap to attention, and stand there stiff as a fence post. It was not easy to get a good and complete history from someone so tense. It seemed these "boots" were capable of saying very little other than "Sir, yes sir" and "Sir, no sir." We first had to spend time getting them to relax in order to get a decent history. In those circumstances, they needed to relate to us primarily as doctors rather than as military officers. In fact, I suggested to a group of nonmedical brass that we doctors would be better off not wearing military uniforms when seeing patients, particularly the new inductees. (That suggestion went over like a concrete cloud.)

This combination—doctors with a less-than-serious view of military protocol and hard-core military types—created odd situations that were reflective of the times.

For example, my good friend Dr. John Ehrhart and I were asked to attend a meeting requested by a group of the chiefs (noncommissioned officers) in charge of training. Apparently, they were not happy with the way we were treating new recruits. The meeting was held two blocks from our medical clinic in a dark, simply furnished room with shaded windows on two sides. The chiefs sat in chairs against one of the uncovered windows. We stood in front of them, almost squinting because of the glare of the light behind them. I suspected that arrangement was not by chance. Most of the chiefs were burly men in their late thirties or forties. Their faces were creased and weathered, fixed in various expressions of discontent. They were not the kind of men you would want to encounter in a dark alley. The executive officer, second in command at the base, stood off to one side of the room, a benign expression on his face.

I was more curious than intimidated by the situation, puzzled as to why the meeting had been arranged. They told us they wanted to talk with us because they felt we were being "too soft" on the recruits. They believed, for instance, that we were hospitalizing patients who did not need it. We explained to them that we tried hard to keep recruits on active duty. If we did have to hospitalize them, we made every effort to get them back to their units within the week. If they were out longer, they would have to be reassigned to a different unit. We knew this was tough on everyone, particularly the recruits, as they would have to adjust to a completely new group.

Some of the chiefs accepted our argument, but others did not, particularly one grizzled old chief. He was stocky, with a short crew cut and reddish complexion. He looked like Hollywood's image of a typical drill sergeant. He had a strong southern accent and a less-than-sophisticated manner. In short, he struck me as being either a redneck or a redneck-in-training.

During the latter part of our meeting, this particular chief angrily said, "You know, Doc, if you were the last doctor in town, I wouldn't come to see you."

I politely asked, "Why not?"

"Because you have a mustache."

This was one of the most ridiculous statements I'd ever heard. He would rather die than accept my help—because of my facial hair? I could feel the muscles in my jaw tense up. For a second, I was speechless.

I took a deep breath and told myself, *Be cool*. Then, in a slow, controlled voice, hoping to sound objective and philosophical, I said, "You know, there are some who don't like people with crew cuts."

He looked at me in dismay and said in a hurt voice, "You mean you don't like me?"

He wasn't kidding. I half expected him to start crying. I just shook my head.

This interchange is an example of the generational and cultural differences that existed during the sixties—not to mention a good example of a macho-acting chief with thin skin and a weak grasp of irony.

The 1960s were decidedly different than the 1940s and '50s. World War II had dominated the 1940s, and the 1950s were characterized, in part, by the former five-star general, Dwight David Eisenhower, who served as our president. It was a relatively stable decade, noted for such things as the spread of suburbia and steady employment. People often worked for the same employer their entire lives. It was a time when America was the undisputed economic power in the world. Authority was widely respected. Modesty and conformity were the norm.

In contrast, some have characterized the 1960s as an era of sex, drugs, and rock and roll, although it was much more than that. It was a time of major conflict and change. It was the time of Martin Luther King Jr.'s "I Have a Dream" speech, race riots, and President John F. Kennedy's assassination. It was a time of sweeping civil rights legislation and the institution of such policies as affirmative action. It was the beginning of "women's lib." There was not only "free love," "flower power" and the peace sign, but also a general rebellion against authority. For the older generation, anyone with a mustache or wearing bell-bottom trousers was likely viewed as a "damn hippie." I suspect that is how the grizzled old chief perceived me. And my perception of him was hardly more charitable. Cultural clashes during the sixties were unavoidable.

In spite of the antiauthority, antimilitary, antiwar feelings of the times, as well as my own rebelliousness and immaturity, I was proud to be serving my country. I was proud to be serving with the Coast Guard. After all, the Coast Guard and I, as a physician, had the same goal: saving lives.

The Coast Guard has always done a wonderful job of achieving this goal, as evidenced by their rescue of 133 men from a torpedoed transport ship off Greenland in 1943, and 520 passengers and crew from a cruise vessel off Alaska in 1980. More recently, in 2005, the Coast Guard rescued 33,500 people during Hurricane Katrina—by far the most effective branch of our government during that disaster. According to the Coast Guard historian's office, the men and women of this heroic service have saved over a million people since it was founded in 1790.

Damn right I felt proud to serve with them.

4

Reality Check

I ENJOYED WORKING AS A GENERAL MEDICAL OFFICER (GMO) AT CAPE May. I learned a number of practical things a general practitioner needs to know—things I typically would not have seen in a hospital setting, like how to remove plantar warts from the sole of the foot and how to tape sprained ankles. Other things were less enjoyable, like assembly-line physical exams of new recruits. Having fifty sailors in a row turn their heads and cough, while checking them for hernias, was something I thankfully only had to do about once a month.

One absolute plus to being a GMO was earning a decent salary. It wasn't a great salary, but it was far more than the $300 a month I had been making as an intern. It was the first time in my life that I had enough money for any kind of luxury item. I bought a powerful Yamaha stereo tuner and amplifier, an excellent record player, and a Tandberg reel-to-reel tape recorder. The high-quality sound they produced was pumped through the two huge speakers I'd purchased, each about the size of a footlocker. I also bought a decent guitar and a surfboard. I appreciated and enjoyed all of these things.

In addition, I also had a reasonable work schedule. Gone was the on-call-every-third-night, twelve-hour-a-day schedule I'd had to cope with as an intern. Some services during my internship were so busy that I'd had to grab what sleep I could on an examination table. In contrast, working a forty- to forty-five-hour week was almost like being on vacation.

Waves and weather permitting, one of the things I enjoyed most was surfing, something I had done only once before in my life. I could even go surfing when I was on call, as long as I surfed at the Coast Guard beach.

The lifeguards there had a telephone. I would leave their number as my contact phone. If I received a call, they would wave at me. I'd throw my surfboard into the back of my VW convertible and rush off to the clinic.

Of course, most patients were not used to seeing their doctor barechested and in a dripping-wet bathing suit, but it never seemed to matter, which surprised me. It was the first time I had ever seen patients when I was not wearing some kind of uniform. It was interesting to realize that instilling confidence in a patient does not depend on what one wears, but rather what one says and does, and what kind of attitude one projects.

⚊⚊

Prior to leaving for Antarctica, I attended a training session for icebreaker-bound doctors in Bethesda, Maryland. The primary aim of the training was to teach us about underwater medicine, as there would be scuba divers on the icebreakers. There also was some training about cold-weather medicine and general conditions in Antarctica. Since I was a certified scuba diver, I was familiar with much of the material. Also, growing up in Minnesota, I had learned a bit about cold-weather medicine.

But I knew nothing about medical problems unique to the Antarctic. For example, I learned that seawater in Antarctica is typically 28 degrees Fahrenheit. The considerable pack ice there "steals" freshwater, leaving behind higher-salinity water, which has a lower freezing point. Anyone unfortunate enough to fall into such waters, we were told, would likely be dead within ten minutes—most likely due to uncontrollable hyperventilation, causing loss of consciousness, resulting in death by drowning. Death caused by hypothermia would take longer, but not by much. Sometimes death could be very sudden if the shock of the icy water precipitated a heart attack.

We also learned about the terrible whiteout conditions that commonly occur in Antarctica. I had been in whiteouts a few times when I was skiing. I knew from personal experience that the disorientation caused by this atmospheric condition not only makes it very hard to see, it also makes it difficult to tell up from down.

Our Antarctica training did not deal with the medical aspects of "wintering over," since that was not part of our mission. Our instructor did tell us a few things about what it was like for the comparatively few people in the permanent land-based stations who remained there during the winter. Essentially everyone during the long, dark winter experienced a condition similar to a depressive episode, mostly characterized by apathy, loss of sex drive, and difficulties concentrating. For example, those who were normally high-level readers ended up reading things like comic books. Those who started out reading comic books typically ended the winter season incapable of reading much of anything. The cause of this syndrome seemed partly due to sensory deprivation, which was not too surprising, given that they were generally confined indoors all winter, surrounded by perpetual darkness outside. And it's not like they were stuck in an igloo or a shack; the permanent American bases were nice, modern, well-constructed buildings.

There was one person, we learned, who typically did not succumb to this syndrome, and that was the weatherman. Most everyone else had little to do during the winter season. Scientific and support personnel had to wait for daylight and warmer conditions in order to do their work. It was simply too dangerous to venture outside for any appreciable amount of time. In contrast, the weatherman always had work to do, as weather conditions were always changing.

The good news was that this depressive syndrome was reversible. As soon as daylight returned, people could get outside, resume their regular activities, and return to their normal selves.

﹏

Knowing that I would be gone for at least six months, and mostly isolated from the rest of the world, I began to gather things to entertain myself. In addition to collecting a bunch of books, I also started taping music on my Tandberg. I hooked up the tape recorder to my stereo receiver and, whenever I heard a song I liked, I would quickly switch on the recorder. This resulted in my having a number of tracks with the initial notes missing, but I knew I would be happy to have those songs later. I saved a lot of money by not having to buy prerecorded tapes. I had a few records, but I assumed a record player would not work too well on a rolling ship—and this was before I knew how much pitching and rolling we would be facing. (Music

CDs and personal computers would not be available to average consumers for another twenty years.) With the addition of a camera, a guitar, and a set of skis, I felt ready for the trip. The only other thing I decided to bring was my surfboard. I could just picture myself riding perfect waves in Hawaii, Tahiti, Fiji, and Australia—all of those places I'd heard were part of the standard itinerary for an Antarctic-bound icebreaker.

The Coast Guard paid to ship all of my things to Long Beach, California. The *Glacier* was in dry dock at Todd Shipyard in San Pedro, just north of Long Beach. I stored my things at my uncle's house in Los Angeles until the ship was ready.

One of the main reasons why the ship was in dry dock was to install an air-conditioning system. This seemed odd to me at first. Why, I asked myself, do we need an air-conditioning system in the Antarctic? The reason, I subsequently learned, was twofold: First, the ship's massive engines put out a great deal of heat. Second, we would be going back and forth across the equator, not to mention all of those warm-water ports the *Glacier* usually visited.

The ship was also in dry dock because it required a number of general repairs. Icebreakers take a beating during polar cruises. Consequently, their home ports are always adjacent to major dry-dock and ship-repair facilities.

Since the ship was in dry dock, I assumed it would be a mess, but nothing as bad as what I saw when I first came aboard in late October 1969. I expected our medical unit to be like a mini hospital, with a coating of dust. As I stepped into what was commonly known as sick bay for the first time, I saw a young man, Danny O'Keefe, standing on a pile of dirty laundry 3 feet high. Danny was one of two junior corpsmen assigned to my unit. He had a towel wrapped around a 6-inch-wide pipe, which he was holding tightly with both hands. His efforts did little to stop water from gushing in every direction. I was stunned. I stood there for a second with my mouth gaping. *This is sick bay?*

With a stricken and helpless look, Danny said, "You must be the doc. Sorry I can't shake your hand right now."

Once the plumbing leak was fixed, I took a closer look at our facility. It consisted of an office, three storage areas, a big treatment room with a surgical table, a dental room, and a cramped hospital ward with four sets of bunk beds. There wasn't enough room for typical hospital beds, but we needed to have sufficient beds in case of multiple casualties. We were also equipped with an X-ray machine, some laboratory equipment, and a bathroom.

The main problem with the equipment was that none of it worked. Not even the toilet. Apparently, someone had cut off the drainpipe to the toilet and welded it shut. I learned that almost two-thirds of the interior of the ship had been torn apart in order to install the air-conditioning system.

We had six weeks to get everything fixed. I wasn't too worried about that particular task, as I knew there were technicians in Long Beach who could handle it. My main concern was determining what supplies and medications were needed—and then obtaining them. Both were big issues. I had never needed to concern myself with such problems before. All the hospitals and clinics I had ever worked in had been fully stocked. Having supplies and equipment at my disposal was something I took for granted.

Fortunately, I had an excellent crew to help me. Danny O'Keefe was a laid-back Midwesterner from St. Louis. He was in his early twenties, medium height, trim of build, with wavy brown hair. His pleasant facial features were often set in a slightly quizzical, not-quite-awake manner. He spoke slowly, with a cross between a Midwestern accent and a Southern drawl. The combination of his manner, speech, and features made him appear a bit slow on the draw, but he was quite bright, with a ready smile and a good sense of humor. And he was calm under pressure—except during one medical emergency, which we'll get to later.

The other corpsman, Joseph Burke, was another Midwesterner, from Wisconsin. He too was in his early twenties, but quite a contrast to Danny. Of average height, dark, trim, handsome, and energetic, Joe's speech was quicker, more intense and precise. He had an eager-to-please sincerity, combined with an eager-to-learn curiosity. (His only serious flaw was that he was, and still is, a Green Bay Packer football fan—a team that has often broken the heart of this hard-core Minnesota Vikings fan.) Like Danny, Joe also had a ready smile and a fine sense of humor. Joe had a double-duty assignment. In addition to being assigned to sick bay, he also had duty as a corpsman with the helicopter aircrew.

William "Sal" Salvatorre was our dental technician. He was a medium-tall, dark-haired Italian who looked like he enjoyed his pasta. He had a corny sense of humor and a goofy laugh. Most important, he was a knowledgeable and skilled dental professional.

Prior to the trip, I had received a one-week course in dentistry. During this mini-course, I learned how to pull teeth and do temporary fillings. I felt sorry for the "boots" who were my patients while I was learning these skills. Fortunately, all of my dental patients did well, thanks to the excellent supervision I received (although I did cause a few near-panic attacks when I disclosed the fact that I was a doctor, not a dentist, before treating them). A one-week course hardly qualified me as a dentist, so I was delighted to have someone aboard with Sal's talents.

The last member of our medical crew—and in many ways the most important—was Chief Petty Officer (CPO) Warren Toussaint. He was in his early forties and of French descent. He had dark hair, was of medium height, and boasted a small mustache and a perpetual twinkle in his eye. I could readily see him in a beret on a Parisian street corner, maybe as a painter who could sell his works based on his charm alone. (I later learned that he had briefly worked as an insurance agent in the past and had been an excellent salesman.) He was a hardworking, smart, roll-up-your-sleeves veteran of World War II and the Korean War. He had graduated from Marquette University, loved to teach, and loved responsibility. Not only did he have good medical skills, but he also knew the ins and outs of working with the Coast Guard. This latter skill became all the more important for me as the trip progressed.

Chief Toussaint had a clever wit. You had to keep on your toes around him. He had a tendency to embellish things just enough so that you thought he was telling the truth, but if he was wearing a sly grin, you could be certain he was pulling your leg. He was a good people person and an all-around great guy.

While Chief Toussaint had had some hospital supply experience, he'd never had the responsibility of supplying a ship for a seven-month deployment in Antarctica. We would be responsible for the lives of two hundred men. If we didn't have what we needed once we were in Antarctica, we would be in serious trouble.

"We need to do an inventory," the chief said.

I totally agreed.

The same day we'd scheduled the inventory, Joe Burke had an opportunity to go to Disneyland with the aircrew. For a young man from Wisconsin who had never seen Disneyland, it was a big deal. He really wanted to go. When he asked Chief Toussaint if he could have the day off, he was told, "There is no way you're taking a day off. We need to do an inventory." He did not need to raise his voice.

Although Joe was quite disappointed, he did not question Chief Toussaint's decision. The chief had a natural ability to lead and command respect. He was never condescending, but he knew how to make his point, and this was an urgent matter.

The inventory did not take long. I was shocked to find that most of our ample supply cabinets contained nothing more than a thick coating of dust. The other cabinets held outdated antibiotics and a limited supply of bandages, wrapped in brittle, desiccated paper. I suspected that some of those packages dated back to World War II. I was shocked.

Chief Toussaint knew how to order supplies from the Coast Guard, but he seriously doubted that the items on our massive list would arrive within the next six weeks. Things looked bleak. In addition, I knew the chief wouldn't be available to help much, as the executive officer (XO) had given him some other assignments. Since the XO was a commander and I was merely a lieutenant, I didn't feel I could ask for much more of the chief's help. For the most part, I was on my own.

The awesome responsibility of my position hit me with full force.

I had volunteered for this cruise because I wanted to travel and see all of those exotic places I had heard were always part of the itinerary for Antarctica-bound icebreakers. Hawaii. Tahiti. Fiji. Australia. New Zealand. South America.

I soon learned that our itinerary would be completely different. The only ports we were scheduled to hit were Punta Arenas, Chile, and Valparaiso, Chile. I was extremely disappointed. I had ignored the adage "Never volunteer for anything" and was going to suffer as a result.

But that feeling of disappointment paled in comparison to my worries about not having the supplies and equipment, not to mention the skills, necessary to take care of all the men, in all conditions, in all the remote areas of our voyage. With almost no forethought, I had put myself in a very scary position.

I didn't know if I could handle it all. I felt overwhelmed. I didn't know where to start. I wouldn't say I was on the verge of breaking into tears and running home to Mommy, but that idea certainly held merit.

After getting a grip on myself, I sat down and started thinking of all the medicines, supplies, and equipment I had ever used or heard about. Some things I could easily eliminate from the list. There were no women in our crew. (Women did not participate in icebreaker deployments until the early 1980s.) I knew we would not be doing certain types of elective surgery. Also, certain types of large medical equipment would be impractical. But just about everything else on the list seemed to fall within the realm of something I might need.

After sending out the supply requisition, I just couldn't sit around and hope the supplies would arrive on time. I was desperate. I had to do something, but I wasn't sure what.

Then the idea hit me. I might be able to get supplies from some of the navy aircraft carriers in port.

About all I knew about aircraft carriers was that they were big and transported airplanes. I had no idea what kind of medical supplies they carried, but I assumed they must have stocked a lot more than our icebreaker. Comparing the size of our ship to a huge aircraft carrier was like comparing a canoe to a large yacht.

The staff of the first aircraft carrier I visited was very helpful. They had a major hospital facility on board, located in a space about the size of a large warehouse or basketball gymnasium. I gaped at their facility like a tourist looking at the interior of a huge cathedral. They kindly helped me fill a couple of shopping carts with some of their surplus supplies, but it wasn't nearly enough. And I wasn't even sure if I was asking for all of the right things in the first place.

With only three weeks to go, I figured we had less than 30 percent of the supplies we needed. I was so worried I could barely sleep. I started getting a dull, burning pain in the pit of my stomach. Worrying made the pain worse, and antacids only partially alleviated the discomfort. I just had to hope it would not become disabling. I didn't have the time to deal with a serious stomach ulcer.

I kept making the rounds of the aircraft carriers. Eventually, I found a couple that were being decommissioned. Many shopping carts of supplies later, I felt we had close to what we needed.

The day before we shoved off, a load of supplies and equipment that we had ordered from the Coast Guard arrived. Although our order hadn't been completely filled, it did supplement what I had already obtained. It was nice to have extra.

The main item I had ordered that was missing was a machine for administering general anesthesia. There was nothing to do but hope—and pray—we wouldn't need one.

5

A Promise

After the shipyard work was completed, the *Glacier* moved to
its regular berth in Long Beach.

When I moved aboard, I remember walking up the long gangway for
the first time. Under one arm, I had a pair of skis. Under the other, I had a
surfboard. The bottom of the surfboard was imprinted with colorful paisley flowers. It was the sixties, after all. I suspect there were crewmembers
on deck scratching their heads and asking, "Who *is* this guy?"

Although I wouldn't be surfing in Antarctica, I knew there were good
surfing spots near Valparaiso. Besides, I thought it wouldn't hurt to have
an extra flotation device with me in case the ship sank. Although I knew
there were no ski areas in Antarctica, I assumed that with all the snow and
ice there, I could find somewhere to ski. I had two good legs for uphill
transportation. Also, if we spent much time in Chile, I might be able to do
some glacier skiing in the Andes. (I later learned that one of the Wind-
class icebreaker captains had once come up with some bogus reasons for
using his helicopters in Antarctica for what amounted to a "heli-skiing"
adventure.)

After reporting aboard, I was shown my quarters. It was a room about
9 feet long and 7 feet wide. It contained a built-in couch, covered in green
vinyl. The back of the couch folded down to form a narrow bed. I also had
a small, beige foldout metal desk and a matching steel closet. The walls
were welded steel plates painted a dull gray. It was more like a glorified
claustrophobia-inducing jail cell than something I'd call "homey."

I said to the sailor showing me my quarters, "But I don't have a
window."

On my paisley flowered surfboard in 1969, Coast Guard Beach, Cape May, New Jersey. (Photo by Sandy Speers)

The sailor told me in no uncertain terms, and with a definite edge to his voice, "Only the captain, the XO, and the engineering officer have windows."

The unspoken message was, "You should be damn thankful for what you have." I was lucky he didn't say something like, "Besides, you asshole, it's not a 'window,' it's a f——g porthole."

At the time I moved aboard I was unaware of the conditions most of the sailors had endured prior to my boarding. The following description comes from David Frydenlund, who was an ensign at the time:

The shipyard availability before deployment was a living hell for the crew. The ship was uninhabitable for months. The watch section lived in trailers in the shipyard and ate cheap catered food. The ship was gutted to the point where the roving security watches had to be careful not to fall when the passageway they were following suddenly had no floor. Daily work for the junior enlisteds consisted mostly of "fire watches," where they sat for hours on the opposite side of a bulkhead

42

being welded to make sure that no fires were set from the construction activity. No fun. Crew were short so work was hard.

Ensign Frydenlund often had to work twenty-four-hour shifts as officer of the day. He went on to note how much the crew was looking forward to a morale-boosting cruise after going through such a difficult period of time.

I felt bad that I might have come across like some kind of spoiled rich guy when I was first shown my quarters, particularly given what the rest of the crew had been enduring. I never expected a spacious suite, just a small berth with a tiny porthole, the latter because I am somewhat claustrophobic. It did not take me long to appreciate and feel comfortable in what I had. By military icebreaker standards, my stateroom was luxurious, and, unlike the ones for junior officers, it was all my own.

⌐⌐

Once I was living aboard ship, it was easier to handle the multiple projects that still needed to be done. I worked almost nonstop trying to get everything in order. I assumed that once we shoved off it would be virtually impossible to get any more of the supplies and equipment we needed. It was a scramble to get all of the broken and malfunctioning equipment repaired or replaced. I could not stop worrying. In the rush of trying to pull everything together, I kept thinking, *What am I forgetting?*

There were patients that came to sick bay for medical attention before we ever left port. One of the first emergencies was a sailor who had amputated about a third of the tip of his thumb. He came in with the small, severed piece of his thumb in his hand. I knew the piece was too small to be reattached by a vascular surgeon, but I thought suturing the severed piece might function like a skin graft. It was an educated guess.

Although it took about a month for the wound to heal—and most of the "graft" didn't take—it seemed that the graft and our ongoing wound care helped to stimulate regeneration of lost tissue. The end result was almost perfect. He ended up with a smile on his face and a slightly beveled, but essentially normal-looking, totally functional thumb. It also left me feeling more positive about handling medical problems I had not previously encountered. I had no doubt those kinds of situations were going to occur.

<hr/>

A week before we left port, a young Black sailor approached me while I was walking on deck. He was a thin, lanky, inner-city lad who apparently had never been on a long voyage—certainly not one to the ends of the earth. With a furrowed brow and shaky voice, he said, "Doc, we're gonna be in the middle of nowhere. If somethin' happens, are you gonna be able to take care of me?"

An honest response would have been, "I hope so."

No doctor knows everything about medicine. Four years of medical school and a year of internship is little more than a good start. But this sailor obviously needed to hear reassuring words, not a list of my doubts.

"Don't worry," I said emphatically, "whatever comes up, I can handle it."

"Thanks, Doc," he said.

He seemed relieved. I seriously hoped that I could keep the promise I had made.

There was no way I could foresee the life-or-death situation I would later face with this very same sailor.

<hr/>

Our first cruise on the *Glacier* after leaving dry dock was within the breakwater of Long Beach Harbor. Although we were sheltered from the open seas, there was a light swell and some rocking of the ship. The motion was not surprising because of our rounded bottom. (Icebreakers are built to ride up on the pack ice and break it by falling through it.) Due to this construction, the *Glacier* did not handle particularly well in open seas, but no one paid much attention to this problem in Long Beach's sheltered harbor. Except for one sailor, who became seasick.

When I learned of this man's mal de mer problem, I strongly recommended that someone without such a predilection replace him. After all, we would be traveling through some of the roughest seas on Earth.

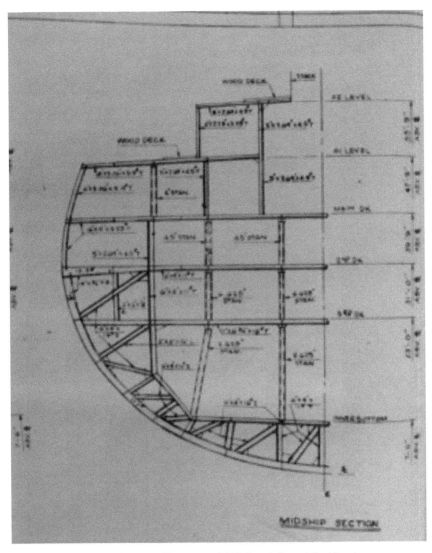

Cross section of *Glacier* hull. (Courtesy of US Coast Guard Archives)

I could only imagine how much trouble this sailor would experience in open seas. The majority of sailors, I knew, would get their sea legs and be able to cope with most conditions, but not this man.

My medical recommendation, I assumed, would be honored. But I was wrong. This sailor, I was told, had certain technical skills deemed essential. My medical advice was overruled.

It was one more indication that this was going to be a long trip for me—and a much longer voyage for this poor sailor.

6

Cast Off

On December 3, 1969, we cast off the lines and began our voyage. While a large crowd came to see us off, there was no one in the crowd bidding me farewell. Most of my family was back in Minnesota, and my girlfriend at the time was in San Francisco. I didn't know if she was going to be the love of my life, but I really cared for her. She was cute, spunky, and witty, and I loved being with her. I wished she had been there waving good-bye.

Part of me was already feeling lonely about being separated from the people I cared about, and I was apprehensive about what lay ahead, but at the same time I was excited that we were finally under way.

As the shore receded, I experienced a wide range of emotions, but to my surprise, the overriding feeling was one of peaceful acceptance. I had done everything I could to prepare our medical department for whatever was to come. There was nothing more I could do. That churning, ulcer-like sensation in my gut had finally stopped.

Our position in Long Beach when we threw off our lines and started south was latitude 33.752° N, longitude 118.227° W. (For non-navigators like myself, *latitude* refers to lines running parallel, or lateral, to the equator, and *longitude* refers to lines running up and down from pole to pole.)

Over the next six months, I would learn a lot more about life at sea. The oceans cover approximately 71 percent of the Earth's surface. Whereas the Northern Hemisphere is 60.7 percent covered, the seas of the Southern Hemisphere, where we would be spending most of our time, cover 80.9 percent. The Coast Guard is often mockingly called "the bath-tub navy" by other military services. Another common jibe is, "You don't have to know how to swim to be in the Coast Guard, you just have to be 6 feet tall so you can wade ashore." But where we were headed was far beyond average coastal waters.

My corpsman Joe Burke kept a daily diary of the trip. He was twenty-three years old when we set off on our adventure. I was twenty-six. After leaving Long Beach, we briefly sailed into San Diego Harbor. In his diary, Joe wrote: "We pulled into San Diego Harbor for about an hour but never went close enough to touch land. It really gave me a hollow feeling when we pulled out because I knew it was the last time I would see the good old U.S. of A [for a while]."

I shared some of Joe's feelings, but they were less intense. Unlike Joe, I had been living away from home for five and a half years, so the tug of a home environment was less. And my feelings about leaving were tempered by another mostly subconscious one: I was looking forward to a great adventure.

We had stopped in San Diego to undergo a process called *degaussing*, in which the ship passes over electrical coils in order to demagnetize it. This was done because there were still World War II–era mines floating around that could be triggered by a ship's magnetic field. Some of those mines could have broken loose and been carried by currents almost anywhere in the world. I knew we would be facing a number of dangers during our voyage, but hitting an explosive device was not one I had considered.

The early part of the voyage was pleasant. The weather was great. I enjoyed the gentle rolling of the boat in calm seas. Great for sleeping. Getting used to walking on a rolling deck took a little longer, but it soon became second nature. The ship was rolling to some degree essentially all the time.

We would soon find out what happened to that gentle rolling motion when we were in rough seas.

———

Life at sea quickly became routine. The only thing a bit different was taking a "sea shower." In order to conserve precious water, one could not luxuriate in a long, hot shower. Instead, we had to turn on the water long enough to get wet, then turn it off, soap down, and then turn the water back on just long enough to rinse off. It was no big deal—certainly not a hardship.

There were no serious medical problems at first, just cuts and colds. Some of the sailors were worried about becoming seasick, but most fared well in the relatively calm seas, except for the poor sailor previously mentioned, who spent almost 25 percent of our deployment in sick bay receiving medications and/or intravenous fluids.

I think it was Napoleon who said "An army travels on its stomach." I would have to say that this holds true for the Coast Guard. Meals were a big part of our daily routine. The food we had in the pleasantly spacious officers' mess was quite good. It was not haute cuisine, but it was well prepared and tasty—at least for the first several weeks after we left port. After that point, we were out of fresh food and the meals became less interesting.

We all sat around one long table, according to rank. Since I was a full lieutenant—because of my medical degree, not my service credentials—I sat on one side of the XO, Commander John Dirschel. He was tall, dark-haired, handsome, and fit—a pleasant, generally upbeat person. In later years, he received an assignment as a liaison officer with the film industry, which earned him the nickname "Hollywood John."

I interacted with him and the other senior officers well enough, but it was hard to feel completely comfortable with them. I was out of my element. The senior Coast Guard officers not only shared a strong bond as members of the same military service; they were also mostly from a different culture and political persuasion than I. During the early days of our deployment, I felt like a visitor at a large family dinner, where 95 percent of the people were blood relatives.

Prior to going on the icebreaker, the only other officers I had spent much time with were my fellow medical and dental Public Health Service officers. Before my assignment to the *Glacier*, I had never even had a cup of coffee with a senior Coast Guard officer. Now I was sitting next to them at every meal.

Directly across from me sat Lieutenant Commander Stansell, the chief engineering officer. He was about forty years old, short, dark, and

WIND, FIRE, AND ICE

wiry. He had difficulty making eye contact, and I never saw him smile. He had a dour personality and conversational skills that made other engineers seem like traveling salesmen in comparison. I found it much easier to relate to the junior officers and the enlisted men.

Captain Eugene McCrory did not sit with us at that long table. As the commanding officer, he was served meals in his quarters, one deck above our wardroom. It was like he was in a different world. The CO was a forty-six-year-old stocky man of medium height, stern-looking, sometimes gruff. He rarely smiled, at least in my presence. He had short, graying hair and a thickened midsection. His speech was clipped, matter-of-fact. I didn't feel comfortable when I was around him. I felt the difference, the separation. It wasn't a good feeling.

There were a number of reasons for my discomfort. He was an older, hard-core military type—a World War II and Korean War veteran, in fact—while I was a younger-generation and nonmilitary type. And for all practical purposes aboard the *Glacier*, he was the absolute ruler.

It wasn't like Captain McCrory was openly hostile toward me, but neither was he overtly friendly. He was usually cordial and acknowledged my presence, but that was about it. I assumed he was a good and competent captain. If that hadn't been the case, I would have heard about it, as this was his second year as CO of the *Glacier* and some of the crew had already served under him.

Corpsman Joe's initial impression of Captain McCrory was not favorable. Chief Toussaint and the corpsmen had busted their butts to get sick bay completely shipshape, particularly after it had been so torn apart. The chief was so proud of the work that had been done that he asked the CO to inspect our gleaming facility. Joe expected Captain McCrory to show obvious pleasure or at least give some kind of compliment about how quickly the work had been completed, but all he offered during the inspection was a cursory acknowledgment.

The conversations in the officers' mess were somewhat stilted. We were advised to avoid any discussions about sex, religion, or politics. I don't recall having a lot of exciting talks around that dinner table; however, about a week after we'd left port, I did have an interesting chat with the XO, Commander Dirschel. I was telling him how stressful it had been to gather all the supplies and medications we needed for the trip, particularly with Chief Toussaint being tied up so much helping him.

The XO gave me a curious look and said, "Why didn't you ask for help?"

I responded with something lame, like "I didn't know I could."

He just smiled and shook his head.

I thought, *You mean I could have avoided a lot of that stress just by asking you for Chief Toussaint's help?*

I came away from that conversation with a couple of realizations. First, I needed to be less intimidated by high-ranking officers. Second, I needed to stop thinking I had to be so independent and self-reliant.

Shortly after we left Long Beach, we experienced our first significant mechanical problem when a part in the fuel oil pressure regulator kept failing. The part was a small bellows, about 1.5 inches in diameter. Sometimes it would fail within five minutes. Other times, it would work properly for two weeks. We had a number of spare bellows, but we were going through them rapidly. When the bellows failed, the boiler burners—which we needed, to produce freshwater from seawater via a desalination process—had to be shut down. If we could not produce our own water, we would have to cancel the mission. We simply did not have enough space to store all the freshwater we would need for our mission.

The water had to be significantly rationed during the time the engineers struggled with this problem. They eventually were able to jerry-rig a hydraulic dampener from a spare piece of pipe, which fixed the problem well enough to carry on with our deployment. It was amazing to think that the failure of one tiny part could have ended our voyage.

One of our first naval exercises occurred about five days after we'd left port. We had a .50 caliber machine gun aboard. (The ship's large, 5-inch guns, a carryover from when the ship was part of the navy, had been removed earlier in the year.) The CO wanted to set up the machine gun on deck and have target practice. The target was a huge float, which we lowered over the side. While the crew was setting up the machine gun, we lost sight of the float.

Captain McCrory was so intent on completing the exercise that he sent up our helicopters to search for the float. The pilots never found it. The CO was furious. It was the first indication that he had a significant temper, and another sign that the trip would not go as smoothly as planned.

On December 8, we came within sight of Clipperton Island, an uninhabited French atoll located at 10° 18' N, 109° 13' W, about the same latitude as Costa Rica. Joe noted in his diary: "The island looked real tiny but it must be loaded with birds, because the birds have been following the ship ever since we got near the island."

As we traveled south into tropical seas, I remembered hearing a lecture about Polynesian voyagers. Tonga, Samoa, the Marquesas, and the Society Islands were colonized by around 500 BC. Hawaii was colonized between about AD 450 and AD 600, which was particularly impressive, since it is 2,000 miles from any of the Polynesian islands—and, at least for the initial voyagers, in a hemisphere of unknown navigational stars. The lecturer said that one of the ways these voyagers kept their bearings was by using their knowledge of the prevailing currents. I later learned that these early voyagers had other means of orienting themselves, such as by the flight of birds at dusk. At that time of the day, birds were likely heading for land. The voyagers also could make predictions based on the physical properties of the water—things like temperature, smell, taste, or color. A cluster of clouds, or a change in the rhythm of waves against the hull, or different kinds of sea life—all could be signs of nearby islands. I wish I had been more aware of these things at the time. It would have made the many months I spent at sea more interesting.

The important milestone that occurred while we were traveling through this tropical zone was crossing the equator. For myself and about two-thirds of the crew, it was the first time we had crossed the equator—a seminal event.

An equator-crossing ceremony has been a British and American sailors' tradition for at least the past two hundred years. Sailors who have crossed the equator are called "Shellbacks" or "Sons of Neptune." Those who have not are called "Pollywogs."

"Baby Neptune" and Neptune's Court. (Courtesy of US Coast Guard Archives)

The initiation rites we Pollywogs had to endure were truly barbaric, but it was done in the spirit of good fun. As the ship's medical officer, I was told I could skip the initiation rites, but I never considered it. I didn't want to come across as someone who was "above it all." Besides, I didn't want to miss out on a once-in-a-lifetime experience.

One of the first things we initiates had to endure was a head-shaving ceremony. Our heads were not totally shaved; instead, someone with electric shears made a cross-shaped mark or a couple of parallel marks on the tops of our heads. All the way down to the scalp. Another part of the ritual was squirting something into our mouths from an oil can. It wasn't oil, however; it was Tabasco sauce. After being blindfolded, we had to squirm and crawl through an inflatable boat and a long tube made of burlap sacks filled with slimy garbage. It would have been worse without the blindfold.

Photo of unidentified sailor receiving his whacks. (Courtesy of US Coast Guard Archives)

For the final part of the ceremony, we had to kneel before "Baby Neptune" on the flight deck, with everyone watching. Baby Neptune was a diaper-clad chief with an ample belly covered in axle grease. As you knelt before him, Baby Neptune would grab your face and rub it on his thickly slathered belly. Then Chief Johnny Johnson, dressed as King Neptune, read off a set of the "charges" for each man.

After hearing this condemning verdict, the victim received a couple of whacks across his bottom with a huge flat paddle. In my case, I was found guilty of being "too nice" to the men. While this charge didn't spare me, the mildly stinging blows I received were gentler than those given to some of my fellow Pollywogs.

Maybe you have to be a guy to appreciate how much fun such a gross ritual can be. It was good for everyone's morale, including my own.

In his diary, Joe noted: "It was really wild. The day was holiday routine and the entire crew participated. It felt really good to see the entire crew joking and laughing and sharing the good time together." He ended his entry by saying: "I am sure I will sleep like a baby tonight. I count flying fish now instead of sheep. The sea is just full of them."

Rather than go around with a big cross on our heads, all of us initiates had our heads shaved completely so our hair would grow out uniformly. Since we previously had been given permission to grow beards—something allowed only during our deployment—I had, for a while, more hair on my face than on my head.

It was about this time that I learned about "Square Knot Sailors." In order to receive this appellation, one must achieve all of the following shipboard milestones:

Crossing the Equator

Crossing the Antarctic Circle

Crossing the Arctic Circle

Crossing the International Date Line

By the end of the trip, I knew I would be at least halfway there.

7

Death at Sea

On December 12, 1969, a man almost died. One of the sailors was looking for something under his workbench in the electrical shop. He didn't know there was a 440-volt, live-circuit junction attached to the bottom frame of the bench. His head touched the junction and powerful current coursed through his body. He went into convulsions. The combination of his convulsions and the forces of gravity no doubt saved his life, as they jerked him away from the electrical contact.

By the time my medical crew and I got to the electrical shop, this sailor was in a semi-comatose state. We admitted him to sick bay to observe him. He soon regained full consciousness, and his condition remained stable for the next twenty-four hours. Other than a minor electrical burn, he was in good shape, and we were able to return him to full duty. It was a close call.

Although our patient made a full recovery, his near-death experience shook me up. We had barely crossed the equator. What was it going to be like when we started sailing in far more treacherous waters?

In 1975 a similar incident occurred aboard another Coast Guard ice-breaker. A young sailor was working in the engine room when his chest accidentally hit a 440-volt contact. He was holding on to part of the engine at the time. The current went through his chest, up his arms, and into the engine. When he was found lying on the deck, it was assumed he had just fainted and passed out from the heat. Temperatures of 120 degrees Fahrenheit or more are not uncommon in the engine room. At first, no one thought it was a critical emergency. It was not until they tried to revive him that they realized he was dead. When they lifted his T-shirt, they saw the electrical burns on his chest. Only then did they fully understand what had happened.

The electrocuted sailor was a devout Mormon. In his pocket they found a copy of the prayer he said each night, in which he asked God to bless and care for his family, as well as his ship and fellow sailors. It was particularly tragic to lose such a caring young man. The ship was deep in Antarctica at the time, and his body had to be stored in a refrigerated compartment until the ship returned to port. His death cast a pall on the entire deployment.

When that sailor died in 1975, there was a physician's assistant aboard, but no doctor. Apparently, someone had made the decision that it was not cost-effective to have a doctor caring for two-hundred-plus men for six months or more, when that same doctor could be land-based and available for many more. Whether or not this sailor would have died if a doctor had been aboard is hard to say. The ship was not carrying a defibrillating unit—the electrical paddles that shock a heart so it can start beating again. (A heart that is "fibrillating" is in spasm and incapable of pumping.) Any treatment other than a defibrillating jolt would have been far less effective.

Based on what I learned during my deployment, it is my professional opinion that a doctor should be aboard any icebreaker sailing to Antarctica. It is the most remote place in the world, and icebreakers are typically stationed there for long periods of time. Odds are that there will be times during these deployments when a doctor's knowledge and hands-on abilities are essential.

On December 16 Joe noted in his diary that the ship had "really been pitching and rolling." He wasn't feeling seasick, but he felt "beat up" from being tossed around. We were at 24 degrees south latitude, in the area of the trade winds—so called because they routinely blow at about 11 to 13 miles per hour, a good velocity for propelling the trading ships of another era. We had a ways to go before we hit the more-dangerous latitudes— the "Roaring Forties," the "Furious Fifties," and the awesome "Screaming Sixties."

"It was something to watch the cooks frying eggs today," Joe wrote. "They would crack the eggs on one end of the grill and [they] would slide just fast as hell to the other end. It was some kind of fun to watch it." Although the cooks no doubt had a rougher go of things when it came to food service, trying to eat a meal in rolling seas was no picnic either. In normal seas, there was enough of a roll that we were only served half a bowl of soup at a time. In heavy seas, it was more like a third. Whereas the enlisted men had tables and seats fixed to the deck, the officers' mess had regular dining-room chairs. Sometimes the seas would be so rough we would have to contain all of the chairs within a large loop of rope.

I vividly remember one occasion where the containing rope broke while we were eating. I went skidding across the deck in my chair, fork poised in my hand, totally out of control, until I slammed into the bulkhead. When the seas were particularly rough, any kind of a normal food service was impossible.

On a couple of occasions while in tropical waters we were entertained by a pod of dolphins. They would swim alongside the ship and leap across the wake formed by our bow. At times they would swim on their backs in front of the bow and look up at us. One definitely got the impression that they were checking us out.

It is well known that dolphins are very intelligent animals. The most remarkable story I ever heard about dolphin intelligence comes from the "Golden Globe Race"—the first nonstop, around-the-world, single-handed yacht race via the three Capes (Africa's Good Hope, Australia's Leeuwin, and South America's Horn). It began in June of 1968 and was completed 313 days later in late April 1969.

Only one of the nine entrants completed the race, and that was Robin Knox-Johnston. He became the first sailor to sail around the world without stopping, and he likely would not have been successful without the help of a pod of dolphins. Much of the sailing took place in the Southern Ocean. Knox-Johnston was slightly off in his directions and unknowingly sailing toward a dangerous, isolated reef south of New Zealand. To his starboard side, he noticed a pod of about twenty dolphins in a long line at right angles to his boat, swimming in the same direction. They repeatedly swam from his stern to his bow—and then abruptly turned right.

After watching them perform this strange maneuver ten times, he began to suspect they were signaling something—namely, to "turn right." It was then that he realized he was heading toward an invisible reef. As soon as he corrected his course, the dolphins swam away. It seemed to be an example of not only intelligence but also of empathy.

The *Glacier* could have benefited from a pod of dolphins of the same ilk in Antarctica.

8

Strait of Magellan

THERE WAS A NOTICEABLE CHANGE IN THE WEATHER AS WE TRAVELED
farther south. On December 19, Joe needed a jacket. In his diary, he wrote,
"It may even look like Christmas when we get to Chile. It still won't be
like home."

In part, the coolness was related to our having entered the Humboldt
Current. We were getting our first taste of Antarctica. That cold-water,
nutrient-rich stream originates in Antarctica and travels along the western coast of South America. This current was named after the greatest
naturalist of the era, Alexander von Humboldt (1769–1859). Besides
being a naturalist, he was also one of the founders of ecological thinking.
For example, he described the interconnections between human activities, such as deforestation, on other natural phenomena, such as lake levels. His natural history writings helped to spur interest in more-scientific
studies of unknown lands.

Scientific studies would be a big part of our deployment in Antarctica. Some of those studies, I suspected, would show how Antarctica
affects the rest of the world.

The first American to write about the concept of broad ocean currents
was Benjamin Franklin. He apparently became interested in the topic
after some discussions with a cousin, who was a whaler. Franklin went on
to commission and collect hundreds of reports about ocean currents from
sea captains, from which he compiled the first accurate sea current chart
ever published—what we now refer to as the Gulf Stream.

We were getting close to the Strait of Magellan. I was excited to see land again. I was also excited to be entering such a famous body of water, although I knew nothing about the historical background of this famous strait, or its significance, or much at all about what is known as "The Age of Discovery." I knew that during much of the Middle Ages it was generally agreed that the world was flat. What I didn't know was that this theory persisted in part because it helped to simplify the religious teachings of the day. If the world was round and a southern hemisphere existed, then one would have to ask if people in that hemisphere also descended from Adam and Eve. And did they have to atone for their sins in the same way? It was easier for religious authorities to denounce such thoughts as heresy.

The first person to accurately determine the circumference of the Earth was Eratosthenes of Cyrene (276 BC–192 BC). This Greek philosopher, poet, and astronomer was able to use geometric principles to determine the approximate circumference of the Earth. Later studies showed that he was off by a mere 8 percent.

In AD 1410, Ptolemy's works from AD 150 were translated into Latin and French. Ptolemy, an Egyptian geographer, agreed with the ancient Greek view that the world was round and probably symmetrical. He speculated that there was a southern continent—generally referred to then as *Terra Australis Incognita*. It was assumed that this landmass stretched from Africa all the way to the South Pole. He, as well as a number of others, believed that this landmass was fertile and populated, but cut off from the known world by a torrid region and a zone of fire. Aristotle had opined that temperatures at the equator were too hot to support life. Others feared that horrible monsters populated the uncharted southern oceans.

These irrationally based thoughts about the world being flat began to change when the Moors invaded Spain in the eighth century. The Arabs had preserved some of the ancient Greek teachings showing evidence that the world was round. Also, Columbus's voyage to the New World in 1492 began to significantly shake up the entrenched ideas of Europeans. After all, there was no denying that he had discovered populated lands covered with exotic flora and fauna.

The Roman Catholic Church had difficulty coping with some of these new findings, such as the suggestion that some of the animals discovered in the New World were different than those reportedly saved by Noah's Ark. But these irrefutable findings, combined with the broader dissemination of information via affordable printed books, gave rise to an inquisitiveness that could not be suppressed.

Our voyage to Antarctica was, in part, an extension of that inquisitive spirit.

When the Portuguese navigator Ferdinand Magellan sailed for South America in September of 1519, he knew that Ptolemy's theories were not totally correct. After all, the Portuguese explorer Bartolomeu Dias had reached Africa's Cape Hope in 1488, and one of his compatriots, Vasco da Gama, later sailed around the cape all the way to India. Thus, there was no landmass connected to the southern tip of Africa. Magellan, however, did not know if the South American continent extended all the way to the pole. Similarly, he and his crew did not know if sea monsters, terrible whirlpools, or other such rumored horrors existed in this region. But he had some reason to believe that a strait existed that cut through South America. And he knew that a fortune could be made in spices if he could find a shortcut to Asia and the Spice Islands.

Spices and other exotic items from Asia, such as pearls, opiates, and diamonds, had always been expensive. But they became much more expensive after Constantinople (modern-day Istanbul) fell to the Turks in 1453. As a result, traditional overland routes between Europe and Asia were cut off. Oceanic routes became much more important.

And it wasn't only captains and merchants who stood to make a fortune in the spice trade. In a relative sense, the same held true for an ordinary seaman. Even the profits from a small sack of cloves or nutmeg would be enough to allow a seaman to buy a basic house and retire on the money left over. (In contrast, no such treasures awaited the crew of the *Glacier* in Antarctica.)

More than half the world was unknown or misunderstood by Europeans at the time Magellan left on his voyage. He sailed into what was then known as the "Ocean Sea." Ancient Greeks referred to it as "The Sea of Atlantis." The odds of his successfully completing his voyage were quite small. For starters, Magellan was Portuguese, but sailing for a Spanish king. Most of his crew was Spanish and distrusted him. And most of them did not believe that the fabled strait even existed. They were more convinced that Magellan was going to lead them off the edge of a flat earth. Mutiny was an ever-present threat.

After surviving a number of fierce storms, Magellan and his five-ship armada made it to a port on the southern coast of Brazil, which they named Port St. Julian. Shortly after arriving in this port, where they planned to spend the winter, a full-scale mutiny broke out. The men on three of the five ships decided they were going to return to Spain. It was only the cleverness and cunning of Magellan that allowed him to survive this revolt. The lead mutineers were brutally tortured. One of them was drawn and quartered, his body parts left on display for several months. The net effect of Magellan's wrath was to make the men more fearful of him than they were of any perils they might face on their voyage.

On October 21, 1520, following a two-year voyage, Magellan's pilot saw for the first time the opening to the strait that would later bear his name. The opening to the east side of the strait was marked by a long spit of sand at S 52° latitude, W 68° longitude.

Traversing the 350-mile-long strait proved almost as difficult as finding it. Magellan had to deal with strong currents, horrendous storms, 24-foot tides, poor anchorages, and heavy kelp beds, which fouled the keels and rudders of his ships. The strait meandered through a confusing maze of fjords. Rocky shoals and dead-end bays were everywhere. He also had to deal with frequent "willywas," the name given to the harsh storms common in this area. These storms occur when air chilled by glaciers surrounding the strait suddenly pour down the mountains, picking up speed along the way.

One of the things Magellan used to navigate was the taste of the seawater. If the seawater started tasting fresher as he headed in one direction, he knew he was headed inland.

It took thirty-eight days for Magellan and his men to find their way to the Pacific Ocean. Magellan named the passage the Strait of All Saints,

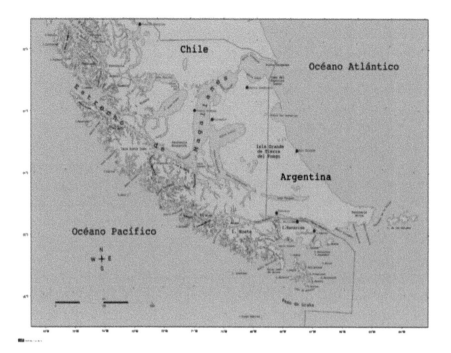

The Strait of Magellan. (Courtesy of Wikimedia Commons)

because it was discovered on November 1, All Saints' Day. In spite of his ego and pride, Magellan never wanted the strait named after him. It was not until six years later that the strait officially became the Strait of Magellan.

The man whose ships were the first to circumnavigate the world did not live to complete the voyage. Magellan made it as far as the Philippines, where he seemed to lose track of his goal of discovering a new route to the Spice Islands. Instead, he became obsessed with the idea of converting all the inhabitants of the Philippines into Christians and loyal subjects of the King of Spain. After achieving apparent success with some of the islanders, he issued an untenable ultimatum to a defiant village, ordering its inhabitants to immediately convert to Christianity. When they refused, he rushed into a battle with the natives, who outnumbered his men thirty to one. He died in this battle. In spite of his brilliance and vast abilities, in the end Magellan's arrogance and foolish pride led to an error in judgment that cost him his life.

When the *Glacier* arrived at the western entrance to the Strait, I expected it to be narrower—more like a wide river. In fact, it is quite wide. It is in an area of multiple islands, peninsulas, and fjords. Magellan would have had a much tougher time finding the opening from the Pacific side.

The Strait is slightly more than a mile wide at its narrowest point. Prior to the opening of the Panama Canal in 1914, it was the favored route for steamships because it was shorter and safer than sailing around Cape Horn at the southern tip of South America and traversing Drake Passage. Sailing ships, however, generally chose to transit Drake Passage because they needed more room to maneuver. Although Chile officially took possession of the Strait in 1843, it agreed to allow all nations free access.

I was excited to be entering this historic body of water and looking forward to setting foot on another continent, which I'd never done before.

We entered the Strait in the morning. Given the harsh weather, strong currents, rocky shoals, and narrow passages, it would have been dangerous to try to enter it at night. To the north, the land was mostly rocky, barren, and gently sloped. Looking south, the low hills of Tierra del Fuego gave way to snow-packed, glaciated peaks. About a third of the hills to the south were covered in trees. They would be the last trees we would see as we traveled farther south.

Shortly after we entered the Strait, the *Glacier* was approached by another boat about the size of a tugboat. It sailed next to us, and a man in a dark uniform boarded our vessel. At first, I thought he was a customs official. However, when he went straight to the bridge, I realized he was a different kind of official. We would not have to worry about getting lost in the many misleading, dead-end channels leading off the Strait (nor would we have to resort to such things as tasting seawater for its freshwater content). A Chilean marine pilot would lead us to port.

9

Punta Arenas

Before we docked at our first port, Punta Arenas, I gave a standard talk about venereal diseases (VD), basing it on what was known about VD in Chilean ports. In a nutshell, the news was not good. Punta Arenas had a number of brothels, and they were linked to a variety of serious venereal diseases. I felt like I was conveying very useful medical information that was going to significantly change the behavior of most of my shipmates once we hit port. While the crew listened with polite interest, I clearly overestimated the impact of my talk.

Fortunately for me, my talk preceded the one Chief Toussaint gave on the same topic. His presentation was far better. He knew how to encapsulate VD information into gems of commonsense wisdom. Moreover, he was far more entertaining. I remember only part of his talk, but what I remember will give you an idea of how he conveyed some very useful knowledge.

Chief Toussaint began simply.

I will give you a list of the most common questions I'm asked about VD, along with my answers.

First question: "But she had a legal certificate on the wall."
My answer: "You have a legal case of VD."
Second question: "But none of my buddies caught it."
My answer: "There's one in every crowd."
Third question: "But she didn't look like she had VD."
My answer: "Where did you look?"

His talk continued in the same pithy, sarcastic, and humorous fashion. It was like *VD for Dummies*. It contained the essentials of what these sailors needed to know—and had us rolling in the aisles.

At ten p.m. on December 23, 1969, we arrived in Punta Arenas, a city of about one hundred thousand people. The city was originally established as a small penal colony. "Problematic" military personnel were also sent there as a form of punishment. Prior to the completion of the Panama Canal, it probably was a much more important city than it was when we docked there.

Even though we arrived late at night, a number of sailors were granted liberty. Joe Burke was one of them. His diary entry for the following day reads: "Went ashore last night. It was out of sight. I'm really beat. They drink some stuff called pisco that would knock King Kong on his ass."

Joe must have been served pisco straight up. Pisco is a form of brandy and certainly potent. A tastier and milder drink is a "pisco sour"—kind of like a South American margarita.

The first thing I learned about being in port was that whatever I did in town, I had to stay sober and be back to the ship early. Excitement in sick bay began later in the evening when drunken sailors staggered back—or were carried back—to the ship. I think the first Spanish word most of the crew learned, and it may have been the only one, was *cerveza*, Spanish for "beer." It seemed that some of our sailors liked their beer with a brawl chaser. I wondered if they thought of facial stitches as a badge of honor.

There seemed to be no limit to the ridiculous stunts some of our drunken sailors tried to pull in port. On one occasion a sailor got drunk, got into an argument with a cabdriver, and started jumping on the roof of the cab. On another occasion, several of the crew started using a chain as a jump rope. The problem was that they borrowed the chain from the front of a local police station. In both cases, the guys were arrested. They were lucky the police were willing to release them into our custody. I suspected the police were glad to get rid of them.

Our third day in port was Christmas. Nothing in particular sticks in my mind about that day. No doubt I was a bit down about being away from friends and family.

Joe wrote, "They had a big feed aboard ship. I guess I'll go on liberty and pretend I am home or forget I am away." Some of the men asked that I go check out the main brothel in town to see if it met with my approval. I told them I did not think I would be able to tell anything from a casual, cursory look. Per Chief Toussaint, I knew where to look. And I had no intention of doing so.

The main brothel in town was Maria Theresa's. The name sounded more like a religious shrine than a bordello. This venerable establishment has been billed "The Southernmost House in the World." Reportedly, it has been in continuous operation since the late 1800s, and is still owned by the same family.

I stopped by Maria Theresa's briefly to check it out. The place was dark and had a large central area where women were sitting. Some people were dancing. The way things worked was a sailor would choose a dance partner, a brief dance probably serving as the extent of their foreplay. If the sailor decided to choose that partner, they would retire to one of the back rooms.

A few of the women were young and fairly attractive, but there also was an assortment of women who were anything but. Several of the women were unusually short, rotund, and disfigured with facial scars. It looked as if they had been victims of a smallpox epidemic. I had difficulty imagining how anyone would be so horny as to want to spend even a portion of their evening with one of these women.

Apparently, I have limited powers of imagination.

Ensign David Frydenlund was directed by the CO to tour the brothels in town with Chief Toussaint. Supposedly, he was to report his findings and issue a list of "approved" brothels. Since his Coast Guard Academy training did not include "Brothel Inspecting," and his Spanish-speaking abilities were limited, it was hardly an easy task. If the ship ever compiled a list of Coast Guard–approved brothels, I never saw it.

A number of the men may have had a hard time finding any brothel that would accept them. Reportedly, some of the veteran sailors went around town telling the ladies of the evening that they should avoid having sex with anyone with a mostly shaved head—those of us who had been Pollywogs only a few weeks before. They convinced these women that a recently shaved head was the Coast Guard's way of designating those with venereal disease.

Shortly after we arrived in Punta Arenas, one of the crewmembers came back to the ship with a ridiculously tall tale. Or so it seemed. He said there was a ship in port that carried a surplus of almost one hundred college women. We, of course, assumed he was suffering from some kind of delusion, probably caused by six weeks of sexual deprivation. We could relate to his condition. We responded with kidding, but kindly, remarks. But then he gave us more details. The group he was talking about was "The College of the Seven Seas." It was a ship chartered by Chapman College, a Southern California institution, and they had something like four hundred students on board, many of whom were young women.

Being men of action, a small group of us hit the streets and canvassed the town for a venue big enough to handle a party of five hundred people. It's amazing what can be accomplished with broken Spanish, a strong will, and a wad of cash.

That night we had a rousing party for our crew and any of the Chapman students who wished to join us. (Allegedly, the women talked the captain of their ship into delaying their departure in order to party with us.) There was no shortage of attention paid to the unattached women who attended the party. One junior officer was totally smitten by one of the women he met, claiming he was going to marry her. And in fact, when he finally made it back to California, he did just that.

While we were in port we needed to purchase laboratory chemicals for certain medical tests. I contacted some Chilean doctors who were genuinely helpful. They gave us the supplies we needed and invited me to lunch. During the meal I noticed a plate piled high with green peppers half the size of my little finger. I went to grab one and they shook their heads. They said the peppers, which they were casually eating, were too spicy for me. I said I would try only a small bite, but they still advised against it.

I said, "But I may never have another chance to try one."

One of them patiently said, "Try putting one in your soup and then take a spoonful of the broth next to the pepper."

I did as he suggested, thinking, *How hot can it possibly be?*

I confidently slurped a tablespoon of the steaming broth. At first I thought, *Spicy, but not too bad.* But then the full effect of the liquid fire hit me. My confident smile quickly disappeared.

Tears started pouring down my cheeks. I wanted to say, "I see what you mean," but I couldn't speak. My throat was on fire. As I grasped at my throat, I gave them a nod of acknowledgment. They smiled knowingly.

This was my first trip to a foreign country, and I swore to myself that in the future I was going to listen to the natives.

One of the doctors I met was particularly friendly. I will call him Jose. He graciously invited me to his home for dinner, which I happily accepted. The highlight of the dinner was meeting Jose's wife. She was one of the most beautiful women I had ever seen. A classic, black-haired, olive-skinned Castilian beauty, with dancing dark eyes and perhaps a touch of Indian blood to give her a more exotic look. And she was perfectly charming.

After a lovely dinner, Jose's wife asked if I would give her a tour of the *Glacier* the next day. I was more than happy to do so. She was just as beautiful in the full light of day as she had been in the soft light of her home. I gave her a complete tour of the ship, trying to communicate with her as best I could in my limited and broken Spanish.

Part of the tour included my tiny quarters. While the two of us were alone in my cabin, I was the perfect gentleman, although the thought of being a less-than-perfect one certainly crossed my mind. I had, after all, gone almost two months without any female companionship. And she was *so* beautiful.

The following day I gave Jose a tour of the *Glacier*. During the tour he asked me a question. I thought he said something like "*Como esta mi espanole mujer?*," meaning "How was my Spanish wife?"

I looked at him blankly. I'm sure I started turning red. I had been raised Catholic, and at the very least, was guilty of having "impure thoughts." I felt I needed to say something like, "Honest, I didn't touch her."

He repeated himself, and this time I understood.

He said, "*Como esta tu Espanol—mejor?*" meaning, "How is your Spanish—better?"

Mejor, not *mujer*.

No, I told him, my Spanish was not getting any better.

⚊⚊⚊

Our first case of VD came into sick bay on December 27. "Poor horny sailors!" was how Joe described the early patients. We could have been more assertive in repeating our warnings about VD risks, but I don't think it would have made a significant difference. And it may have harmed the rapport we were trying to develop with the crew. Apparently, the doctor who had preceded me during the previous deployment to Antarctica had gone so far as to post graphic photos of VD infections. He placed these photos on the bulkhead next to the chow line. Some members of the crew were reluctant to warm up to us until they realized we weren't going to resort to this type of scare tactic.

On December 28, we received mail for the first time. I had letters from my mother, my sisters, and my girlfriend. Receiving those letters was like finding an oasis in the desert.

Joe wrote, "Today was about the most delightful day so far for the crew. I sure wish we got mail more often." He added, "The year and the decade are almost gone. I will never forget the '60s."

Nor will I.

We were going to be in Punta Arenas for New Year's Eve, so I asked Jose if there was any type of New Year's celebration a small group of our crew might be able to attend. He immediately suggested we arrange a party with some women from Maria Theresa's. I was rather shocked. The impression he gave me was that it was perfectly acceptable to party with the town prostitutes—even if one was married. With a wife as beautiful as his, I could hardly imagine him being involved. It was clearly a different culture than the conservative Catholic one in which I had been raised in Minnesota. (Most of the Scandinavians in Minnesota are Protestant, but my mother was an Irish Catholic.)

Ensign Frydenlund had the same impression about the cultural differences. As he was checking out the various brothels, he noticed that men would come to pick up some of the women after their shift was over. He was surprised to learn that many of these men were, in fact, husbands of these working women.

Another example of cultural differences occurred during one of my last days in port. I met with Jose in order to give him a parting gift, to thank him for his generosity. It was a very simple gift—a pair of Bic lighters. He marveled at their clever and functional design, and thanked me profusely. Then he asked me how he could refill this amazing invention, once the fuel was gone.

Without a second thought, I said, "You don't refill them. You throw them away."

With jaw agape, he said, "You throw these away?"

I was embarrassed to say that it was true. It reflected badly on our wasteful, consumer-oriented culture.

When New Year's Eve came, one of the junior officers, Ensign Howard Waters, heard that there was an Argentinean passenger ship in port. Howie and I put on our best uniforms and tried to join the party. Some Chilean naval officers had the same idea. We all went up the gangway of the Argentinean ship and tried to talk our way aboard. Our requests were flatly denied. It looked hopeless.

Then the man in charge of the entrance motioned for Howie and me to move to one side, where he told us in a soft whisper to hang around for a while. He was going to let us join the party. His adamant refusal apparently was meant for the Chileans. In retrospect, it occurred to me that his allowing us to attend the party was probably not so much due to our American charm, but rather a case of ongoing animosity between two South American neighbors. The Argentineans and the Chileans have had border disputes that remain unresolved to this day.

When we finally got on board, the New Year's Eve celebration was in full swing. The wine and champagne flowed freely, we feasted on hors d'oeuvres, and we had our pick of lovely dance partners. We definitely felt like a couple of very lucky sailors. I spent the latter half of the evening with an attractive woman from Buenos Aires. She worked as a travel agent and appeared to be quite sophisticated. By the end of the evening, we were dancing more like lovers than strangers.

When the music stopped, I politely asked if I could escort her to her stateroom. She looked at me sharply with a wide-eyed, almost horrified look, as if I had just made the most indecent proposal imaginable.

It seemed as if she was ready to slap me. I assured her I would not step beyond her threshold, and I meant it, but it made no difference. Once again, I realized that I was quite clueless about the cultural norms of this foreign land.

Joe was in a more-reflective mood on New Year's Eve. He wrote: "New Year's Eve and I don't even feel like going ashore. It is strange, but I just don't feel like going out and having a good time. Next year will hopefully be different. . . . This is the end of the decade. Earlier I argued about who the greatest and most influential man of the decade was. In these final lines of a decade I know that to me it was a man named Dad."

10

Drake Passage

On January 3, 1970, we cast off the lines, sailed east through the Strait of Magellan, and then headed south by southeast toward Antarctica and the Antarctic Peninsula. We left with sixty-five new passengers. Three were US Navy officers who were going to be stationed in Antarctica, along with seven enlisted men to relieve men who had wintered over. There were also twenty-seven scientists, including nine scheduled to remain aboard the *Glacier*.

The largest single group was made up of twenty-eight Navy Seabees, members of the US Navy construction battalions. Their simple motto is "We build. We fight." There is a soft place in my heart for them. My father was a Seabee during World War II, and fought on Iwo Jima. He never spoke about the war, but he had a box of photos. I found them one day when I was snooping in his closet. The pictures were mostly of wounded and dead soldiers. I understood why he never wanted to show them to me. The box also contained a medal, a Purple Heart.

The Seabees were not going to Antarctica to fight. They were going to Palmer Station on the west side of the Antarctic Peninsula, just north of the Antarctic Circle, to do more construction work. The main part of this American base had been completed only the year before, and there was still much work to be done.

Antarctica is the only continent that has never seen a war. It has, however, been the subject of warlike ambitions. During 1938 and 1939, for example, there was a mostly secret Nazi project called "The National Socialist Antarctic Expedition." Germany lost their colonial empire following World War I, and Hitler was determined to change that. He wanted to acquire territory in Antarctica and start his own whaling fleet.

The Nazi-backed expedition sent to Antarctica a large, ice-rated ship called the *Schwabenland* and two Lufthansa-owned flying boats, the *Boreas* and the *Passat*, which could be launched from a ship by a pneumatic catapult. Under the cover of doing scientific mapping of a portion of the continent east and north of the Weddell Sea, these two airplanes were able to photograph 150,000 square miles of previously unmapped Antarctica. The planes also carried dart-like bombs one and a half meters long, embossed with a swastika, which could penetrate a foot deep into the ice. The plan was to release these darts every 15 to 18 miles as "sovereignty emblems." The mission was mostly successful from Hitler's point of view. A number of geographic features were given German names. After the defeat of Germany, though, most of these names were removed. A more-detailed land survey by the Norwegians later resulted in this same area being given the name Queen Maud Land.

Germany was not alone in desiring to acquire territory in Antarctica. In fact, most of the countries involved in Antarctica have had designs on acquiring territory. Many countries have officially declared possession of different sections of Antarctica. Britain and Argentina have come close to having military battles in Antarctica, with both periodically occupying Deception Island and declaring it their own.

On one occasion in the 1950s, a British warship was greeted by an Argentinean ship off of Deception Island, just north and west of the Antarctic Peninsula. The official message the British initially received was "Welcome to Argentina." The captain of the British vessel was invited to board the Argentinean ship, at which time he was told his ship was in Argentinean territory—without permission. This could have ended in open battle, but the British decided it was not worth it, whereas they did go to war over the Falkland Islands, where they badly defeated the Argentineans.

All territorial acquisition plans changed—at least in principle—when the Antarctic Treaty went into force in 1961. The treaty became a model of international peaceful cooperation. Some have suggested that if we ever populate the moon, it should be governed by a similar treaty. So far, the signatories to this treaty have mostly behaved themselves. But Antarctica is rich in such things as coal, oil, and marine products. It remains to be seen how well the treaty will hold up. The treaty specifically rejects all territorial claims, but if it is allowed to lapse, preexisting claims could become valid, which could become a major problem, as most Antarctic territories are claimed by two or more countries.

The Antarctic Treaty covers the area below 60 degrees south latitude. It declares that Antarctica shall only be used for peaceful purposes. Military operations are allowed only for the support of peaceful activities, such as providing logistical support for scientific projects. The results of all scientific studies are to be shared with the forty-eight (as of 2020) signatory nations.

The Antarctic Treaty guarantees free inspections by the signatory nations of all the stations and equipment of other nations. The disposal of nuclear waste is prohibited. No new territorial claims are allowed. A key principle is "preservation and conservation of living resources." Periodic meetings among the nations are required "at suitable intervals and places, for the purpose of exchanging information, consulting together on matters of common interest."

Scientific research studies of areas in and around Antarctica was one of the *Glacier*'s major missions. Our initial research projects were aimed primarily at studying the penguin and seal populations, including metabolic studies.

Scientific studies performed in Antarctica have been important for the rest of the world, including one where ice core samples from Antarctica allowed us to study atmospheric changes dating back as far as 800,000 years ago. These studies, along with oceanographic research, wildlife studies, and weather recordings, have given us a better understanding of such things as global warming.

As we passed Cape Horn and left the tip of South America behind, we entered the most treacherous and infamous body of water on Earth: Drake Passage. I had always thought that Sir Francis Drake discovered this dangerous stretch of ocean because he had missed the Strait of Magellan and inadvertently sailed around the tip of South America. In fact, he had successfully traversed the Strait from east to west in September of 1578. But shortly after exiting the Strait, he was blown 300 miles south by a fierce storm—comparable to a ship leaving San Francisco Bay and being pushed all the way to Los Angeles. It was like a verse from Samuel Taylor Coleridge's "The Rime of the Ancient Mariner":

> *And now the Storm-Blast came, and he*
> *Was tyrannous and strong:*
> *He struck with his o'ertaking wings,*
> *And chased us south along.*

One of the ships in Drake's convoy, the *Marigold*, was lost in the storm, along with the entire crew. By the time the storm had abated, Drake was at 57 degrees of latitude, which is about 1,500 miles (2,414 km) south of Buenos Aires. It was a place where the Atlantic and Pacific, in his words, "meet in a most large and free scope."

He also wrote, "no traveler hath felt, neither hath there been such a tempest so violent . . . since Noah's flood."

Drake's discovery confirmed for the first time that South America—specifically, Tierra del Fuego—was not part of the hypothesized Terra Australis Incognita, the temperate and habitable land near the South Pole rumored to exist for centuries. Drake was also the first captain to sail around the world—and survive the voyage. Magellan did not survive his fleet's circumnavigation, but a number of his crew did.

When it comes to the history of Drake Passage, there is a competing Spanish version. Some Spanish and Latin American historians call this area the Mar de Hoces. The name derives from a voyage in 1525 by a Spanish navigator, Francisco de Hoces, who thought he saw land's end.

There is a common thread to these competing versions. In both cases, the ships were blown south from the Strait of Magellan by incredible storms. Perhaps historians should just get together and call it something like "Blown Off-Course Passage" or the "Passage of Storms."

For a long time, particularly prior to the building of the Panama Canal, Drake Passage was known simply as the "graveyard of the sea." If

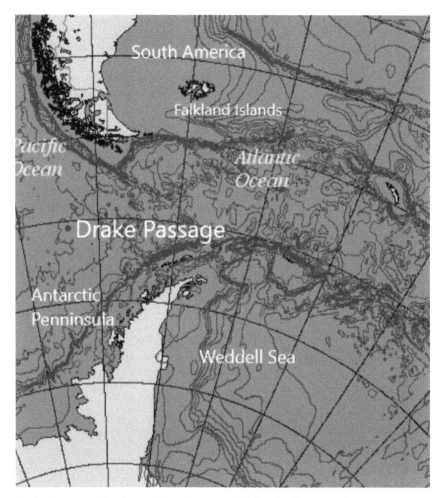

Drake Passage. (Courtesy of Geo Swan and Wikimedia Commons)

I had known we would be crossing it six times during our deployment, I would have asked myself whether it would end up being our graveyard.

There does seem to be some agreement about the name for the southern tip of South America: Cape Horn (*Cabo de Hornos*, in Spanish). The first recorded sailing of Drake Passage was in 1616 by Dutch captain Willem Schouten, in the *Eendracht*. He gave the cape the Dutch name *Kaap Hoorn*, after the city of Hoorn in the Netherlands. The city of Hoorn helped to finance Schouten's voyage, hoping to find a route to the Far East free of the monopolies held by the Dutch East India Company.

Drake Passage became famous, in part, because it was the preferred route traveled by clipper ships, particularly those coming from the West Coast of the United States heading for the East Coast and ships carrying grain from Australia bound for Europe. The Strait of Magellan is not only narrow in places, but it can also become icebound. In contrast, Drake Passage is 500 miles (805 km) wide—the distance between Cape Horn and the northern tip of the Antarctic Peninsula. It allows plenty of room for maneuvering wind-driven ships, but at a cost.

We would learn much more about this perilous passage, and the price one pays for traversing it.

In olden days, sailors from the Pacific Ocean who rounded the Horn were allowed to wear an earring in their left ear—the ear facing the Horn during the favored west-to-east route. These sailors were called "Cape Horners," and were allowed to put one foot up on the table when they dined. (I have not yet attempted to convince my wife of my privileged status based on this little-known historical tradition.) Sailors who also rounded Africa's Cape of Good Hope could wear earrings in both ears. I don't know if this meant they could put both feet on the table. (My view is that this would have made them more vulnerable to their wives or girlfriends kicking their chairs out from under them.)

When Charles Darwin first saw Drake Passage, he wrote, "The sight is enough to make a Landsman dream for a week of shipwreck, death and peril."

There are many reasons why Drake Passage and the area around Cape Horn are so dangerous and have such powerful waves. The height of a wind-driven wave is affected by three different factors: the velocity of the wind, the duration of the wind, and the fetch. The latter term refers to the distance wind blows over open water, which is essentially infinite in the case of Drake Passage.

There are almost constant westerly winds (winds coming from the west and blowing toward the east) in this passage. According to the US Navy's *Sailing Directions for Antarctica*, the winds in this area "are often of hurricane intensity and with gust velocities sometimes attaining 150 to

200 miles (241 km to 322 km) per hour." Other than tropical hurricanes, the navy noted, "winds of such violence are not known elsewhere."

Unlike other oceans, there is no land to stop wind-blasted waves from becoming progressively larger. The North Atlantic is awe-inspiring during a storm but at some point, the waves there will crash onto a continental landmass. In contrast, waves in Drake Passage can travel, without hindrance, around and around the Antarctic continent, which is why the fetch is essentially infinite.

The duration of storms in Drake Passage is quite variable, but storms generally last a few days rather than a few hours. If the winds are strong and steady, they will continue to pump energy into the waves. The waves can become progressively higher, thicker, and more powerful. The higher the waves become, the greater the grip the wind has on the surface of the waves. In addition, the power stored in a wave is proportional to the square of its height; thus, a 4-meter-high wave is sixteen times more powerful than a 1-meter-high wave.

The estimated distance between the crests of waves—the wavelength—in this stretch of ocean can be up to a mile. The longer the distance between the crests, the more power contained in each wave and the faster the wave moves. A 60-knot wind, sustained for twenty-four hours, produces waves traveling about 60 miles per hour (97 km/h).

The most powerful waves are tsunami waves, created by the massive forces present in earthquakes. The distance between their crests can be 100 miles or more, and the speed of these waves in deep water can be as fast as a jet plane. Tsunami waves are different, though, in that the force of the wave is transmitted through the water, rather than on top of it—much like a sound wave traveling through water. In shallow water, these waves slow significantly because of the resistance created by the ocean bottom.

Some awestruck sailors have reported waves up to 200 feet (60 m) high in Drake Passage, but maximum heights of 80 to 90 feet (24 to 27 m) are more likely. As waves increase in size, their speed increases dramatically as well. Sailors refer to these waves as "Cape Horn rollers" or "graybeards."

Waves traveling around Antarctica get "pinched" between the opposing tips of Cape Horn and the mountainous spine of the Antarctic

Peninsula. It is like the higher wind forces experienced in many cities created by winds funneled into the narrow "canyons" formed by rows of large buildings. In some areas, the waves are also forced up by sea bottom shoals. Furthermore, the easterly-moving Antarctic Circumpolar Current adds power to the force of the prevailing winds.

Sailors also have to worry about hitting icebergs. Even in summer, icebergs can be found as far north as Cape Horn. During the winter, icebergs can be found north of 40 degrees south—almost as far north as Uruguay.

The English poet and writer John Masefield captured the dangers of sailing around Cape Horn in these lines: *Cape Horn, that tramples beauty into wreck / And crumples steel and smites the strong man dumb.*

11

The Southern Ocean

OUR FIRST CROSSING OF DRAKE PASSAGE WAS PRETTY TYPICAL FOR that stretch of ocean, meaning, treacherous. Twenty-foot waves are common in Drake Passage even on a good day, so we considered ourselves lucky with just a 10- to 15-foot swell in the choppy seas, a misty gray sky overhead, and a blustery breeze.

When the Seabees reported aboard, there was not enough storage room for their olive-green duffel bags, so they were stowed in the enlisted men's mess. Early in the crossing, I happened by this stack of duffel bags and saw a moaning Seabee in the middle of it. If I had not heard him, I might not have spotted him—his complexion was about as green as the surrounding bags. I heard another Seabee say, "I'd rather be in Vietnam getting shot at than be on this damn ship."

As we approached the islands off the Antarctic Peninsula, we sailed into what is today the world's newest ocean—the Southern Ocean. In the year 2000, the International Hydrographic Organization officially declared that the seas between Antarctica and 60 degrees south latitude merited its own name. So what had changed? In fact, some of the oceanographic studies done aboard the *Glacier* contributed to this declaration.

Intensive scientific studies began in Antarctica as part of the International Geophysical Year (IGY) which began in 1957 and ended eighteen months later. Sixty-seven countries took part in the IGY. Multiple cooperative international studies thereafter revealed that the Southern Ocean was a separate, distinct body of water—not just the southernmost Atlantic and Pacific oceans. One of the things that made it truly unique was its own current, the Antarctica Circumpolar Current (ACC).

The unit of measurement used to express the volume of water transported in a current is called a sverdrup (symbol, Sv), after the famous Norwegian oceanographer, Harold Sverdrup (1888–1957). A sverdrup equals one million cubic meters per second. Whereas the Gulf Stream's flow is about 55 Sv, in Drake Passage, the flow is almost twice that amount, and six hundred times the flow coming from the Amazon River. The ACC is the largest current in the world and the only one that flows completely around a continent.

The waters in the Southern Ocean are colder and have a different composition when compared to other oceans. They have a lower salinity—34.65 PSU (practical salinity units) versus 35.5 PSU for the global ocean average, because of the diluting effect of melting ice. The deep waters off Antarctica are the densest in the world, 1.0279 grams per cubic centimeter. The cold has a greater effect on density than it has on salinity. Dense cold waters sink to the bottom and push up nutrients from the ocean floor, and cold water can absorb more oxygen than warm water, which tends to expel oxygen. These cold, oxygen- and nutrient-rich waters are about four times more productive of plant and sea life than other oceans. During the Antarctica summer, when sunlight hits this ocean, there is a veritable explosion of sea life.

The marine life that is so abundant in Antarctica is composed primarily of one-celled plants called diatoms. These plants can absorb the sun's energy through the sheets of ice. Their numbers are so great that they often stain the bottom of the ice a dirty yellow. In open waters they cover areas so vast they can be seen in satellite images.

We experienced one of these massive blooms of diatoms during our deployment. The seas were covered with a yellowish-green to bluish-green film almost as far as the eye could see.

Collectively, the diatoms and other small floating plants are called phytoplankton. These tiny plants are, in turn, eaten by animal plankton, known as zooplankton. Tiny shrimplike creatures, called krill, feed on the plankton. Some scientists have postulated that the protein contained in krill together with their massive numbers could be enough to solve world hunger.

Moving up the food chain, krill are eaten by small fish, which are eaten by larger fish. Penguins and seals feed on the fish. These larger animals are eaten by leopard seals and killer whales. Blue whales—the largest animals that have ever existed, weighing up to three times more than the largest dinosaurs—are filter feeders who feed directly on zooplankton and other types of plankton, typically straining more than three tons a day. The top predator is the killer whale. Pods of killer whales will attack other whales, even blue whales.

On January 5, 1970, we reached Deception Island, which is part of the South Shetland Islands. This island is actually the caldera of a semi-active volcano, but a gap in the caldera wall allows ships to enter into a sheltered harbor. In the early 1900s, it was the site of a whaling station. The British set up a permanent station there in 1944, but temporarily vacated it

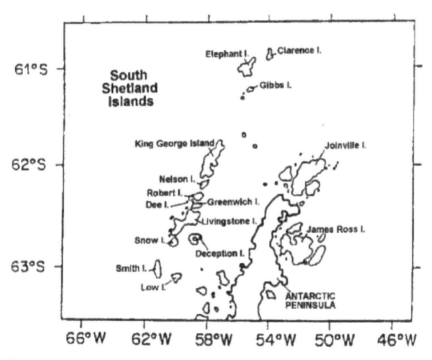

(Courtesy of Paula De Soussa, Commonwealth Scientific)

because of an eruption in December 1967. They permanently abandoned their base in February of 1969 after further volcanic activity. Vestiges of the old whaling station and other old buildings remain. The island continues to be a popular tourist stop for ships going to Antarctica because of its thermal waters, as well as several populations of chinstrap penguins.

On January 21, 1964, the USCGC *Eastwind* ran aground at Deception Island, but was able to float off in a high tide. It is probably the only time an American military ship has ever run aground inside an active volcano. I don't know if the *Eastwind* was there for some official reason or just for the crew's entertainment. Because volcanic gases bubble up from the ocean bottom in places, it's a great place to swim. No doubt the Coast Guard brass would have been upset if the ship got into trouble merely because they had stopped there for a dip.

The danger of another eruption like the one in 1969 must have been quite low when we were there on January 5, 1970, as we dropped off several scientists for an extended stay.

The same day we dropped off the scientists, Joe noticed thousands of fast-swimming penguins and a number of icebergs. Ship records indicate there were thirty large icebergs in the vicinity, mostly detected by radar. There were many times when we were in a dense fog, surrounded by icebergs. It was a scary sensation to stand on deck and hear waves break on the base of icebergs we could not see.

The following day we attempted to land some scientists on nearby Gibbs Island. The three-man party, headed by Dr. Ian Dalziel, was beginning its "Structural Studies of the Scotia Arc" that included research on continental drift theories. Other scientific studies planned for our deployment included such things as biological productivity, seal physiology, magnetic variability, bottom sediment, and deep current studies. Knowledge about these factors—particularly in the Weddell Sea east of the Antarctic Peninsula, where we would spend much of our time—was quite sparse.

The initial plan was to carry the scientists and their gear to the island using one of our two Sikorsky HH-52A Seaguard helicopters; however, visibility was poor, so the group was transported to the island by our LCVP (Landing Craft, Vehicle, Personnel). The attempted landing was a

Botched LCVP landing, Gibbs Island. (Courtesy of US Coast Guard Archives)

near catastrophe. The LCVP broached (turned sideways) in the surf and dumped almost everyone into the icy waters. The LCVP had to be abandoned. In spite of the bad weather, the landing party, a total of seventeen people, had to be rescued from the island by helicopter.

Aboard ship, all I knew at first was that something had gone seriously wrong. I feared the worst. People could have easily suffered fractured bones, dislocated shoulders, severe hypothermia. Fortunately, there were no serious injuries—only a handful of people suffering from moderate overexposure. We treated them with "cold weather rations," the cheap mini-bottles of liquor we stocked in sick bay. They are an effective treatment for mild cases of hypothermia in that the burning taste of the liquor going down makes the patients temporarily forget about their shivering. The important thing was that they were standing in a warm room while sipping the liquor.

If they had actually suffered severe hypothermia, the treatment would have been quite different. Alcohol causes slight dilation of peripheral blood vessels, which is not what you want when you are trying to warm critical organs. If they had suffered from major hypothermia, we would have dressed them in dry clothes, wrapped them in blankets, and given them warm fluids to drink. We would not have immersed them in warm water, because rapid warming can trigger a heart arrhythmia.

The botched landing was a bad sign—at least, it was for me. It was essentially our first mission in the Antarctic, and it had been a disaster. Was this a harbinger of things to come?

12

Elephant Island

On our way to resupply Palmer Station, we briefly stopped at Elephant Island, just north of Gibbs Island, to off-load Dr. Dalziel's crew and supplies. Although the Gibbs Island landing had been an abysmal failure, Dr. Dalziel and his crew could still do meaningful geological studies on Elephant Island. This time men and supplies were successfully transferred with our helicopters. The *Glacier* did not attempt to land them with its boats.

Elephant Island was tremendously important for Shackleton and his twenty-eight-man crew. It was the first solid land they had touched in 497 days—after being at sea, losing their ship, and living on the unstable ice pack for 156 days.

Shackleton and his crew had had no choice. The Antarctic summer was ending in late March of 1916, and the ice pack, which had drifted to the north and warmer temperatures, was breaking up beneath them. After abandoning it, they took to their three whaleboats. They spent six days exhausting themselves while rowing in icy and treacherous seas. After continuous rowing—totally exposed to the elements, battling currents, and dodging pack ice that easily could have destroyed them—they finally reached Elephant Island. Had they not reached the island when they did on April 15, 1916, several men likely would have died from overexposure and hypothermia.

If the *Glacier* had sunk in open water near the Antarctic Peninsula and we'd been able to transfer to our auxiliary boats, we would have had an easier time than Shackleton and his crew, as we would have had motorized boats, including a 39-foot Arctic Survey Boat (ASB) and a Zodiac inflatable with an outboard engine. These two crafts could have towed the additional inflatable life rafts we would have needed to accommodate the entire crew. However, our ASB did not have a double hull, which meant we would have faced dangers similar to what Shackleton and his crew faced in their rigid-sided whaleboats. We would have had to be very careful about dodging pack ice and icebergs, particularly smaller car-sized pieces that can be hard to see, yet still cause significant damage. If we'd had to use our survey boat to land on an island, I hope we would have done better than we did trying to land on Gibbs Island.

It surprises me to learn that many people have either never heard about Sir Ernest Shackleton or know very little about him. I will give readers a thumbnail sketch of what Shackleton did after reaching Elephant Island, in hopes that they will want to read more about this incredible story of survival. It is also an example of superb leadership, and the sea conditions we faced—both relevant to my story.

Shackleton converted one of his whaleboats, the *James Caird*, into a semi-enclosed, 22-foot sailboat in which he and five crewmembers sailed northwest 650 miles (1,050 km) to South Georgia Island. One of the

The *James Caird* leaving Elephant Island. (Courtesy of Library of Congress and Wikimedia Commons; photograph probably taken by Frank Hurley)

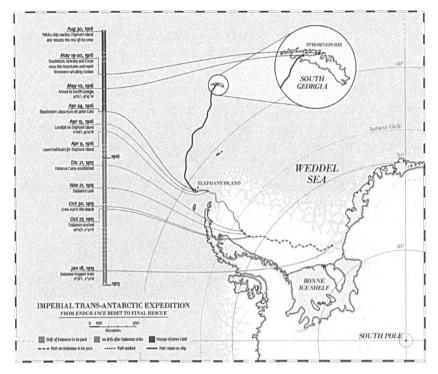

(Courtesy of Wikipedia and Lucca Ferrario of Density Design Research Lab)

sailors he took with him was a man he felt would be bad for the morale of the people remaining of the island. His overall concern for the entire crew was paramount. The three-week voyage aboard the *James Caird*, which was beyond heroic, ended on May 10, 1916. During the voyage they encountered multiple horrific storms and severe icing. During one of the storms they were flipped end over end after being struck by a rogue wave—the kind of wave that killed a sailor on the USCGC *Polar Star* (see chapter 25), and of particular concern for us aboard the *Glacier*.

After landing on South Georgia Island, Shackleton and two crewmembers hiked 29 miles and climbed 10,000-foot peaks, without climbing gear, for thirty-six hours, over an uncharted expanse, in order to reach the whaling station on the other side. (See *The Pursuit of* Endurance: *On the Shoulders of Shackleton* by Luc Hardy, listed in the bibliography.) Upon reaching the whaling station, Shackleton and his men were taken to see the manager of the station. Although Shackleton knew the man rather well, by that time he was in such sorry shape he was unrecognizable. When Shackleton had to tell him who he was, the manager reportedly broke into tears.

After reaching the whaling station, it took another three and a half months and multiple attempts before Shackleton was able to get a ship to Elephant Island to rescue all of his men. He was so relieved to see that they were all alive that according to one of his crewmembers, "years literally seemed to drop from him."

Two years after losing their ship, camping on the ice pack, rowing and sailing in open boats, and living on a barren Antarctic island, they had all survived—largely due to the strength and quality of Shackleton's leadership.

I did not get a chance to set foot on Elephant Island myself. I would have felt privileged to have walked the same shore as Shackleton and his brave men.

Dr. Dalziel and his crew were there to do geological studies. Apparently, some of the work Dr. Dalziel and his men completed provided additional evidence that Antarctica was once part of the South American continent, during a time when it was much warmer, and habitable. In a sense, the fabled Terra Australis Incognita once existed, although it preceded the myth by millions of years.

13

Antarctica

Prior to seeing Antarctica, I had no clear idea of what to expect. I'd not given the matter much thought. After all, I'd volunteered for the trip primarily because I wanted to see all of those exotic places—Tahiti, Australia, New Zealand, etc.—those ports "always" visited by Antarctica-bound Coast Guard icebreakers. My preconception was that Antarctica was going to look something like Minnesota in the winter, only without the lakes and the trees. In fact, about the only macroscopic plant life you'll find on the Antarctic continent are low-growing lichens and mosses in the far northern regions.

In one sense, I'd imagined Antarctica being little more than a large block of ice. My preconceptions were ridiculously wrong. When we reached the Antarctic Peninsula, one thing was patently clear: The continent's natural beauty is breathtaking.

The Antarctic Peninsula is rugged, mountainous, and majestic. Approximately 1,000 miles long, it is a continuation of the Andes mountain chain. The seas along it do not roll onto sandy beaches; they crash onto sloping or vertical faces of rock and ice. Your eyes naturally follow the path of broken patches of sea ice until your gaze fixes on the soaring walls of ice or dark rock, often lined with brilliant streaks of snow and glacial ice. Only 2 percent of Antarctica is exposed rock, but a good portion is on the Antarctic Peninsula. Even where snow and ice cover the ridges and mountains, there remains a contrast between fractured and fissured ice, next to subtle gradations of angular whiteness. The soaring peaks are backed by ever-changing skies. And when the weather is fine and clear, the skies are cobalt blue—deep, rich, and pure.

A northern portion of the Antarctic Peninsula. (Photo by Gail Bunes)

Everywhere you look there are fantastic formations of ice, ranging from fields of broken sea ice to icebergs larger than Rhode Island. In 1956, *Glacier* spotted an iceberg 60 miles wide and 208 miles long (100 by 335 km). Imagine being in a car, traveling at 60 miles per hour on top of an iceberg, and needing an hour to cross it the short way. It would require a propeller-driven plane the same amount of time to traverse it the long way.

The large icebergs typically have sheer faces rising 100 feet or more. The continental ice shelves, in turn, dwarf them. At the edge of the continent, these ice shelves float on the surface of the sea and extend outward for many miles—so much so that they increase the size of the continent by about 25 percent. Their fissured, layered, and faceted walls look like abrupt cliffs, rising up to 150 feet or more above the sea. The ice shelves are the terminal portions of glaciers forming in the center of the continent, some of which can be up to 10,000 feet thick.

Eventually, the edges of these ice shelves break off into the ocean in a process called calving. The sound of this rupturing can echo like the shot from a cannon. Each year over 300 cubic miles of ice break off and

A tourist ship off the Antarctic Peninsula. (Photo by Gail Bunes)

join the armada of bergs circling the continent. The water contained in these bergs is equal to about one-half of the world's annual drinking-water usage.

The surface of the sea is a constantly changing dance of ice forms. Sun, wind, and water constantly reshape the icebergs. An almost endless variety of shapes occur as a result. When the bottom of a berg melts away sufficiently, the berg turns upside down, revealing forms like the turrets of a castle, or the curves and contours of a modern sculpture. Contrasting layers graphically stripe the sides of some of the bergs. At times, one can see broad blue and white stripes, almost zebra-like, arranged vertically or diagonally. Or one can see more-realistic sculptures, like the one seen at right in a photo taken by my

(Photo by Bea Weingart)

(Photo by Gail Bunes)

mother-in-law. (What was she thinking?) An intrepid traveler, she first traveled to Antarctica when she was seventy-five, and liked it so much she went again a few years later.

Just as there are no two snowflakes alike, the same holds true for icebergs—though you don't need a magnifying glass to appreciate their intricate beauty. Every shade of white, blue, gray, green, and black is part of their color palette, as well as any reflected color in a sunset. And the character of the light can vary from opaque fog to arc-light brilliance. What cannot be seen is the underside of the iceberg, which may be five to six times larger than the visible portion.

The *Glacier*'s captain from 1980 to 1982, Captain James W. "Bill" Coste Jr., told me that he felt the two most beautiful places in the world were Antarctica and the Grand Canyon. I have rafted the entire length of the Grand Canyon, and would agree that it's one of the most beautiful places in the world. Beauty, of course, is in the eye of the beholder. In my view, Antarctica's beauty is world-class, just like that of the Grand Canyon. Antarctica differs in that it has so much more readily visible wildlife in its coastal portions, particularly the many kinds of birds, seals, and penguins. The combination, to my mind, is unbeatable.

Antarctica is the coldest place in the world. Its lowest temperature ever reliably recorded is -129.3 degrees Fahrenheit (-89.6 degrees Celsius), noted in July of 1983 at Vostok, one of the Russian bases. At that temperature, carbon dioxide begins to freeze. In temperatures anywhere near that level, it is necessary to breathe through a heated snorkel tube in order to protect your lungs.

Having been born and raised in Minnesota, I was no stranger to extreme cold weather. One day during a 2014 cold snap, it was actually colder in Minnesota than it was at the North Pole. When it gets to 30 below zero Fahrenheit in Minnesota, it is tolerable for five to ten minutes, assuming one is warmly dressed. After that, it gets really uncomfortable. But 30 degrees below zero would be unseasonably mild during the middle of an Antarctica winter.

Antarctica is also, by far, the windiest continent, the site of the highest sustained winds ever recorded, at 199 mph! According to the *Guinness Book of World Records*, the place with the highest average winds on Earth is Commonwealth Bay in Antarctica (close to where the Russian icebreaker, the *Akademik Shokalskiy*, discussed in the introduction, was trapped). Steady winds there often blow at 150 miles per hour (250 km/h). One of the reasons why Antarctica is so windy is because the cold, dense air in the 9,000-foot-high central plateau descends along the sloping glaciers, picking up speed as it goes, creating the infamous katabatic winds. From the Greek word *katabasis*, meaning "descending," these are essentially drainage winds powered by gravity that reach average speeds of 50 miles per hour (80 km/h).

On average, Antarctica is the highest continent. The mean elevation of Antarctica is 7,500 feet. This is due to the vast ice cap covering the continent. Ice sheets 13,000 to 15,000 feet thick cover large parts of East Antarctica. The deepest ice is 15,669 feet (4,776 meters). The ice is so thick and heavy that it pushes large parts of the continent below sea level. The average elevation of the continental landmass in West Antarctica is 1,444 feet below sea level. Were it not for the weight of all the ice, this same land would be above sea level.

If all of the ice in Antarctica melted—on a continent larger than the United States and Mexico combined—the sea levels worldwide would rise approximately 160 to 200 feet (50–60 m). Low-lying states such as Florida would virtually disappear. Given that many of the world's major cities are seaports, the effects would be catastrophic.

Despite all of the snow and ice on Antarctica, it is surprising that it is also the world's driest continent. Large central portions of the continent receive slightly more moisture than the Sahara Desert. It does not snow very much in Antarctica, but the majority of snow that falls does not melt. As a result, most of the snow one sees in Antarctica is wind-blown rather than newly created. This type of snow has the consistency of talcum powder because of the dryness and low humidity. It gets into everything, as the fierce winds will blow it through the smallest crack. The remainder of the snow accumulates and turns into ice.

The people who work in Antarctica, or spend a good deal of time on the continent, call it "The Ice." Having grown up in Minnesota, I thought I knew a fair amount about ice; I can easily name half a dozen different kinds, including "black ice"—that almost invisible coating on roads responsible for more than a few fender benders. But the variety of ice found in Antarctica is truly staggering. Stephen Pyne's book about Antarctica, titled *The Ice*, lists eighty different kinds, including forty-seven types that either touch the sea or are part of it. And this overwhelming list doesn't even include the kinds of ice with which we are most familiar, like ice cubes and icicles. I'm not surprised that Pyne failed to mention black ice, as there are no roadways in Antarctica.

If you want to see penguins, go to Antarctica. They are there by the tens of thousands, particularly along the coasts and in the ocean. Of the seventeen different types of penguins known to exist in the world, seven are found in Antarctica. That group includes king, emperor, gentoo, Adélie, chinstrap, rockhopper, and macaroni penguins. We mostly saw Adélie penguins, named by French explorer Jules Dumont d'Urville for his wife, Adélie. The coast of Antarctica is the only place where Adélie penguins

98

(Photo by Gail Bunes)

reside, whereas others, such as rockhoppers, are also found in South America and South Africa.

Penguins are amazing and delightful creatures. Although they are almost comically awkward on land, they are incredibly graceful in water and can reach swimming speeds of 25 miles per hour (40 km/h). Some can reach depths of 1,000 feet (300 m) or more, although they prefer shallower dives. They can stay submerged for up to twenty-five minutes. They may spend 75 percent of their lives at sea, but they have a homing instinct that enables them to return to their original breeding ground year after year.

I did not spend much time trying to differentiate between the various types of penguins. With their diverse antics and talents, I found them all entertaining to watch. You see them flying out of the water, like salmon jumping a dam, trying to get up onto a low ice shelf. On land they waddle along with their Charlie Chaplin–like gait, in the tuxedos Mother Nature gave them, or you see them tobogganing along on their bellies, their little feet pinwheeling the ice behind them.

Since adult penguins have no land-based predators, they do not have a natural fear of humans. Although it is illegal to approach or bother them, if you stand or sit quietly in one place, there's a good chance they will approach you, as they are quite curious.

Antarctica is also a good place for birdwatching. Including penguins, there are forty-five different species of birds found there. The southernmost include Wilson's storm petrel, the snow petrel, the Antarctic petrel, and the south polar skua. The latter bird has been seen as far inland as the South Pole.

You can also find five different types of albatross in Antarctica. Of these, the wandering albatross is the most common. It has the largest wingspan—up to 11.5 feet—of any bird in the world. Albatrosses spend most of their life in flight. They can remain airborne for several hours at a time without flapping their wings.

For myself, and I think for most sailors, albatrosses are special birds. When one is on a lonely stretch of ocean, far from land and home, it is very comforting and engaging to be joined by an albatross. It's a pleasure to be with another natural being in the middle of nowhere. Watching a soaring and gliding bird helps break up the monotony of a seemingly limitless ocean. I think the albatross feels the same way. I frequently marveled at how a single bird would parallel our path for such long periods. They did not fly with us merely because we were throwing them scraps of food; they obviously liked it for reasons I can only assume were rather similar to our own.

Once we reached the Peninsula, we headed southwest through Bransfield Strait, the passage between the northern tip of the Antarctica Peninsula and the South Shetland Islands.

This strait bears the name of Edward Bransfield, an Englishman who captained a brig called the *Williams*. On January 30, 1820, he sighted land at latitude 64 degrees, which he thought was the Antarctica continent, but he did not attempt a landing. While he was probably the first to see that portion of the continent, he wasn't the first to see Antarctica. That honor goes to Thaddeus Bellingshausen, the Russian captain who, only three days before Bransfield, reached 69° 21' S, 2° 14' W, within 20 miles of the continent. Bellingshausen described "an ice field covered with small

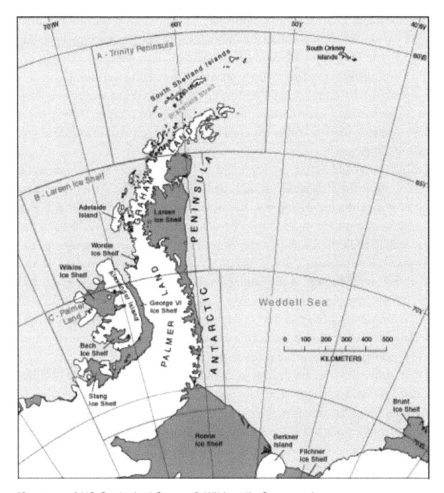

(Courtesy of US Geological Survey & Wikimedia Commons)

hillocks." At the time, he did not realize that he was seeing a continent. In fact, it was not until the 1950s that Bellingshausen finally received official credit for his discovery.

Americans like to claim that the sealer Nathaniel Palmer first sighted the continent, but his sighting reportedly occurred on November 16, 1820. Less than three months later, John Davis, an American sealer who said he was "on a cruise to find new Lands," was probably the first person to actually set foot on the continent. Davis wrote in his logbook, "I think this Southern Land to be a Continent." It was more than one hundred years later, in 1935, that the first woman set foot on Antarctica—Caroline Mikkelsen, the wife of a Norwegian explorer.

Since sealers tended to be a secretive bunch, Davis likely did not know about Palmer's claims, nor could he reasonably justify that what he had seen was a continent rather than a group of islands. It took more than a century before it was conclusively determined that Antarctica was indeed a continent.

When we were there in 1969 and 1970, we referred to the Antarctic Peninsula as the Palmer Peninsula, which had been the American name for over a century. In England, the peninsula was called Graham Land, the name given to it in 1832 by a British sealer, John Biscoe. What I did not realize back then was that the official name had been changed to the Antarctic Peninsula in 1964, based on an agreement between the UK and the USA, with the tip of the peninsula designated as Graham Land and the base of the peninsula as Palmer Land. In Chile, the official name of the peninsula is O'Higgins Land. Argentina, which has more bases on the peninsula than any other nation, including bases with families, children, and schools, calls the area Tierra de San Martín.

In order to avoid major territorial disputes, the general policy of those countries—and certainly the US policy—has been to neither officially grant nor deny any territorial claim to the continent. It is kind of a "Don't ask, don't tell" policy. If it is ever formally decided to partition Antarctica, the nearest neighbors, Argentina and Chile, will probably aggressively assert their territorial claims.

The weather was clear and mild as we sailed through the northern portion of the Bransfield Strait. I spent a good deal of time on deck watching the magnificent scenery and enjoying the warmth of the sun. I was wearing a jacket, but if we had been anchored and there wasn't much breeze, I would've been comfortable in a light sweater. It was such a peaceful and idyllic setting. On days like these, sailing in relatively clear waters, it was hard to imagine a ship ever getting into serious trouble.

14

The Mighty *Glacier*

As we traveled farther south toward the US base at Palmer Station, the *Glacier* started to encounter heavier concentrations of ice pack. It was early January 1970, and the beginning of our most important mission: heavy-duty icebreaking to create a channel through the ice pack wide enough to allow vital supply ships to reach Palmer Station. The path we cut had to be secure, as the supply ships coming after us were not heavy-duty, ice-rated vessels. If we were unable to create this channel, the base would have to wait at least another year for fuel, supplies, and new personnel.

Luckily, we had an ice-busting behemoth made for the job.

The *Glacier* was commissioned on May 27, 1955. At the time—and for many years afterward—it was the free world's largest and most powerful icebreaker. It was designed to break sea ice up to 20 feet (6 m) thick. Built in Pascagoula, Mississippi, by Ingalls Shipbuilding, it was considered a prototype in icebreaker construction—but not because of its curved steel bow. This thick curved bow, which enabled the ship to ride up on the ice and break through it with its weight, was commonly found in other icebreakers.

In fact, the curved shape of *Glacier*'s hull was based on an earlier design by Norwegian explorer Fridtjof Nansen. His ship, the *Fram*, launched in 1892, was designed so that it would be forced up and out of the ice pack if confronted with crushing pressure. The design proved effective during a three-year drift of the *Fram* in the Arctic ice pack. The *Fram* was the ship Nansen's fellow countryman, Roald Amundsen, used to sail to Antarctica when he became the first person to reach the South

USCGC *Glacier*, circa 1980. (Courtesy of Captain James Coste Jr.)

Pole on December 14, 1911. The *Fram* still holds the record for the combined farthest north to farthest south voyages. (Full disclosure: I have a bias toward Norwegian and/or Viking exploits, as by my ancestry, I am three-fourths Norwegian.)

What distinguished the *Glacier* from other icebreakers was its power. With almost a 9,000-ton displacement and maximum propulsion of 21,000 horsepower, it had almost twice the power of most other icebreakers of its era. Her twin propellers, each two stories high, were driven by a pair of 108-ton, 900-volt motors. When built, these 15-foot-tall propulsion motors were the largest single-armature, direct-current motors ever put into a vessel. The two propulsion motors were driven by electricity produced by ten generators. In turn, the generators were powered by ten Fairbanks-Morse, opposed-piston, 12-cylinder diesel engines, each developing 2,400 horsepower. Her top speed was 18.6 knots.

When she was launched in 1954, the *Glacier* carried the largest diesel-electric plant "afloat in the free world." The power created by its generators was enough to light a small city. The fact that a pair of large DC motors drove the propellers meant there was much finer and quicker delivery of power to the props than if they had been driven solely by direct connection to diesel engines. That electrically generated power is why a 2011 Tesla roadster 2.5 S can go from zero to 60 in 3.7 seconds—or why a slow-moving icebreaker in tight conditions can quickly deliver torque power in order to stop, reverse, turn, or accelerate forward. Also, using an electromagnetic force to spin the driveshaft—rather than a totally mechanical linkage—helped to protect the ship's drivetrain from the shocks caused by large chunks of ice jamming the propellers.

For a 310-foot-long ship with a 74-foot beam, the *Glacier* was incredibly maneuverable, particularly important for following twisting leads in the ice pack. The steering gear enabled her to move her rudder hard over—from 30 degrees on one side to 30 degrees on the other—within

In the foreground, the USS *Glacier,* along with the USS *Burton Island* and the USS *Atka,* pushing an iceberg blocking the channel at McMurdo Station, December 1965. (NavSource Online)

twenty seconds. At a speed of 17.1 knots, a hard turn created 7,500,000 pounds of rudder torque, although the steering gear was designed to handle almost three times that amount of force.

In addition to her pioneering, diesel-electric propulsion, *Glacier* also had a number of other features not previously found in icebreakers. She was the first to have an enclosed conning tower with total pilothouse functions. One person, 74 feet above the waterline, could have the same control over the ship as someone on the bridge. Previous icebreakers had had to rely on communication between the helmsman, often on the bridge wing, and the conning officer, who had engine controls.

Earlier-model icebreakers had an exposed helicopter pad where maintenance crews would have to do their work. In contrast, the *Glacier* had an insulated, steam-heated hangar large enough for two helicopters, as well as a complete workshop. For scientific work, she was the only icebreaker equipped with the tools needed for doing deep-sea coring and various other oceanographic studies.

The *Glacier*'s welded outer hull was 1.625 inches thick at the bow—almost twice as thick as the steel plating of an average ship. Specially designed, low-carbon steel was used in the hull. It had excellent low-temperature strength as well as good tensile and fatigue properties. Furthermore, it was easy to weld, given the foregone conclusion that the ship would take a beating and require periodic repairs. The lighter interior hull was joined to the heavier exterior hull by strut framing as well as transverse and longitudinal bulkheads. The tanks for fuel and water storage occupied the space between the two hulls.

In addition, some of the tanks could be used for "heeling" operations. If the *Glacier* became locked in the ice, she could use this heeling system to transfer approximately 320 tons of seawater from one side to the other in eighty-five seconds, rolling the ship back and forth 10 degrees.

The *Glacier* was the only one of its kind ever built. The 120,000-member American Society of Mechanical Engineers (ASME) nominated it a "Historic Mechanical Engineering Landmark." To qualify for such an award, the recipient must, among other things, "represent a progressive step in the evolution of mechanical engineering and its significance to society in general."

When first commissioned by the US Navy, the USS *Glacier* (AGB 4) was painted gray and equipped with large deck guns. In 1966, she was painted white and transferred to the Coast Guard, by which time most of her armaments had been removed. Three years later, her 5-inch guns were also removed. In 1973, the USCGC *Glacier* became the first icebreaker to be painted red to improve its visibility.

Whether she was painted red, white, or gray, with the US Navy or the Coast Guard, the *Glacier* made history. In 1955, during her maiden voyage, she served as the flagship for Admiral Richard Byrd as part of the first Operation Deep Freeze, the name given to US operations in Antarctica, operations that have continued every year since. She played a critical part in establishing a baseline camp at McMurdo Sound in the Ross Sea of Antarctica in 1955. In subsequent years she helped the McMurdo base become the biggest on the continent.

Over the years, the *Glacier* transported many scientists to field stations and permanent stations, including those that helped to discover the Van Allen radiation belt in Earth's upper atmosphere. Due to her advanced capabilities, the ship functioned as the platform for a number of pioneering oceanographic studies. And because of her size and power, she made a number of significant Antarctic penetrations and landings—sailing deeper into Antarctica than any icebreaker had ever gone before.

The *Glacier* could steadily sail through sea ice 3 to 4 feet thick without much difficulty. That kind of ice would be pushed aside as the ship plowed straight through. Thicker ice sometimes required a backing and ramming operation—backing the vessel two to three ship lengths and then accelerating forward into the ice.

The sailors at the controls during typical icebreaking activities usually loved it. Captain Coste, commanding officer of the *Glacier* between 1980 and 1982, gave one reason why it was so enjoyable: "It's so fricking much fun to hit something as hard as you want." He described it as being so different from normal sailing, when he had to be careful not to hit anything. This long-ago-retired CO added, "I would go there again in a flash if I could bust ice."

Glacier rescuing the Belgian *Polarhaf*, Breid Bay, Antarctica, 1959. (NavSource Online)

Ensign David Frydenlund, a science officer aboard the *Glacier*, said, "Breaking ice, with such huge horsepower in your control, it gives you a surge." Sometimes "balls to the wall" acceleration was required to smash into the ice. Captain McCrory described the feeling as being like "driving a high-powered sports car." Ensign Frydenlund was complimentary about the thorough and patient teaching he received from Captain McCrory about icebreaking techniques.

Although sailors at the helm generally love to bust ice, they have to be careful when breaking heavy ice. If they just plow straight ahead as hard as they can, they run the risk of getting the ship hung up, or "fetched up," on the ice. A wave of water can be pushed forward onto the ice by the bow and then suddenly freeze. The bottom of the hull can stick to the ice, just like a wet tongue sticks to a frozen window. If this happens, the helmsman has to somehow shake the ship loose. Moving water from one heeling tank to another, like swishing water from one full cheek to the other, often allows the ship to rock and tilt enough to break loose. Alternating power to the props, from hard right to hard left, is another technique. This gets the vessel "fishtailing," and usually breaks it free. Whichever technique one uses, it is important to react quickly, because the longer one takes, the more freezing can occur between the ice and the hull. Sometimes the only way to free a ship is to bury "deadmen" ice anchors into the ice pack and then use winches or towing engines to break the seal enough so the ship can back out.

One of the ways to avoid getting stuck is to cut into the ice at a 45-degree angle in one direction, back off, cut into the ice pack at 45 degrees in the opposite direction, back off, and then go straight forward. This triple-cut technique follows a "chicken foot" pattern. This method typically breaks the ice pack into two pieces. In addition, this procedure, also called "herringboning," creates a wider channel, making it easier to displace and move adjacent ice.

Two ships working together can employ a different technique known as "railroad tracking." The ships work in unison about 50 yards apart. Ship A rams into the ice a short distance and then stops; then Ship B rams into the ice. Typically, this technique cracks the ice between the two ships and gives them both more room to maneuver. After repeated backing, ramming, and freeing each other, the ice pattern behind them looks like a railroad track with ties.

One of the common problems *Glacier* and other icebreakers experience is damaging their props while backing out of the ice. According to Captain Coste, the best way to protect the props is to make sure they are going forward. "The trailing edge of the prop is thin when you're in reverse," he said. The obvious question then is, "How do you back out of freshly broken ice pack without going into reverse?" The short answer is "technique and gravity."

The basic technique is to thrust forward just far enough up onto the ice so that the ship will slide backward—propelled by gravity after the power is decreased, even with the props going slightly forward. When done properly, the ship progresses in an efficient rhythm.

The *Glacier* had an advantage over the smaller Wind-class icebreakers because the sailor up in the conning tower, 74 feet above the ocean's surface, could see whether there was significant ice behind the ship. In contrast, the Wind-class icebreakers, with controls only on the bridge or bridge wings, needed a deck watch officer with a view of the ship's stern to relay information. If there were no "growlers" (car-sized berg chunks) or shelf ice behind the ship, then the conning officer could safely reverse the engines.

In his book *Polar Operations*, Captain Edwin A. MacDonald described another prop-protecting technique for icebreakers. Captain MacDonald was the former captain of the icebreaker *Burton Island* when it was with the navy. He also served as deputy commander of Antarctica Operation Deep Freeze and task group commander of the Weddell Sea Group. After retiring from the navy, he became director of ship and polar operations for Lindblad Travel, Inc. Given his vast experience, I felt comfortable relying on him as an expert in his field. In his book, he wrote: "The conning officer, after determining that the ship is not 'stuck,' may decide to keep the bow against the ice and turn the propellers over at moderate speed ahead. This action will provide more open waters astern through which to back down before the next charge, as the powerful prop wash can drive an appreciable amount of ice aft."

Busting ice with an icebreaker is an art form. However, unlike most art forms, doing it poorly or improperly can leave one stranded or disabled in the middle of a hostile environment—like deep in the Weddell Sea.

15

The Weddell Sea

On January 8, 1970, we arrived at Palmer Station, located on Anvers Island (64.46° S, 64.05 W) on the west side of the Antarctic Peninsula. It is the only US research station in Antarctica north of the Antarctic Circle. Initially built in 1968, there were a number of unfinished construction projects for our Navy Seabee passengers.

Palmer Station is small compared to the main US station at McMurdo Sound. During the summer the Palmer Station can hold up to forty-six people, but only about fifteen to twenty remain during the winter. When we were there in 1970, it consisted of several dark green buildings that

Palmer Station, 1970. (Courtesy of US Coast Guard Archives)

appeared to be simply but solidly built. The buildings rest on a barren rocky slope. Unlike McMurdo, it did not have a landing strip for airplanes. Most of the science research done at Palmer Station revolves around marine biology. It also has year-round monitoring equipment for measuring atmospheric, seismic, and ultraviolet radiation changes.

I wondered what it would be like to spend the winter there. It did not look very inviting. At least it was a permanent site; some of the other US bases in Antarctica were built on inland ice pack and were in constant motion, albeit at a glacial rate. Eventually, some of the older bases sank into the ice and drifted out to sea long after they had been abandoned.

Our focus at Palmer was the off-loading of about 23,000 pounds of supplies and most of our new passengers. We transferred passengers and supplies with the aid of our helicopters and a small research ship, the *R/V Hero*. The crew worked ten- to sixteen-hour days for three full days to get the job done.

Palmer had a good bulkhead pier. Ernest Hemingway's wife had used that same pier for fishing. I heard that the one fish she caught was small, bony, and not good to eat. I also heard that there were not that many different kinds of fish in Antarctica, which is not true. Apparently, not much was known about fishing in Antarctica at that time. In fact, there are over one hundred different kinds of fish in these waters, but most are small and not fished commercially. But there are exceptions, like the Patagonian toothfish, which can weigh up to 220 pounds. In restaurants, this same fish, or its close relative, the Antarctic toothfish, is generally called Chilean sea bass.

Corpsman Joe was impressed with all the seals in the area of Palmer Station. Seals are a common sight in Antarctica, often lying on ice floes in small groups. Different types include Ross, crabeater, and leopard; the Weddell seal is the only one that spends the entire year in Antarctic waters. It can dive up to 2,000 feet (600 meters) in search of food and stay underwater for as long as forty minutes. Unlike humans, it does not suffer from "the bends"—nitrogen bubbles blocking capillary blood flow, following deep and prolonged dives. Studying Weddell seals could help us understand how our bodies might better utilize oxygen.

(Photo by Gail Bunes)

While we were at Palmer Station, rumors started circulating about the *Glacier* going to McMurdo Station, because one of the other Coast Guard icebreakers had broken down. If we did go there, it meant a longer deployment, or maybe a short stop in New Zealand—a place I longed to see.

We later learned that the damaged icebreaker was going to New Zealand under its own power to get a prop replaced, and that its crew would have a long layover there. I was envious. I had heard many stories about the Kiwis' legendary hospitality. They typically would be at the docks waiting to treat our sailors to a good home-cooked meal. And then there were the welcoming young women—in fact, one of our helicopter pilots married a fair lassie he had met there on a previous trip.

After resupplying Palmer, we again headed north, departing on January 11, 1970. We traveled on a course parallel to the spine of the Antarctic Peninsula. Our main goal was to provide support for additional scientific missions, including a "Status and Population Dynamics of Antarctic Seals" study headed by Dr. Albert Erickson of the University of Minnesota, and a "Biologic Productivity of Antarctica Waters" study headed by Dr. Sayed El-Sayed of Texas A&M.

Dr. Erickson, or "Al," as he was known to his friends, was a particularly delightful shipmate. He had a great sense of humor and a jolly disposition. Although he was a serious scientist, he also knew how to have a good time. One of the secondary experiments in which he was involved was testing out a new, superthick wet suit. The designers of this wet suit claimed it would keep divers comfortable for an hour, even in subfreezing Antarctic waters.

Twenty minutes after this experiment had begun, I saw Al back on deck.

"What happened?" I asked him. "I thought the suits were good for an hour."

"That's what they said, but . . ."

"But, what?"

"After about fifteen minutes, I could feel my balls shrinking to about the size of a pea, and, well, I just started thinking . . ." He had a big sheepish grin on his face. This former marine was willing to make certain sacrifices for science, but there was a limit.

⌐ ⌐

The following day, we transited Antarctic Sound—the gap between the northeastern tip of the Antarctic Peninsula and the Joinville Island group—and entered the Weddell Sea. We encountered the northern edge of the Weddell Sea ice pack at 64 degrees south. The ice pack was dense—six to eight "oktas" of ice. An okta is a unit of measurement used to indicate the percentage of surface coverage, but it is not a measure of thickness or density of the ice. Imagine a pie cut into eight equal pieces: The surface of one piece, or one-eighth of the surface, is equal to one okta. Four (out of eight) oktas represents 50 percent of the sea surface covered in ice. We were in an area that was 75 to 100 percent covered, compared to the edge of the ice pack by Palmer Station, which was three to five oktas. Thus, the dense ice pack of the Weddell Sea extended all the way to the northern tip of the Antarctic Peninsula, far north of the Antarctic Circle, giving us our first indication that the Weddell Sea was a far different area than the seas west of the Peninsula.

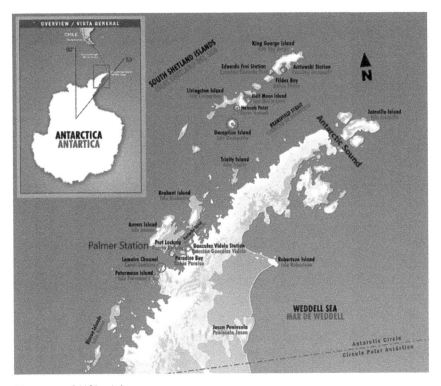

(Courtesy of UCI.edu)

The Weddell Sea is named after James Weddell, a Scottish sealer, who in 1823 was the first person known to have sailed into this body of water. He picked a good year because it was incredibly free of ice. He and his twenty-two-man crew aboard the brig *Jane* reached 72 degrees south latitude in February. In his log he noted how the surface of the sea was covered with birds and spouting whales. In large print, he exclaimed, "NOT A PARTICLE OF ICE IN ANY DESCRIPTION WAS TO BE SEEN."

Weddell had sailed enough to know how unusual it was to see so little ice in Antarctic waters. He continued sailing south, and two days later reached 74° 15' S latitude, 34° 16' W longitude. This exceeded the record previously set by Captain James Cook in 1773 by over 200 miles.

Nearly one hundred years would pass before anyone exceeded Weddell's "farthest south" record in the sea bearing his name. In fact, one historian, William Herbert Hobbs, wrongly called Weddell a "fake explorer." Hobbs, an American geologist, described as "colorful" and "ever happy and enthusiastic in controversy," felt Weddell's southern penetration record was impossible. Hobbs was the author of an article, "The Pack-Ice of the Weddell Sea," written in 1939, so it can be assumed he knew a fair amount about the topic.

Due to the heavy ice concentrations created there every winter—and lasting through much of the summer—the Weddell Sea is known as "The Cold Factory." Ice-free waters deep in the Weddell Sea are about as common as snow in Miami (where it has snowed only twice in recorded history).

Rare things do happen, however.

Although Weddell and his crew had amazingly good fortune in 1823, their attempt to penetrate the same region the following year proved far more typical. Weddell was halted almost 100 miles short of his destination by heavy pack ice. He searched for an opening for several weeks but failed to find one, and then was caught in a gale-force storm. There was a high swell, dense fog, and heavy ice. He wrote, "We fell in with many ice islands, some of which, by the heaviness of the sea around us, were rolling with the noise of an earthquake." The winds increased to hurricane force and everything not firmly secured was swept from the *Jane's* deck, which quickly became coated with thick layers of ice.

Weddell and his crew survived the storm, but one week later, while skirting the edge of the pack ice, they struck an iceberg with considerable force. Much to Weddell's amazement, he could not find any signs of leakage in his wooden hull, which was only 2.5 inches thick. Later, when the ship went into dry dock, he found that the berg had shoved the bottom planking inward, where it lodged firmly between two thick timbers that were part of the vessel's sturdy wooden frame. Had Weddell not had this stroke of good fortune, the blow undoubtedly would have sunk his ship.

In 1838 a French explorer, J. S. C. Dumont d'Urville, attempted to penetrate the Weddell Sea. When he first encountered the ice conditions there, he described them as being "austere and grandiose beyond words." He added that the sight "filled us with an involuntary feeling of dread." He was able to make some headway into the ice pack, but it quickly started closing in on him. His sailors had to use picks and crow-bars to escape. They did not come close to crossing the Antarctic Circle.

Not long after d'Urville, an American expedition under the command of Charles Wilkes hoped to sail into the Weddell Sea. After nine days of trying to deal with dense fog, fierce gales, massive icebergs, and dense sea ice, Wilkes had to turn back. His failure was even worse than d'Urville's.

The lessons of history indicated that the odds of completing a voyage in this formidable sea, without encountering major problems, were simi-lar to going through a lifetime without ever having a minor car accident.

On January 13, 1970, Joe recorded, "It was hard sleeping last night because of all the noise the ship was making while breaking through the ice."

Light sleepers do not do well on a ship crunching and crashing through heavy pack ice. For the most part, I slept rather well—in spite of the noise—because of an earlier experience. During my first year of medical school, I shared a one-room efficiency apartment in a converted pickle factory, next to eight sets of railroad tracks. Switching engines worked those tracks night and day. They shuffled around large freight cars—certain cars, for a certain track, for a certain locomotive, going to a certain place. All of this shuffling created a wall of sound. Sometimes the sound of freight cars colliding boomed like an explosion. The whole apartment would shake. I found it very hard to sleep the first week in that apartment. Then I got used to it, and slept like a baby. Who knew that this would be good training for life aboard an icebreaker?

The noise created by icebreaking varies according to the kind of ice and where one is located in the ship. Sometimes it sounds like you're inside of a 50-gallon steel drum being pelted with hard snowballs. Churn-ing through long stretches of solid ice pack creates a different sound.

Joe often slept in sick bay, which was close to sea level, as the beds there were more comfortable than his bunk. Joe said it sometimes sounded "[l]ike having an ice crushing machine next to each ear."

Two days later, while still near the edge of the Weddell Sea pack ice (approximately 64° 00' S, 56° 15' W), we had a fantastic day—the kind few people ever have the chance to experience. Joe penned: "Wow! What a day ... the ship pulled into the ice and stopped. The loudspeaker then announced that liberty and beer rations could be had on the ice. ... It was like a dream come true. The weather is just beautiful. ... The crew acted like a bunch of kids seeing snow for the first time. It was so much fun today. I wish today would last and last."

The guys were acting like a bunch of kids who had not been let outdoors to play for six months. Only these "kids" were also celebrating their freedom with a couple of beers. Nearby, there were small icebergs frozen into the ice pack, some with good slopes. It didn't take long before guys were sliding down these slopes on their bellies. Others used the cardboard boxes from Pabst Blue Ribbon cases as sleds. At one point, I saw a circle of eight sailors, their arms locked like a human bracelet, sliding down the steep face of a large berg on their butts—whooping, spinning, shouting all the way. Some of the less athletically inclined turned to artistic pursuits, such as building a pyramid out of empty beer cans. It was heartwarming to see my shipmates experiencing such spontaneous joy.

Weddell Sea ice pack, 1970. (Courtesy of Bob Beck)

Joe Burke, with sailors in the background, Weddell Sea ice pack, 1970. (Photo courtesy of unknown shipmate)

I took advantage of this opportunity to go skiing. I didn't know if I'd have another chance, and I wasn't going to pass this one up. One of the junior officers, Ensign Howard Waters, joined me.

On such a sunny day, khaki pants and our regular jackets were warm enough. We put on our ski boots, snapped on our skis, and poled across the ice pack. We found a berg around 100 feet high with approximately a 30-degree slope. The surface of the berg was slightly coarse and granular, but no moguls. My Minnesota skiing experience served me well. Skiing

"Downhill skiing" on a Weddell Sea iceberg. (Courtesy of Joe Burke)

on solid ice was nothing unusual. The "artificial snow" the ski areas made back home then worked about as well as spraying slopes with a fire hose. And the vertical drop on the berg was not a whole lot different from a number of the ski runs in my home state. (One of the sayings about skiing in Minnesota is, "It's the only place where the lift lines are longer than the slopes.")

Howard and I sidestepped up the berg's icy face. After climbing up and skiing down about a half-dozen times, we were pooped. But it was a blast—not just because of the joy of skiing, but also because of the extreme novelty of being able to downhill-ski in the middle of a frozen ocean, on a perfectly sunny day, with a view of the open sea on the near horizon. Everyone on Earth who can truthfully say *I've skied the Weddell Sea* probably could be packed into a Volkswagen Beetle.

While I was having a jolly time, a medical emergency occurred. One of the scientists was walking along the side of an open stretch of water when the ice gave way and he fell in. Ensign Frydenlund was on the spot and jumped in to rescue him. Between Frydenlund's pushing and one of the muscular crewmembers pulling, the scientist was quickly extricated. Frydenlund was not in the water more than a minute or two, but it was long enough for his legs to grow numb, and he was beginning to hyperventilate.

In 28-degree F water, it doesn't take long for muscle rigidity to occur because of the loss of blood flow to the limbs. Within eight minutes, heart and respiration rates slow, and ventricular fibrillation—spasms that prevent the heart from pumping—may occur. If the core body temperature drops below 80.6 degrees, cardiac function ceases.

Ensign Frydenlund admitted that it would have been hard to extricate himself if there hadn't been someone else there to give him a strong pull.

Ice more than 2 inches thick is usually strong enough to support a man's weight, but it's not thick enough for safety, particularly in Antarctica. That is because there are so many killer whales there during the summer season. If they see something walking on the ice above, they may think it's a seal and crash through the ice to grab it. This is easy for them to do, as they weigh up to 18,000 pounds and grow up to 32 feet in length. If their prey turns out to be a human being, they will not eat the person, but in rare cases, they have been known to inflict minor injuries before realizing they are attacking something other than their normal prey. It may be the case that humans are safe from killer whales because we simply don't taste good, or, that as very intelligent animals, whales have learned it is wiser to leave us alone. However, a killer whale's "innocent mistake" could easily result in a fatality as a result of hypothermia or drowning.

Leopard seals will also knock people off an ice shelf, and they have also been known to aggressively attack and, albeit rarely, kill humans. These solitary predators—weighing anywhere from 440 to 1,320 pounds, and up to nearly 12 feet long—seem to view man as just an overgrown penguin. They have been known to chase after people on top of the ice pack, including one of Shackleton's crew, who barely escaped.

Fun and games on the ice pack is a naval tradition, dating back to the time of early polar explorers. Coast Guard captain James Fournier, one of the captains of the *Burton Island*, told me an interesting story about his crew playing a game of touch football on the ice. The "audience" was a group of emperor penguins. Before the game started, the penguins saw the football lying on the ice. They had to first come out and inspect it. I guess they thought it was some kind of odd-shaped penguin egg. Once they had determined it was not, they were satisfied just being onlookers.

After briefly skirting the edge of the ice pack, we returned to Elephant Island to pick up the three-man field party we had left there, plus 2,000 pounds of cargo and geologic samples. We transferred the party to Hope Bay, where they stayed at the Argentinean base, Esperanza.

Hope Bay (see X) faces Antarctic Sound and indents the northern tip of the Antarctic Peninsula. The Swedish Antarctic Expedition discovered this bay in 1902. The expedition was under the leadership of Otto Nordenskjold, a Swedish explorer and geographer. (His uncle, Adolf, was the first to discoverer and transit the Northeast Passage above Siberia.) Hope Bay was named in honor of the three men from the Swedish expedition who spent the winter there and survived. They not only survived their time at Hope Bay, but also an almost 200-mile trek the following spring to locate Nordenskjold, who, along with five scientists, had spent two winters on Snow Hill Island, a small island farther south in the Weddell Sea.

Nordenskjold and the others were stuck on this remote island because the ship that was supposed to pick them up, the *Antarctic*, had been crushed in the ice. The crew of that ship was forced to winter over on Paulet Island, just east of the Antarctic Peninsula, after their ship sank. All three groups from that expedition were rescued in 1903 by an Argentinean ship, the *Uruguay*.

The *Antarctic* was under the command of Norwegian captain Carl Anton Larsen, an experienced polar sailor. The Larsen Ice Shelf, which is

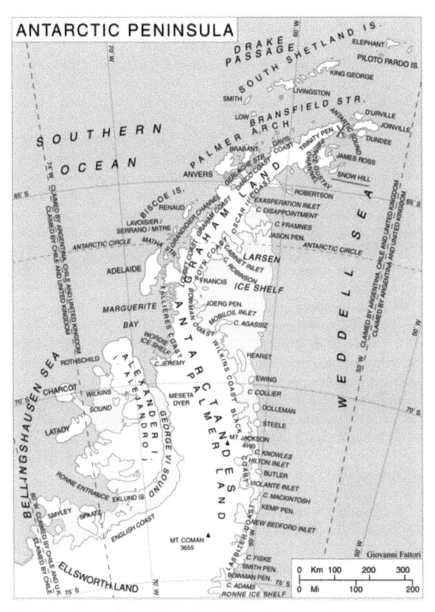

(Courtesy of Apcbg, Giovanni Fattori, and Wikimedia Commons)

fixed to the eastern edge of the Antarctic Peninsula, is named after him. He was the first person known to have skied in Antarctica, when he skied on the ice shelf which bears his name.

Captain Larsen demonstrated his polar experience early in the voyage of the Swedish Antarctic Expedition when he successfully maneuvered through the ice pack in order to drop off Nordenskjold and his scientific party on Snow Hill Island. He then returned to the Falkland Islands, where he spent the winter.

Things did not go so well for Captain Larsen when he returned to Antarctica the following summer. On November 17, 1902, he was caught in a four-day raging storm—the same kind of storm the *Glacier* would likely experience if we spent much time in the Weddell Sea. On November 21, the *Antarctic* was trapped within three or four ship lengths of the sheer face of an iceberg, which was, Larsen wrote, "considerably higher than our mainmast and about three times as long as the vessel. . . . We were in evident danger of being carried by the pack . . . right onto the ice-mountain."

With his engines going full speed and with the additional help of sail power, Captain Larsen was able to make headway into the ice pack. They barely escaped being crushed against the berg. After surviving this close call, they continued on to Hope Bay, where they dropped off the three-man party previously mentioned.

Captain Larsen then attempted to penetrate the Weddell Sea ice pack in order to rescue Nordenskjold and his scientific party. He did not get far before he was caught in another storm. He drifted with the ice pack for several days before finally reaching some open water near Paulet Island. He waited for several days for the pack to open up, but once again it closed in on him.

On January 10, 1903, one of the scientists on the ship, Carl Skotts-burg, wrote: "The pressure on the sides of the vessel—which had begun yesterday—could scarcely be marked . . . the ship began to tremble like an aspen leaf, and a violent crash sent us all up on deck. . . . The pressure was tremendous; the vessel rose higher and higher, while ice was crushed to powder along her sides."

As long as the *Antarctic* was lifted above the pressure of the ice pack, it seemed that they would be safe, but then the ship collapsed back into the ice and started to list to starboard. The hull was leaking, but a single pump contained the leak.

For almost two weeks the ship drifted with the ice pack in a southeasterly direction, until a fissure opened up and she was again afloat. But then the leak increased. All of the pumps were started. Captain Larsen hoped to be able to beach the ship on the shores of Paulet Island, but the vessel again became trapped in the ice pack. They could no longer control the leak. They had to abandon ship.

Skottsburg wrote: "We stand in a long row on the edge of the ice and cannot take our eyes off her. . . . The pumps are still going, but the sound grows fainter and fainter. . . . She sinks slower, deeper and deeper. . . . Now the name disappears . . . the waters are up to the rail, and, with a rattle, the sea and bits of ice rush in over her deck. That sound I can never forget, however long I may live."

I could not imagine how horrible it would be to be standing on the ice and be forced to watch the *Glacier* getting crushed by the ice pack, or by towering icebergs. It would be a slow, agonizing catastrophe that, although unlikely, very well could happen. No ship is strong enough to resist some of the worst hazards in the Antarctic.

The *Antarctic* sank 25 miles from Paulet Island. The off-loaded stores had to be ferried from ice floe to ice floe by whaleboat. They had to camp on ice floes, endangered by icebergs. After fourteen days and six hours of rowing, they finally made it to Paulet Island, where they were forced to winter over. Their situation was in many ways like a condensed version of the first half of Shackleton's expedition.

Shackleton's *Endurance*, Weddell's *Jane*, and Larsen's *Antarctic*—three examples of what the Weddell Sea can do to ships that dare to penetrate its massive, relentless, unforgiving ice pack.

16

Titanic

On January 16, 1970, after completing our delivery of supplies and scientific personnel to the Argentinean base, the *Glacier* departed Hope Bay and headed for King George Island and the South Shetland Islands to continue our scientific programs. Among other things, we completed helicopter seal surveys in the area, where some of the seals were tranquilized so fat samples could be extracted to test for DDT concentrations. (The use of DDT for commercial agriculture in the United States was banned in 1972.)

I had the opportunity to go on several helicopter flights during this time, and on one of them, I remember looking down on the *Glacier* as we climbed and veered inland. Looking back, the ship, which seemed so substantial when I stood on its decks, looked more like a toy boat in a bathtub, surrounded by floating marshmallows. My gaze shifted from the ship to the intricate patterns in the snowpack, the rugged glaciated peaks and the patchwork quilt of icebergs in the distance. I was awestruck by my bird's-eye view. I would have loved to stay up there for hours, but this flight and the few others I took were all short ones.

Every time I was on one of the "birds," I sat in the middle of the back seat. As a result, when it came time to land and we were hovering somewhere over our small landing pad, I could not see the ship beneath us. All I could see was open ocean on both sides, which meant I could never be sure if we were over the ship or the water. Since the deck was small and often rolling, the helicopters had to follow a strict procedure in order to land safely, without its long rotors striking a tilted deck. The pilots would hover about 5 feet above the deck—a deck that I could not see in my mid-seat position—and wait for a landing signal. As soon as the deck crew thought the deck was relatively level, they would give the signal to land. The helicopter would immediately cut its engine and we would drop like a stone. From my perspective, there was always that half-second of concern: *Are we going to have a good landing, a crash landing, or a plunge into the ocean?*

Fortunately, the *Glacier* had top-notch pilots and a skilled flight crew, both particularly important, as they faced a number of problems apart from landings, including difficulties with radio communications, visually sighting a white ship, and flying in marginal and unpredictable weather conditions. In spite of these multiple complications, there were 101 helicopter flights during our deployment, covering more than 12,000 miles—and an equal number of safe landings.

Following the seal survey work, we sailed via the Bismarck and Gerlache Straits to a point east of the Antarctic Peninsula, where we planned to rendezvous with the USNS *Wyandot* cargo ship. This navy ship carried the bulk of the cargo necessary to supply Palmer Station for the year. Arthur Harbor at Palmer Station was too clogged with ice blocks, berg ice, and brash ice—the latter, ice fragments less than 6 feet (2 m) in size—for the *Wyandot* to safely enter the harbor. We needed to clear out the harbor and the channel into Palmer Station that we had previously created. The channel had to be significantly wider and straighter than one sufficient for the *Glacier*, as the *Wyandot* was 150 feet longer and less maneuverable.

It took the *Glacier* thirty-five hours to clear the harbor—and the passage into it—well enough for the *Wyandot* to safely enter. Using two of its LCM landing craft and our combined crews, we off-loaded almost 450,000 pounds of supplies and took back on almost 100,000 pounds. The *Glacier* also received some much-needed fresh provisions and, of almost equal importance, we exchanged movies. The whole operation took forty-eight hours of intense activity.

On January 24, we shoved off, bound for Livingston Island and the South Orkney Islands, in order to continue the scheduled scientific programs. Our final destination for that leg of our trip was Punta Arenas. Joe

Glacier landing deck. (Courtesy of US Coast Guard Archives)

was anxiously looking forward to getting there and receiving mail, noting in his diary: "The morale aboard ship hit an all-time low today. There are some very fine young men aboard and I sure hope spirits pick up. Everyone is getting edgy."

Joe did not mention why the morale was so low at that point, but there could have been multiple reasons. Homesickness. Being separated from loved ones. Confined quarters. Missing fresh food. Limited leisure activities. Lack of privacy. My guess is that morale was particularly poor at that time not only because of the previously listed factors, but also because of the combination of no exciting liberty ports on the immediate horizon, long working hours, and being stuck in one place for a while. Morale typically was better when we were under way and heading for new destinations.

It was clear on the day we left Palmer. The weather was mild, seas were calm, visibility was good. We were in the Bismarck Straits, south of Palmer Station and west of the Antarctic Peninsula, sailing through open waters mixed with light brash ice. It looked like it would be a day of easy and uneventful sailing.

It was not.

We were cruising in relatively open waters (64° 50' 18 S, 64° 09' 14 W) when we struck the submerged tongue of a tabular iceberg (one that has broken off from an ice shelf). The visible portion of the berg was about 100 yards off our starboard side. It was a glancing blow, which caused the ship to lurch up a few degrees before it settled back down. I was standing on the fantail deck at the time, and absorbed the blow with my legs—an instinctive reaction, much like something I would have done if I was surfing or skiing. I did not know what to think. After being tossed around in heavy seas, it seemed like a minor event; however, others experienced the force of the blow more strongly.

One of the crewmembers, Jim Irving, wrote on the "Reunion Hall" blog site: "I was in the Oceanographic Crew and was in one of the labs listening to 8-track tapes when we hit the iceberg—threw me off the stool."

Joe was in sick bay at the time of the collision. He felt the ship jerk upward, without much noise, but then he heard the bilge alarms go off. He immediately knew that the hull had been punctured.

After the impact, Captain McCrory ordered the ship to a full stop. It was so calm that we barely drifted. I watched as two of the sailors qualified to scuba-dive donned their superthick neoprene wet suits, hoods, boots, and diving gear and slowly descended a rope ladder into the frigid waters.

Having been scuba-diving myself in the depths of Lake Superior, where the water is 36 degrees F, I had a rough idea of what they would be feeling in 29- to 30-degree F water. Even with heavy wet suits, the initial shock of the cold water takes your breath away. For people who are unfamiliar with wet suits, they are not waterproof. Water seeps in, hits your skin, and then is slowly warmed up by your body temperature to a more-tolerable level. The icy waters often give one a headache. In waters this cold, you can see your breath inside your mask.

The divers were in the water for about half an hour. I was glad they did not have to dive much deeper than the bottom of the hull, roughly 30 feet below the waterline. If they had had to dive deeper and for longer periods, they ran the risk of developing the bends, which can cause things like nerve damage and strokes. In a normal diving situation, the diver partially ascends and then does a decompression stop, to prevent nitrogen bubbles from forming in his blood; but in Antarctica, too long a stop can cause serious hypothermia. The bends can also be treated with a decompression chamber, which we did not have on board.

We anxiously awaited the divers' return. A small crowd had gathered by the time they slowly and stiffly climbed the ladders back onto the deck and started to remove their gear. One of the divers said there was a gash in the hull "2 feet wide and 20 feet long." The damage was mostly in the area called the "sea chest," where there was an intake port for water to cool the engines. Neither of the divers took underwater photos, so we had no way of knowing exactly what they saw, but the mental picture I had was terrifying.

The *Glacier* had suffered the same kind of below-the-waterline glancing blow that sank the *Titanic*, except our ship had a double hull. Even so, the damage to the *Glacier* was so severe that it tore portions of the framing, damaged several compartments, and buckled our second, more-vulnerable, inner hull. Part of the inner wall was torn and could not be repaired. The bilge pumps ran continually thereafter. It was as if we were in an armored vehicle, with a huge tear in our thick armor, and the only thing left to protect us was a damaged, thin wall of tin.

Lieutenant Pitt was at the helm at the time of the collision. Thereafter, the iceberg was known as "Pitt's berg."

At the time, I assumed no one was at fault—that the accident was merely one of the inherent risks associated with any Antarctic voyage. It was not like there were ships doing icebreaker patrols to track and follow all of the bergs in Antarctica. That would have been an all-consuming, essentially impossible task. However, a formal investigation might have concluded that we were partially at fault.

When a passenger ship, the MS *Explorer*, sank off the Antarctic Peninsula in 2007, the captain was officially criticized by a review board for traveling at approximately 5 knots when it hit something—probably a piece of a submerged iceberg. We were traveling at an estimated 8 to 10 knots when we hit the tongue of an iceberg in an area that contained several. Thus, I suspect, a formal inquiry could have concluded that we were cruising at an excessive speed, given the prevailing conditions. However, an inquiry would also have taken into account that a reasonably safe speed for an icebreaker is greater than that of a typical tourist ship. It would have been essentially impossible to complete the rest of our mission if we had had to travel at speeds considered safe for passenger ships.

The consensus of the *Glacier*'s officers was that the accident occurred either because the lookout and/or the officer at the helm did not keep a "sharp eye" on the situation; or because the officer of the day (OOD) had selected a course too close to the icebergs. Alternatively, it could have been a "no-fault accident." To my knowledge, no one aboard blamed Captain McCrory. In any case, it was a harsh reminder that the helmsman and the lookouts had to remain ever vigilant.

Were it not for our double-hulled construction, the *Glacier* probably would not have survived the damage. Nevertheless, it was frightening to learn that even with a double hull, it had been a narrow escape. We became acutely aware of how vulnerable we were to even glancing collisions with invisible berg extensions—particularly when we were in areas surrounded by so many mountainous blocks of ice.

In fact, we were more vulnerable than I realized at the time. I was under the impression that a double hull meant there was an inner hull for the entire ship. Based on research I did for this book, I learned that only about 80 percent of the hull at the waterline had that double hull, which was nothing more than the wall of the diesel fuel tanks and heeling tanks adjacent to the outer hull. The inner metal walls of these tanks were far thinner than a typical inner hull of a ship with a true double-hull construction. If the *Glacier* had been punctured in areas with just a single hull, such as the bow, the stern, or much of its bottom, the flooding would have been serious and instantaneous.

Captain Coste, the CO of the *Glacier* between 1980 and 1982, sent me an e-mail vividly describing what happened when the *Eastwind,* another Coast Guard icebreaker on which he served, punctured her bow. (The ship was not under his command at the time of the accident.) He wrote:

> On Eastwind, *we were traveling way too fast in broken ice—growlers [ice the size of a small car], bergy bits [the size of a small cottage], and hummocked floes [tented ridges of ice]—careening from one chunk to another like a billiard ball. Breakers aren't designed to break ice while going sideways. Anyhow, sliding off one big chunk and hitting another on our starboard bow, we ripped a couple of frames and opened a sizable gash, flooding the forward chain locker. For repairs, we drove her hard into the ice, to bring the bow up, and then used the heeling tanks and transfer pumps to roll to port and get the hole above the waterline. The Damage Control team welded a cofferdam across the damaged area and then filled it with cement.*

For a good while after our collision, anytime the *Glacier* bumped into something, we had reason to fear the worst. The feeling I had then was similar to what I would experience years later, following the massive 1994 Northridge earthquake, which significantly damaged our suburban house in Los Angeles. For several months after this major quake, anytime the ground shook, either from a small shaker or vibrations caused by heavy equipment, I would think, "Here comes the big one!"

After hitting the iceberg, one thing was certain: No one could tell for sure how much pressure the hull could withstand if we continued with our mission, particularly if we sailed back into the dense ice of the Weddell Sea. As far as we knew, the *Glacier* had been significantly impacted by this incident. The only way to completely assess the damage would be to put the ship in dry dock. Some of the crew suggested that we might be going to a dry dock in Buenos Aires, Argentina.

The hull damage did not prevent us from continuing with our immediate mission. We traveled on to Hope Bay to extract the scientific party doing geological studies there. Seal surveying and biological studies, including the first-ever population survey of leopard seals, continued as we made our way through a group of islands in the South Orkney chain.

As we continued toward Punta Arenas, rumors started to fly about what we were going to do about our compromised hull. Either we would be going into dry dock to repair the ship, or we were going back to Punta Arenas to get resupplied, after which we would return to our icebreaking duties.

We soon learned that the only dry dock big enough to handle the *Glacier* was in Rio de Janeiro. If we went to Rio, we would be there for about a month—during Carnival. On January 28, 1970, Joe scribed: "We still don't know if we will be going to Rio or not. If we do, we will arrive there one day before Mardi Gras . . . it would be an experience of a lifetime." The following day he wrote: "We are supposed to run into 50- to 70-knot winds tonight. I sure hope this tub holds together. Also, Rio looks worse every day. I don't think we will go there after all. This trip is getting to be 100 percent disappointment."

The extremes were too much for the crew to handle. Either we would be experiencing a glorious time in Rio or we would be back in Antarctica, breaking ice with a damaged and leaking hull—a hull that some worried might not even be able to handle a decent storm.

The uncertainty of our situation seemed to be the worst part, and being exhausted by pounding seas in Drake Passage did not help. The crew became noticeably irritable, edgy, and temperamental, more so than at any other time on the trip. For the first time, fights were breaking out. I was left with the distinct impression that we as humans are better at coping with a clearly defined bad situation rather than an ambiguous one—particularly one like ours that could turn out to be either incredibly fantastic or seriously horrible.

We arrived in Punta Arenas (PA) on February 2, 1970. Liberty there was better than being on the ship, but the novelty of this small town had worn off. And there were no passenger or college ships to brighten our stay. An old-salt Coast Guard chief I met in 2014 told me, "If the world needed an enema, they'd stick the tube into PA."

While we were in port, attempts were made to repair the damage to our hull, but to no avail. Short of going to a dry dock, there was no way to significantly improve upon the makeshift partial repairs we had already completed; we just had to hope that would be good enough.

The ship was stocked with fresh provisions, and we also picked up seven members of a Coast Guard oceanographic unit, as well as the chief scientist for the Weddell Sea Expedition, Dr. Thor Kvinge, from the University of Bergen in Norway. He had served the same role aboard the *Glacier* the previous year (and the Kvinge Peninsula in Antarctica bears his name).

On February 7, five days after our arrival in Punta Arenas, we left port and headed back to Palmer Station. Rumors started to fly that the Coast Guard brass had given us orders to avoid any situation where we would be in more than four oktas of ice. Even though crewmembers were nervous about going back into the ice with a damaged and torn hull, they seemed better off knowing the certainty of the situation. In addition, we were pleased to hear that we would not be traveling into ice pack with more than 50 percent surface coverage.

As we were traversing the Strait of Magellan, Joe noticed something very unusual: black and white porpoises. Instead, what he observed were the smallest members of the dolphin family, Commerson's dolphins— also known as panda dolphins, because of their distinct black-and-white features. They were first sighted in 1767 in the Strait of Magellan by a French naturalist, Dr. Philibert Commerson.

Crossing Drake Passage again, we hit some rough seas that almost made Joe seasick for the first time. If you have ever been seasick, you know what a miserable feeling it can be. And it can be fatal. People who are constantly vomiting eventually get dehydrated. If they are not rehydrated with intravenous fluids, they can die. There is a huge variation in one's susceptibility to seasickness. People do not become seasick because they are weak-willed or physically unfit. Given enough chaotic motion, almost everyone will become seasick.

Joe and I were among the lucky ones. Neither one of us suffered from significant seasickness the entire trip. It probably has something to do with our genes. Since I am three-quarters Norwegian, I have to thank my seafaring predecessors. There must have been some natural selection favoring Norwegians who did not become seasick. They probably caught more fish, conquered more territory, had more children, and generally had better chances of surviving.

The following day, we continued to experience significant pitching and rolling. It was so bad that we could hardly work, but we had no choice, as sailors were suffering injuries. Imagine what it's like trying to suture a laceration in a rolling sea. It's not easy. Aboard the *Glacier*, a 20- to 30-degree roll in each direction was not unusual. Trying to put a suture into a moving target at that angle was not something I had learned in medical school.

I quickly had to adopt a technique that I found to be successful. First, we had to strap patients tightly to the surgical table so they would not roll off; that way, at least they wouldn't roll any more than the ship did. I then had to stand next to the operating table with a wide stance in order to maintain my balance. The next step involved timing. In the middle of the roll, the patient was relatively flat and I did not have to strain too hard to keep my balance. I would start the stitch just before the midpoint of the roll in one direction, and then finish it right after the midpoint. I had to be quick. Port-to-starboard rolls were a bit easier, but I found that I could handle rolls initiating from the opposite direction, as well. It didn't take long before it became almost as easy as suturing someone on terra firma—it just took a bit more time.

On February 10, we arrived at Palmer Station again and anchored in Arthur Harbor.

The following day, Joe got a chance to practice his suturing skills. "I had a chance to do some suturing late this evening," he recorded in his diary. "I really enjoy suturing people up. They really feel a great amount of gratitude and respect for you after that."

I would second Joe's opinion. There are few things in medicine that are "quick fixes," but the transformation of a bloody, jagged wound into a tidy patch of solidly joined flesh is one of them. As a junior corpsman, I'm sure it was good for Joe to get a chance to show his shipmates that he knew his stuff. He had learned a lot from our old-salt corpsman, Chief Toussaint, whose wound sutures made the rest of us look like amateurs.

17

Hump Day

AFTER DROPPING OFF SEVERAL CIVILIANS AT PALMER STATION, WE
again turned north. It marked the end of the Antarctic Peninsula Scientific Program and the beginning of the Weddell Sea Oceanographic
Expedition. Our first stop was at King George Island (see map on page
123), where we dropped off a scientist, John M. Croom, who was going to
winter over with the Russians at USSR Station Bellingshausen. He was
going to study protozoa found in Antarctic waters.

This stop gave us an opportunity to visit with crewmembers of the
Russian station. The station was made up of a small central structure and
several smaller separate buildings, which looked like prefabricated trailers,
rectangular structures with flat roofs. We met in their dining hall in the
main building. Captain McCrory and I, along with our scientific officers
and the civilian scientists, joined about fifteen members of the Russian
crew.

It is important to understand the context of this meeting. It was during the Cold War, when the United States and the Soviet Union were the
two major nuclear powers in the world. We posed a constant threat to
each other. It was not as if we were concerned about Russia taking over
pieces of adjacent, mostly Russian-speaking territories, such as Putin's
incursion into parts of Ukraine in recent years. The threat at that time was
total annihilation by nuclear strikes. I had grown up during an era when
people built bomb shelters stocked with survival rations in anticipation
of a nuclear holocaust. We had drills in school to practice taking cover
in case of a nuclear attack. It was the era of the Cuban Missile Crisis,
an event that took the United States to the brink of a nuclear war with

Visiting with crewmembers of the Russian station, c. 1970. (Courtesy of *Glacier*
Photography Crew)

Russia. And it was long before the fall of the Berlin Wall, a stark symbol
of the East–West divide.

There we were, sitting around a long table, with our archenemy. On
one wall was a large picture of Lenin. On another, a large picture of Marx.
In the center of the table sat a stern-looking man in a wool suit. The rest
of us were wearing our everyday uniforms.

It quickly became obvious that the man in the center was the Communist Party representative. He sat there stiffly, facing forward, but with
eyes constantly scanning the room. He never spoke, nor did I notice anyone else trying to speak to him. We tried to communicate with the other
members of the Russian station as best we could, but it was difficult. Only
John Croom spoke a bit of Russian, while several of the Russians spoke
broken English.

The common language was Spanish, given that all of us had recently spent some time in South America. Admittedly, our Spanish was quite limited, but we all more or less understood a single phrase—loosely translated, the Spanish drinking toast, "Bottoms up!" In front of us were water glasses filled with Russian vodka. Of course, we did not want to cause an international incident by refusing their hospitality and their libations, particularly the latter. We all drained our glasses, except for the Communist Party apparatchik. I've never had better vodka in my life.

The atmosphere quickly became very festive. We sat around the table laughing, drinking, and eating—mostly pickled food (which I thought went very well with the vodka). By the second glass, we were all pretty well smashed.

After a delightful lunch, we went for a brief tour of their compound. I toured the station with a Russian doctor, who proudly showed me the small trailer that was their medical facility. He was a ruggedly handsome fellow, about thirty years old, with dark wavy hair and a ready smile. He was particularly proud of his EKG machine. It was a box about the size of a small oven, easily three times larger than any comparable American EKG. No doubt it was made of vacuum tubes and more-primitive electronics. Although the Russians had put the first satellite into orbit, it seemed to me that most of their technology, while functional, was not up to our standards. Between their trailer-like buildings, their antiquated equipment, and their apparent reliance on pickled food, I was left with the impression that Soviet Russia was not a particularly prosperous country.

While touring the compound, beyond the prying eyes of the Communist Party representative, the doctor said to me, "I am not a communist," but adding, with strong emphasis, "I am very much a Russian."

It was an epiphany for me. I guess I had naively thought that most Russians were communists, or at the very least, strong supporters of communism. Clearly, this doctor was not someone who fit into that arbitrary category. I thought, *Of course Russians love their country, but they're not necessarily all dreaded "Commies."* In fact, I thought, they're regular guys, just like us.

Ensign Frydenlund had a somewhat similar experience. One of the Russian scientific officers said to him, "Let's take a walk." Once they had

Sick bay. Left to right: myself, the Russian doctor, the Russian station head, and Captain McCrory. (Courtesy of *Glacier* Photography Crew)

walked to the point where they were "far from any microphones," the Russian officer asked him if there was "any chance" for reconciliation between our two countries. Ensign Frydenlund agreed that there was a chance, but we all realized that major changes would be unpredictable, and unlikely in the foreseeable future.

Our mini détente continued, with all of us staggering out to the courtyard in front of the base's main building, where we raised both national flags. Then we welcomed them aboard the *Glacier* for a tour of our ship.

After such a wonderful shared experience, it seemed to me that more wars could be avoided, or at least minimized, if people had the opportunity to get to know people for who they really are, rather than assuming that the majority of people of any given nation fit into a negative narrow stereotype.

While we were in the area of the Russian station, we visited a nearby old whaling station. It was interesting, but depressing. All around this large lagoon were rusted pieces of equipment and large piles of whale-bones bleached by the sun and the elements. One of our pilots took one of the bones as a souvenir. This whale vertebra was large enough that he could use it as a footstool. I could only imagine how many whales had been slaughtered in this area that was once teeming with these magnificent creatures.

In 1970, only a few thousand humpback whales were still in existence. In 1938 alone, more than 40,000 whales had been killed. I only saw one distant whale the entire time I was in Antarctica.

By 2014 there were about 80,000 humpback whales in the area, but that was only 30 percent of the total that existed before the beginning of commercial whaling operations. And we certainly would not have these increased numbers today were it not for the coordinated efforts of the International Whaling Commission, which in 1994 approved a Southern Whale Sanctuary. This sanctuary covers most of the waters from 40 degrees south (including the area north of Punta Arenas) all the way to Antarctica.

February 14 was "Hump Day," the day when supposedly half the trip was over. We celebrated the event with a special meal and a talent show. Everyone participated, including the CO and the XO. The acts were not exactly ready for *America's Got Talent*, but we made up for the lack of ability with good-natured enthusiasm.

Several of the Coast Guard Academy grads had been part of a singing group, and they were looking for a fourth guy who could sing bass. They were desperate, so much so that they settled for me. Fortunately for them, I had only a one-line solo. They had composed lyrics set to the folk tune, "They Built the Ship *Titanic*." Their version was titled, "They Built the Mighty *Glacier*." It was filled with good-hearted mockery and satire. They had plenty of good material from which to draw; after all, like the *Titanic*, we had struck an iceberg. And that was only one of our misadventures.

I wish I could remember the lyrics, as there were many clever lines. In the original version of the folk song, there is a line that describes loading the lifeboats. The line ends with "women and children first." That line was changed in our version to "officers and chiefs first," which elicited a chorus of laughter and booing from the enlisted men. There were also lines gently poking fun at Captain McCrory, who was sitting in the front row. He accepted the jibes with apparent good humor. The whole event was a much-needed boost to our morale, and showed me a lighter and more-personable side to our CO. It seemed there was more to the man than I had realized.

Although we were "over the hump," in reality it was more like we had just entered a "Destruction Derby" event. We were pushing into the heart of the Weddell Sea, which routinely produces more and denser sea ice than any other area in the Antarctic. It's also an area that features a major clockwise current, or gyre, which pushes masses of ice up against the eastern edge of the Antarctic Peninsula and the Larsen Ice Shelf. This gyre creates compacted, multiyear, tented ridges of ice. As a result, the western portion of this body of ice is generally considered impassable, even for heavy-duty icebreakers.

Captain Edwin MacDonald, author of *Polar Operations*, advised against any central penetration of the Weddell Sea. In fact, he advised entering it no farther west than 12 degrees west longitude. That entry point is essentially the farthest eastern portion of the Weddell Sea, where the ice pack is generally much less dense.

We crossed the Antarctic Circle (66° 33' S latitude) in the Weddell Sea on February 16, 1970, at 34° W longitude, about *1,500 miles west* of the 12° W longitude recommended by Captain MacDonald. Assuming a normal distribution of ice pack, this meant we would be plowing through some of the thicker ice in the Weddell Sea.

The first person to cross the Antarctic Circle was Captain James Cook on January 17, 1773. Although Cook was a brilliant explorer, navigator, and captain, he occasionally suffered from lapses in judgment—something of particular interest to me, as it relates to the general issue of leadership.

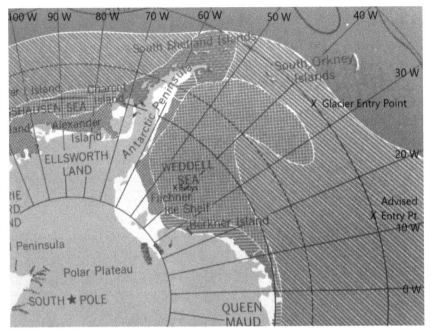

Pack ice density map, with the dotted area representing the densest; the cross-hatched area, moderate density; and the lined area, the least dense. Glacier entry point is marked with an X. (Courtesy of *Polar Operations*)

Captain Cook was killed in 1779 when he decided to hold the King of Hawaii for ransom when some of the natives stole one of Cook's small boats. The enraged natives killed Cook when he went ashore to take the king as a hostage. Obviously, the natives—who had weapons and far outnumbered him—thought that protecting their king was much more important than giving in to the demands of a foreigner who was upset about losing a boat. This episode strongly suggests that there were times when Captain Cook's ego interfered with his judgment and common sense—similar to the flaws in judgment that led to Magellan's demise.

Like the Arctic Circle, the Antarctic Circle is the farthest place from the South Pole that has at least one complete day of sunlight. Thus, it is a somewhat arbitrary designation. Many places north of the Antarctic Circle, such as the northern portion of the Weddell Sea, certainly have the weather, ice, and other conditions typically seen in a polar region.

For example, in January, Joe described having difficulty sleeping because of the noise created by heavy-duty icebreaking. At that time, we were in the Weddell Sea, about 150 miles *north* of the Antarctic Circle. Joe noted in his diary that it was getting "colder outside every hour."

The increasing cold, however, had nothing to do with one of the crew fracturing a bone. One of the things I had worried about prior to the trip was having to treat a complicated bone fracture—the kind that could only be treated properly with rods and pins and traction. In the rough conditions we commonly faced, a severe fracture easily could have occurred. About the only kind of fractures I had treated up to this point were easily treated broken fingers and toes, as well as a few broken ribs, which typically are treated with just pain medication and "tincture of time."

One of the older enlisted men suffered a fractured hand. He came into sick bay one day while I was sitting at my desk, holding his wrist and in obvious pain, a sheepish expression on his face. While standing in the doorway, several feet away, I made the diagnosis. I said, "Looks like you have a boxer's fracture."

He gave me a strange look, but didn't say anything. I wondered if he thought I was either incompetent or some kind of an orthopedic genius who could make a diagnosis without the aid of an X-ray or even a physical exam. More than likely, he thought the former.

I didn't tell him that I knew all about boxer's fractures—a fracture of the bone supporting the base of the little finger—from my experiences as a patient following my swimming pool accident. I knew exactly how to give him the local anesthetic required. I knew how to reduce the fracture, and how to cast it. And I knew the kind of physical therapy he would need for a complete recovery. I was lucky.

I asked this sailor, "How did it happen? Did you punch someone?"

He hesitated and said, "Nah, I slammed a hatch cover on it."

Given the sheepish look on his face, I thought, *He did something stupid. He's just not telling me.* It was only later after he had made a complete recovery that he admitted what had actually happened: He'd lost his temper and smashed his fist into a bulkhead.

Most of the medical problems we faced were routine—colds, minor injuries, simple cases of venereal disease, and so forth. For the most part, these problems could be handled by my very capable corpsmen. I had lots of time to roam around the ship, taking photos or generally goofing off. Nonetheless, I was always "on call." Having ultimate medical responsibility for the crew was constantly on my mind.

The enlisted men and I had a good symbiotic relationship. They had a double food ration, meaning they were eating things like filet mignon and lobster, while I was eating the equivalent of Hamburger Helper, which we officers were required to pay for out of our own pockets. But I was the one with the key to the liquor locker, so we would periodically have small parties in sick bay. The enlisted guys provided the food, and I provided the liquor, but only one bottle per person. I could not have crewmembers running around the ship drunk. It was fun, and helped to build rapport with the crew.

The previous medical staff did not have good rapport with the crew, partly because of inappropriately displayed photos of VD lesions. The only thing we did even remotely similar to that kind of scare tactic was brief, voluntary, and confined to the sick bay. We had an outbreak of pediculosis pubis, more commonly known as "crabs." We attached one of these bugs to a microscope slide and anyone who was interested could come and look at it. The bug looked quite fearsome under the microscope, and suitably impressed the few crewmembers who came to look at it. Our little slide show probably gave us an extra measure of cooperation when we had to "delouse" the affected area of the ship.

A much more serious medical case arose when we were deep in Antarctica. A senior chief came to me with excruciating abdominal pain. He had what is known as a "surgical abdomen." The hallmarks of this syndrome are extreme abdominal pain, accompanied by board-like rigidity of the abdominal muscles. The rigidity prevents a doctor from being able to palpate or feel an abdomen properly, which makes a definitive diagnosis more difficult. A typical cause of a surgical abdomen would be something like a ruptured appendix.

The first thing I did after putting this distressed sailor in a bed was to look at his medical chart. Based on what I saw, it was highly likely that he was suffering from a ruptured stomach ulcer. His chart showed that he had already had two duodenal ulcers, both documented by good X-ray studies. I knew a ruptured duodenal ulcer was always a surgical problem, but did not know if it was a problem that could be treated conservatively. I was hoping that a combination of antibiotics and intravenous fluids would control his condition well enough—at least until we could get him to a proper hospital for the surgery he would need.

Previously, I had been able to use conservative treatment for a suspected case of appendicitis, but that particular patient had had milder symptoms and no record of any other potential surgical problems. The general advice we polar-bound doctors had been given during our pre-deployment training was to avoid all but the most urgent and absolutely essential surgeries.

I looked up the details in one of my medical texts, and the treatment recommendation was unequivocal: If the rupture was not surgically repaired within twenty-four hours, the patient would die. The nearest hospital was three days away—assuming we did not get caught in heavy weather crossing Drake Passage. If he needed emergency surgery, I was going to have to do it myself.

Although my surgical experience was limited, I had seen the required surgery on one occasion. I had not scrubbed in on that particular procedure, but I understood the basic principles involved. So, even under the best of circumstances, I would be performing a surgery I had never actually done.

Unfortunately, the circumstances were horribly less than ideal.

For starters, we were on a moving ship. Although I had learned how to do basic suturing on a rolling ship, doing major abdominal surgery on a less than stationary surface was an entirely different matter.

There was a much more severe problem, however, and that was the fact that we didn't have an anesthesia machine. The one I had ordered from the Coast Guard never arrived. The only general anesthetic we had was open drop ether. From my perspective, using this method—which requires the patient to inhale ether through a gauze-soaked pad—was akin to Stone Age medicine. I had never even seen anyone use open drop ether, other than a scene or two in old movies, nor had I ever read about the technique. It certainly was not something I had been taught in medical school.

If I went ahead and used ether—and did not use it properly—I feared I could cause an anesthetic death. Or if I used it improperly, I could cause an explosion, as it is a notoriously volatile compound. And if I tried doing surgery with only local anesthesia, I was afraid the patient would be writhing around in excruciating pain, making an already difficult surgery almost impossible. It was a nightmare.

Of course, I was not going to do any surgery until I was certain I had made the correct diagnosis. I inserted a thin flexible tube through the patient's nose into his stomach and withdrew a small amount of blood through the tube. It was bright red. If the blood was coming from his duodenum, where stomach acids would have affected it, it would have been darker. It seemed more likely that I had created some bleeding secondary to the tube slightly scraping the back of his throat or esophagus.

We also started some blood studies. I tried to get a urine specimen, but he could not provide one. He did not have a fever, which was a good sign. I tried to gently palpate his abdomen, but, as I expected, it was rock-hard and uniformly tender. None of the tests were definitive.

We started an intravenous drip. Although our patient was moaning in pain, my instincts told me it was too soon to start him on narcotics. I had not completed the studies I needed. I did not want to mask the pain until I had a good idea of what kind of condition I was treating. I vividly remember huddling with my corpsmen and discussing our various options, none of them good. They looked as worried and tense as I felt. I had never been the lead surgeon on any type of abdominal surgery. I had assisted on a few, but there is a huge difference between assisting a knowledgeable surgeon in a hospital versus flying solo for the first time on a remotely isolated, pitching ship.

I was thinking, *He's been here about half an hour. He'll be dead by tomorrow if I don't do the surgery. If he's got a ruptured ulcer, I don't have a choice.*

And if I screwed up the surgery—well, I didn't even want to think about that possibility.

Then the patient stopped moaning. He said, "The pain is gone."

I didn't need any more diagnostic tests to rule out the possibility of a ruptured stomach ulcer. Ruptured ulcers do not suddenly heal themselves. Whatever his problem was, it was something else. He was finally able to provide us with a urine specimen, which was filled with red blood cells. He had just passed a kidney stone.

Kidney stones can present with extreme abdominal pain. In other words, a "surgical abdomen," but not one that typically requires surgery. I don't know who was more relieved—the patient or myself. Since I had not told the patient about my tentative diagnosis, or the likelihood of his needing primitive abdominal surgery, I think I was the one who was more relieved. I felt like I had just dodged a potential disaster.

18

Icebreaker Life

IMAGINE BEING WARMLY SNUGGLED IN YOUR BED, SOUND ASLEEP, IN THE middle of a pleasant dream, then suddenly awakening in a state of panic as you realize that you have been vaulted out of your bed and are about to fall onto a cold hard surface. That is a slice of icebreaker life. Our round-bottomed ship was not built for comfort in the all-too-frequent storms we encountered. It was difficult for anyone to get a good night's sleep when the *Glacier* was pitching and rolling like an amusement park thrill ride.

My particular sleeping arrangement was far less than ideal. My bed was a sofa during the day; at night, the back of the sofa hinged down and made a narrow single bed. Unlike the bunks for most of the crew, I had no railing to contain me, or to grab. Consequently, I could easily fall out of my bed if the ship took a big roll.

In an attempt to prevent becoming airborne, I would prop something under the outside edge of my bed in order to give it a shallow V shape. If the ship rolled in a starboard direction, I slid toward the back of the sofa. If the ship rolled toward the port side, I tilted into the elevated angle of the bed, which held me in place. The problem was that sometimes the V angle was not as steep or as deep as it needed to be. If the ship did a hard roll to port, I'd be launched into the air.

It was very disconcerting to awaken in the middle of the night in midair. You might think I wouldn't have woken up until I actually hit the deck, but that was never the case. Being vaulted into the air was enough to set off my internal alarm system, probably some panic-inducing, survival mechanism we inherited from our simian ancestors. And it was that brutal awakening, combined with feeling a total loss of control that was most disturbing. Actually hitting the deck never hurt that much. (I was young then.)

After a while, I got better at setting the depth of the V angle to compensate for whatever storm condition prevailed, but it was impossible to get it right every time. I suppose it was because things like rogue waves are unpredictable. Maybe I would have my bed set up for a 20-foot swell, but then along would come a 40-foot rogue wave, and I'd go sailing—with enough time aloft to have a thought like *This really sucks!* flash through my brain, just before crashing onto the cold deck.

Being in such a remote location for months at a time was another problem.

I recall an occasion that was more humorous than frustrating. A bunch of us were sitting around the officers' mess one night. We had been out to sea for about four months and were deep in the middle of nowhere when one of the pilots made a suggestion.

"What do you say we go into town for beer and pizza?"

It was such a ridiculously impossible thought that you couldn't help but laugh. At the same time, though, it reminded us of all the simple pleasures we could easily enjoy if only we weren't so incredibly removed from our normal lives. One of the people who wintered over on the continent even described "missing the smell of dirt."

Except for a few of our stops, we were socially isolated. That was one of the reasons why the mail we received was so important. We tried to remain in phone contact with family and friends back home, but it wasn't easy. There was a shortwave radio available to the crew, but it didn't always work. Establishing radio contact had something to do with being able to bounce radio signals off the ionosphere. If atmospheric conditions were not right, it wasn't possible to use our radio, sometimes for three or four days in a row. And when atmospheric conditions were good, the radio operator still had to locate a ham radio operator in the United States who was willing to do a phone patch to the party you were trying to reach. Then you had to worry about the party being at home or the line being busy, as well as the audio quality of the connection, once established. And there were no conveniences like automatic redial or call waiting back in those days.

Being out of touch with the world for several days at a stretch could feel like a lifetime for someone waiting to hear critical news, such as the delivery of a first child or the outcome of a loved one's major surgery. If you were able to make a good connection, there was no such thing as a private conversation, as you would be sitting in a cramped space with a radio operator and usually a few other sailors, waiting their turn.

This lack of readily available communication was generally tougher for the married guys. Deployments involving long periods of separation were difficult on relationships—not only on girlfriends and spouses, but also on family relationships in general. For example, children would get used to life without their fathers around. When fathers returned, children didn't necessarily like having their established routines upset. Some marriages did not last because of these prolonged separations. And even if the marriages were solid, the wives still had to worry about what misfortunes might befall their spouses during a hazardous-duty cruise. Chief Toussaint referred to the wives at home as "The West PAC [Pacific Area of Command] Widows."

Prior to extended deployments, sailors were advised to give their spouses limited power of attorney. According to Captain Coste, one radar man aboard the *Eastwind* icebreaker failed to follow this advice and gave his wife unlimited power of attorney instead. When he came home seven months later, she had sold his house and his car and had run off with his neighbor.

During the latter part of our deployment, rumors started circulating about homosexual encounters apparently occurring between guys who were not gay. This sort of thing certainly happens in prisons, but it can also happen during long, isolated cruises when sexually frustrated males look for alternative sexual outlets. The sailors called it "sea pussy."

I don't know whether such liaisons actually occurred aboard the *Glacier*. During the latter part of our cruise, when these rumors were bandied about, I was approached by a grizzled old chief—someone who obviously was not gay. The chief gruffly said to me, "Doc, I think I got lesbian tendencies." I had to laugh. I knew exactly what he meant. At that point in the cruise, we would have been happy with a woman of any shape, look, or persuasion.

Life can get pretty damn boring during a long polar cruise. There were not a lot of recreational opportunities for the crew. There was always card playing, letter writing, and reading, but that was about the extent of it for most crewmembers. Some of the Filipino crewmembers were into playing mah-jongg. I was lucky in that I had my own room, where I could play my guitar—certainly not well enough that anyone else would want to listen to it—or I could listen to my musical tapes. Of course, those activities did not fill much of a day.

Although we had 16-millimeter movies to watch, we didn't have many titles. One of the favorite films for the enlisted men was a movie starring Paul Newman, called *Cool Hand Luke*. For those of you not familiar with this movie, it's a story in which Paul Newman plays Luke, a perpetually defiant man, unfairly imprisoned and assigned to a chain gang. Given that we were living in the rebellious sixties, it was not too surprising that the theme of the movie resonated with the crew. Some of the best parts of the movie had to do with Luke's multiple escape attempts, and the way he was treated after being recaptured. The character playing the head of the prison, Strother Martin, delivered some of the best dialogue. One of his most famous lines, delivered in a slow Southern drawl, was, "What we've got here . . . is a . . . failure to com—mun—i—cate."

The enlisted men had seen the movie so many times that they had memorized the lines. They would turn off the sound on the projector at the beginning of a particularly memorable bit of dialogue and then a crewmember would stand up and try to imitate Strother Martin's lines, to the laughter, cheers, and jeers of his shipmates. Every night they watched this movie, they would let a different crewmember deliver the lines. These sailors sure knew how to entertain themselves.

The guys also enjoyed playing practical jokes on each other. In one case, it was a very "practical" one, in that it served a badly needed purpose. The sailors who worked in the galley bunked next to a guy who refused to take a shower at decent intervals, no matter what anybody said. According to Joe Burke, his fellow bunkmates came up with a plan. They dusted the inside of his sleeping sack, also known as a "fart sack," with copious amounts of flour. This odiferous shipmate climbed into his sleeping sack, totally unaware of their intervention. It only became apparent when he climbed out of bed the following morning.

"He looked like the Pillsbury Doughboy," Joe recalled.

The man finally took a shower, and was much more conscientious about his cleanliness thereafter.

Chief Toussaint loved to play practical jokes. Chief Johnny Johnson, the sailor who was "King Neptune" during our equator crossing, was one of his many victims. Johnson's problem was trying to figure out some way to outwit someone as clever as Toussaint. He finally came up with a plan, but he needed Joe Burke's help.

Joe was more than happy to be an accomplice, walking up to the chief's quarters, knocking on the door, and asking for Toussaint, who quickly came to the door.

"What is it?" said Toussaint.

"It's Chief Johnson," Joe said. "He's passed out in the galley."

Toussaint rushed to the galley, obviously concerned that his over-sized, Black buddy had suffered something serious, like a heart attack. He reached the galley, with Joe close behind, to find his friend lying on the deck, apparently in a coma.

He got down on the deck, gave Johnson a little shake, and said, "Johnny, Johnny—are you okay?"

For a couple of seconds Johnson didn't respond; then he reached up, grabbed Toussaint's head, pulled him down, and planted a juicy kiss on the chief's cheek.

"Gotcha," he said, a big smile on his face.

Toussaint, knowing he was overdue for some payback, and no doubt relieved it was all just a joke, said, "Not bad, Johnny," then looked over at Joe, and with a twinkly-eyed grin, said, "You too, Burke."

A group of the officers decided to hold a bridge tournament. They needed to have sixteen players. The idea was that everyone would chip in ten dollars and the winners would earn a portion of the pot. They asked me if I wanted to join, but I told them I had only played a few hands in my life; I was no bridge player. However, I said, "If you get fifteen players and need a sixteenth, I'll give you my ten dollars as a charitable contribution, and I'll play."

It turned out they were desperate for that final player, so I ended up participating, certain that I would come in dead last.

The tournament was structured so that partners changed after every complete game. I liked this format. Whichever partner I ended up with, I knew he would be a better player than me. Plus, it gave me a chance to get to know some of the guys better, including some of the scientists, with whom I had not spent much time.

In order to keep from getting bored playing a game I hardly knew, I decided I would try to win the bid whenever I could. It was more fun to play a hand than be the defensive player, or the "dummy"—the partner of the winning bidder who just lays his cards on the table when the hand begins.

Utilizing this strategy, I had lots of fun. I got to play a lot of hands. Of course I lost a number of hands because I overbid, but then I won my fair share because I was lucky enough to get some good hands. When I did win, it was often on a hand where I had made a big bid, one worth "game," which is much more than a typical lower bid.

When the tournament was over, they totaled up the points for each individual. To my utter amazement, I was the winner. I was flabbergasted. I knew I did not deserve to win. This really angered some of the good bridge players, who knew full well that I was the worst player of the bunch. Bridge is almost like a religion to some people—and I was a heathen. (Admittedly, a richer one.)

It was not until years later when I finally took up bridge in a serious way that I realized how I'd won against all odds. Bridge is in large part a game where you communicate with your partner in a seemingly illogical code. Experienced players understand this code-speak. This mutual understanding allows them to get the most points out of their combined hands. But it takes partners playing together a while before they understand their own particular style of bidding.

Since the tournament I played in Antarctica was designed so partners would split up and gain a new partner after every game, no one ever had a chance to build significant communication rapport. For someone like myself, who didn't know how to communicate accurately anyway, it didn't matter. Sometimes it helps to be clueless.

The enlisted men had occasional bingo games, which Joe described this way: "It was fun. The guys had a ball. It was like a bingo game at a Catholic Church—only the language was different."

On payday there was usually a floating crap game that sometimes got so loud the paymaster would stop handing out checks until the roaring had stopped.

⸻

It was not hard to get exercise of a sort. After all, the ship was almost constantly rolling. One had to use a number of muscles just to keep from falling over. Getting good aerobic exercise was another thing, particularly for guys like me, who rarely lifted anything heavier than a stethoscope. Anticipating this sort of problem, I had brought a good jump rope with me. I could work up a sweat almost anywhere, as long as I was somewhere with enough overhead space for a swinging rope and my 6-foot-2-inch frame. The place I used the most was the fantail—below the flight deck on the back of the ship. The deck above sheltered me from rain or snow, and it was a relatively open area.

There was one night, though, when I decided to jump rope on one of the small quarterdecks. We were deep in the Southern Ocean. It was a rolling sea—misty, cold, and almost dark. There I was skipping away when the XO, Commander Dirschel, cut through the quarterdeck. He did a double take when he saw me, then just shook his head and walked on. He probably thought, "Oh, it's just that weird doctor."

Of course, in the scheme of things, I was sort of an oddball. No one else jumped rope for exercise. No one else had a surfboard covered in paisley flowers. But that was only a small part of it. I was the antithesis of a career military type. And I was not afraid to admit it.

For example, one night in the wardroom I was having dinner and talking with the XO when he said, "You know, Doctor, sometimes you sound just like a civilian."

I quickly responded, "Why, thank you."

Again, he just shook his head.

———

We occasionally put out a ship's newspaper, and I wrote an article for one of the editions. It was at a time when the crew's morale was low. We had put together a small weight-lifting room in one of the compartments, which I encouraged my shipmates to use, in an effort to get some regular exercise. One of the lines in my article was, "Life is what you make it."

Most of the sailors had gotten into a rut. I was basically trying to tell them to get off their collective butts and do something—the old "pick yourself up by your bootstraps" sort of thing. Although I am a firm believer in that particular saying, over the years I have become an even stronger believer in a rather different saying: "Life is 10 percent what you make it and 90 percent how you take it." Too often in life things happen that are totally beyond our control. That's when how you take things becomes critically important.

One thing was a frequent source of delight, and that was the ever-changing view. Even when we were mostly in one spot, the view always changed. The sea ice would move. Patches of brilliance and shadows would shift with the arc of the sun. Fog or snow would soften the view. Slight movements of the ship could significantly change viewing angles, making one facet of a berg look quite different from another. New bergs would drift into view. Just as no two bergs are ever alike, the same holds true with mountains, bays, and sunsets.

We traveled far enough south to see the "midnight sun," but our timing was off. By the time we were south of the Antarctic Circle, the Southern Hemisphere had started its tilt away from the sun. We were getting closer to the dark polar night.

I vividly remember, however, gazing at a distant horizon after the sun had set. There were the red and orange and golden colors of a beautiful sunset, the fading rays silhouetting a collection of icebergs that covered the ocean as if some deity had randomly placed them. Loose bits of gently waving brash ice gave the surface an interesting patina. The temperature was cool, but comfortably pleasant. I was the only one on deck at the time, so it was also a treasured moment of privacy. The seas were unusually

Icebergs in a polar sunset. (Photo by Gail Bunes)

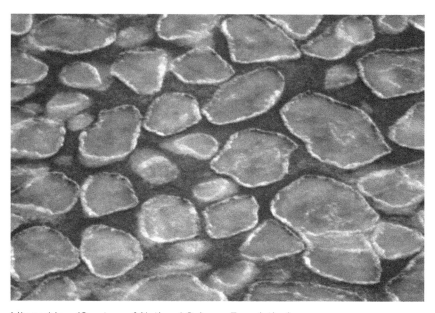
Lily pad ice. (Courtesy of National Science Foundation)

calm, and I was equally relaxed. Off to one side of that same horizon, perhaps 25 degrees or so, were the early blues, violets, and soft-filtered grays
of an early dawn. In effect, it was like simultaneously viewing the early
phase of both a sunset and a sunrise. It was breathtaking.

Another night, we had a beautiful sunset over an almost flat ocean.
The striking thing about the ocean was the film of lily pad ice covering it.
Each segment was about the size of a large dinner plate, only a geometric,
multifaceted one, about 2 inches thick. The edges were slightly raised.
Each "lily pad" was connected to the ones around it by a thin film of ice,
known as "grease ice," so called because the congealed ice crystals give it a
smooth and greasy appearance.

As far as the eye could see, there extended a tapestry of these repeating forms, bathed in the golden afterglow of the sun just below the horizon. They gently undulated in a slow-moving swell that did not disrupt
the continuity of the surface—a mesmerizing sea of luminous magnetic
plates that could not be torn apart.

19

Trapped

ONE OF THE REASONS—IF NOT THE PRIMARY ONE—THAT THE *GLACIER*
sailed deep into the Weddell Sea was to retrieve four oceanographic buoys
that had been submerged and anchored to the ocean floor in 1968. I did
not know much about the Weddell Sea at the time, other than the fact
that it was a place icebreakers rarely went in comparison to other parts of
Antarctica. In 1950, the historian Thomas R. Henry wrote in his book,
The White Continent: "The Weddell Sea is, according to the testimony of
all who have sailed through its berg-filled waters, the most treacherous
and dismal region on earth."

I don't know why Captain McCrory chose to travel to the buoy site
through the area of historically thicker ice in the central portion of the
Weddell Sea, rather than the longer but comparatively ice-free eastern
route. It was not a matter of his simply being reckless. According to one
of the junior officers with whom I spoke, the CO carefully maneuvered
the ship through some of the thicker ice on the way to the buoy site. He
apparently felt the ship could handle the extra stress, in spite of our compromised hull, as long as he was cautious. Most likely, he just wanted to
get to the buoy site by the most direct route possible, even if there was an
extra element of risk.

The buoys had been submerged and anchored about 700 feet below
the ocean surface, at roughly 74° S, 39° W. The exact location of each of
them could not be determined. In 1968, there were some satellites available to aid with positioning, but the process was difficult and not entirely
reliable. About the best satellite navigation systems could do at that time
was to localize an object within about 0.25 mile to 2 miles.

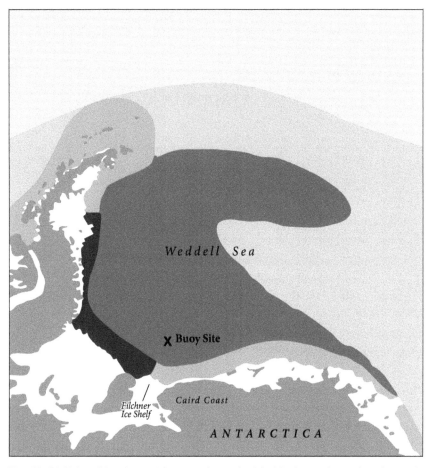

The Weddell Sea (the densest ice area is marked in black, moderate ice, in gray).

The buoys, according to *Glacier*'s official deployment summary report, "Operation Deep Freeze 1970 Report" (ODF70), were designed to "record on magnetic tape the speed and direction of current flow and water temperature for a period of twelve to fourteen months." One of the buoys "included a device for sampling bottom water and storing it every ten days."

I will be referring to the ODF70 report frequently in this book because of all the important information it contains. This 100-plus-page report was compiled sometime after the completion of our deployment.

Its eighteen chapters include summaries of pertinent details related to the ship's operations and its personnel, as well as a chronological overview of our voyage. This latter part most likely was written by Captain McCrory. In any case, he had to review the entire document and give final approval before it was sent to central and regional Coast Guard headquarters, as well as to the captains of all Coast Guard icebreakers. I did not learn of the contents of this summary report until I started doing research forty years after completing my assignment aboard the *Glacier*.

The previous year, Captain McCrory and the *Glacier* had attempted to retrieve the buoys, but they were, according to ODF70, blocked by heavy ice concentrations 57 miles short of the retrieval site. A rumor circulated among the crew that Captain McCrory was determined to succeed this time. Supposedly he believed that retrieving the buoys would be a major feather in his cap—and a giant step toward his becoming an admiral. If that was the case, he must have felt under some pressure, as officers promoted to this level usually received the promotion in their late forties or early fifties. Captain McCrory was forty-six.

Most Coast Guard captains never receive a promotion to such a high rank, but this CO was ambitious and thought he could do it. One of the senior officers who had previously worked under him knew of his ambitions, but was skeptical. When I interviewed him as part of my research, he said, "Some people, you can tell right away. They have what it takes to become an admiral." Captain McCrory, he thought, "was not that kind of person."

As far as the crew knew, the CO was under orders to avoid any heavy ice concentrations, specifically concentrations greater than four oktas (50 percent). It became clear during my research that he was not under any such orders. However, he very likely was cautioned to be more careful than usual, given that the hull was damaged—and no one knew for certain the extent of the damage. All I knew was that as we traveled farther south, we rarely saw open water. I started to feel uncomfortable about our situation. We were getting into areas of six to eight oktas of ice. I kept thinking, *This could be trouble.*

On February 19 we had liberty on the ice. We did not mind being in solid ice when it gave us a chance to "go outside and play." The temperatures were in the low 20s, but it did not stop a bunch of the sailors from playing football and drinking beer.

I never saw Captain McCrory drinking beer, but he was no teetotaler. And he apparently felt he could hold his liquor. The thing is, drinking in Antarctica, at least in some situations, is different. As the story goes, the CO was drinking at the officers' club at McMurdo during an earlier deployment. The senior officer who told me the story said that he had cautioned Captain McCrory not to drink too much, because once they stepped outside to go back to the ship, the cold air would make him more inebriated. Captain McCrory apparently scoffed at the idea, perhaps an indication that the CO didn't take the advice of others too seriously.

Reportedly, he was handling his liquor well—until he left to go back to the ship. Once he stepped outside and the frigid air hit him, he quickly became so drunk he could barely walk, probably because the icy air constricted his skin capillaries and sent more alcohol-rich blood to his brain. The CO was so plastered he had to be hoisted aboard the ship by a crane. Luckily for him, it was not an era when a bunch of sailors were standing around with their iPhones.

Playing football on the ice. (Courtesy of Joe Burke)

While we were out on the ice on liberty some curious emperor pen-guins were in the area. None was curious enough to come and check out our football to see whether or not it was a strangely shaped egg. Emperor penguins are quite remarkable animals. They are the only penguin spe-cies that breeds in Antarctica during the winter. In order to reach their breeding colonies, they have to walk or slide on their stomachs over the ice, sometimes for 70 miles. A colony may contain thousands of penguins. During heavy storms, they huddle together in a tight mass in order to survive the brutal winter conditions.

The female lays but one egg. As soon as she lays the egg, her male partner immediately transfers the egg onto the tops of his feet and incubates the egg by covering it with his lower belly. If the egg is allowed to rest on the ice for even a few minutes, the egg will not hatch and/or the chick will not survive. The female then travels back to the open ocean to feed. The father-to-be has to keep his egg-balancing act going for a number of weeks while the mother is gone. Understandably, this greatly restricts the male's mobility. In a very real sense, his "feet are tied." After the mother returns, they take turns, one caring for their chick egg while the other makes the long trek to open waters in order to feed.

Penguins feed mostly on fish but also eat other species, such as krill and squid. They can dive to depths of more than 1,700 feet and remain submerged for up to eighteen minutes. They are capable of doing this because of the special type of hemoglobin they have, as well as their abil-ity to shut down their blood supply to non-vital organs.

Emperor penguins are only found in Antarctica. They weigh from about 50 to 100 pounds and grow up to 4 feet tall. Their tuxedo-like black-and-white coloration gives them their very distinctive and elegant look.

Besides looking fashionable, the emperor penguins we saw did not seem to be afraid of us. One penguin came very close to where two of us were standing. He did not make any squawking noises like I had heard on previous occasions. He just stared at us for a minute and then slowly waddled away. Since they live for about twenty years, we may not have been the first men to get close to this particular creature, but given how few men ever travel deep into the Weddell Sea, we very well could have been.

The emperors felt comfortable approaching us because they are naturally curious and do not have any land-based predators. A couple of sailors—likely two who had more than their quota of beer—mistook the curiosity of one penguin as a sign of friendliness. They thought it would be cute to have a photo standing shoulder to shoulder on either side of one. They quickly realized the error of their ways after being slapped around a bit by the bird's powerful flipper wings.

While we were parked in the ice, both of our helicopters went searching for open sea lanes that might allow us to reach the submerged oceanographic buoys, which were located about 180 miles north of the continental Antarctic ice shelf. We were eventually able to sail within 20 miles of the buoys. Given that the *Glacier* was so much closer than it had been the previous year, I can imagine Captain McCrory was starting to salivate about a successful retrieval. However, the helicopters returned with very disappointing information. Per ODF70, the pilots reported, "close ice, 7 oktas concentration composed of giant and medium floe, multi-year ice with hummocked [tented] pressure ridges. The adjacent water was refreezing with the formation of young ice."

After assessing the severity of the ice conditions, which hardly could have been worse, Captain McCrory did not give up. Instead, he decided to make what he described as a "temporary withdrawal," and sail farther south, toward the Filchner Ice Shelf and the Antarctic continent.

According to Ensign Frydenlund, the lead scientist for the oceanographic buoy project, Professor Thor Kvinge was not particularly upset about the failed retrieval. He described Kvinge as being "philosophical" about the failure. Kvinge basically told Captain McCrory to "forget it." From a scientific point of view, Kvinge obviously did not feel that it was worth taking any major risks to retrieve the data contained in the buoys.

According to one of the officers I interviewed later, the CO attempted to release one of the buoys from its anchorage while we were in the area.

Perhaps Captain McCrory was frustrated at not being able to retrieve the buoys and hoped he could seize at least one. The buoys could be released via an audio signal. This signal was supposed to set off an explosive charge which would sever the tether that anchored the buoys to the ocean bottom. When Captain McCrory tried to detonate the release, it didn't work. Maybe we were too far away.

If the explosive disconnect had worked, I don't know how we would have retrieved the buoy, unless it could have been hauled back by one of our helicopters. Given the density of the ice at the time, it seems more logical that a released buoy would have floated toward the surface but remained trapped below the almost-solid ice pack. If so, it could have eventually drifted to some distant position where there would have been no hope of finding it, either because it would have lodged underneath the impenetrable ice closer to the Antarctic Peninsula, or because the batteries in the buoy would have weakened to the point where its tracking signal would have been undetectable.

Even though we were traveling farther south, there was a better chance of finding open water along the continental ice shelf. During the summer, strong currents commonly move out some of the ice pack. Also, the infamous katabatic winds help to blow floating ice from the edge of the continent. Cold masses of air descending from the higher central portions of the continent create these winds. However, even these partial shore leads tend to close off the farther one travels west toward the Antarctic Peninsula.

On February 20, Joe noted, "[I] didn't get much sleep last night because of all the noise the ship was making going through the ice." We went through a good deal of heavy ice before we reached the relatively open waters along the continental ice shelf.

There was no mention of a storm during that time in Joe's diary. Perhaps this was because the main portion of the storm was 100 miles or more northeast of us. The storm started on February 20, 1970, and did not die out until February 24, 1970. It drove the ice pack against and all around us. The pressure of the wind tented and buckled the ice pack for

100 miles. We valiantly tried to break loose from its iron grip, including using backing and ramming techniques.

All of that effort was in vain. The ship was taking a beating and burning through huge amounts of fuel. Every time I went out on deck, I could see we were barely creeping forward. Most of the enlisted men did not get outside as often as I did, but every time they did they saw the same iceberg in about the same place. They started calling it the "duty iceberg."

Even when I was not on deck, I could feel the *Glacier* bucking and heaving against the densely packed ice. We were like a goat encircled by a python. We could wiggle around a little, but there was no way we could escape. I had the sinking feeling that it was just a matter of time before we were completely locked in.

On February 23, 1970, Joe's diary entry began with three words: "We are stuck."

The *Glacier's* ODF70 summary report, either written by Captain McCrory or approved by him, described our icebound situation the day before Joe's pronouncement as follows:

Glacier *proceeded to within 8 miles of the Luitpold Coast ice front in position 77-28S 35W at 220712Z Feb 70. There was no evidence of any shore lead along the continent. The deepest western penetration of the pack ice was made to position 77-30S 38-11W at 221300Z Feb 70. There was no indication of any leads in the direction of Belgrano Station.*

In other words, the *Glacier* traveled south from the buoy site to within 8 miles of the continental ice shelf on February 20. Within two days there were no leads toward our intended escape route to the east, nor, for that matter, in any other direction. We were trapped.

Beset.

There is no mention in this ODF70 paragraph of attempting to return to the buoy site. I assumed this meant that Captain McCrory had given up on that idea and was solely concerned with either escaping the Weddell Sea or getting ready to winter over.

The first meeting Captain McCrory held after announcing that we were beset in the ice was on February 23. It included the XO, the chief engineering officer, me, and about six of the senior chiefs. It was during this meeting that he told us we all would be among the key personnel wintering over with the ship.

As I looked around the officers' wardroom, all I saw were grim-faced men, almost all of them fifteen to twenty years older than me. These were tough men and seasoned sailors. I could see their jaw muscles tighten and their foreheads crease, but I did not hear a single word of complaint or dissent. Even though I was by far the most junior member of the group, and not much of a sailor, I didn't feel out of place. I knew I had a critical role to play, and I was not about to shirk my duty. To a man, we all expressed our resolve to do our best to deal with the inevitable situation we faced.

During this meeting, the CO laid out his basic plan. Forty essential men would be selected to stay with the ship for the winter. If indeed possible, the other men were to be evacuated. Not being able to do so would compound an already difficult problem. A survival situation is a lot easier to manage with forty people than a group five times larger. We were close to a huge ice shelf. The plan was to have a C-130 Hercules plane land on the ice shelf and then ferry the evacuees to the ice shelf with our helicopters. The alternate plan was to ferry the nonessential crew to a Japanese icebreaker. However, that icebreaker was nowhere near us at the time and probably could not get closer to the *Glacier* than the distant edge of the dense ice pack.

While both plans had significant problems (discussed in more detail later), in either case, there would be at least forty of us facing a frigid, lonely, dark Antarctic winter.

On February 24 Joe penned: "It is cold and snowing. This is a wonderful place to be if you like [a] white Christmas 365 days a year. We are still stuck in the ice. The big shots running the show are telling everyone not to worry, and still they are worried stiff themselves."

Joe's diary entry corresponds with my memory of that time. The "big shots" were indeed worried, and they had every right to be, in spite of their telling us there was no need for concern. We were burning up thousands of gallons of fuel and getting essentially nowhere. The ice pack continued to drift toward us, blown by winds coming from the northeast. Everywhere you looked, you could see solid ice interspersed with tented pressure ridges of buckled ice.

The temperature was dropping.

The ice was getting an inch thicker every day.

Open water was 100 miles away.

We were caught in the Weddell Sea gyre, the same current that carried Shackleton's ship, the *Endurance*, for ten months before it was crushed to splinters and abandoned. The current was carrying us closer to the continent every day, where it would be colder still. And it was taking us farther west.

We were heading into an area that was impassable even for the largest icebreakers.

After finding out I had made the "top forty," I had mixed feelings. While I felt proud knowing I was considered an essential crewmember and believed I could be a positive influence on the crew, I wasn't looking forward to spending a winter in Antarctica cooped up on a ship. The guys with whom I enjoyed spending my free time—the junior officers, airmen, scientists, and my medical crew—were not, as far as I knew, on the list, although it hadn't yet been released in its entirety. I had to hope that some of them would make the list, but the odds were slim.

The most essential personnel were more likely the crewmembers with whom I least wanted to spend my free time. However, I knew I had the ability to get along with just about anybody, and that was what I intended to do. I was just going to have to suck it up, take one for the team, and do the best I could to maintain harmony among the crew. I thought the best I could reasonably hope for were months of dreary monotony—assuming nothing catastrophic occurred.

As the head of the medical department, I had to make an important decision of my own. I knew there would be medical situations requiring an extra pair of hands. I had to choose an assistant who would winter over with me. It was a difficult decision. Chief Toussaint was the logical choice, because he had the most experience, but he was a married man with children. I ended up choosing Sal, my dental tech. He at least had some medical background, and could handle any dental emergencies.

Sal took the news better than I'd expected. I could tell he was disappointed, but he clearly understood the logic of my decision. He rose to the occasion. I was proud of him.

Many of the sailors scheduled to leave us behind had mixed feelings. Joe, for example, had been looking forward to going home for a long time, yet he didn't feel at all good about leaving. *But I'm part of the crew,* he thought. *And what about my job?*

Similar feelings were shared by many. Those who would leave the ship, if that was possible, would be assigned elsewhere, but no one knew where. Odds were high that they would be split up and separated from shipmates with whom they had formed a bond. Some did not yet know if they would be among the forty people who would remain aboard. The multiple levels of uncertainty weighed heavily on everyone.

We did not hear anything about other icebreakers coming to our rescue. There was a smaller, less-powerful, Wind-class Coast Guard icebreaker in Antarctica at the time, but it was in the Ross Sea. A similar Wind-class icebreaker was in New Zealand undergoing repairs. Apparently, there was no hope for any available icebreaker to come and save us, either because they were not powerful enough or because it was too late in the season. Or both.

At the time, I did not know how hard it was for an icebreaker to reach the general area of the Weddell Sea where we were trapped. In 1960 an Argentinean icebreaker, the *General San Martín*, was unable to reach the coast near us in order to provide supplies and transportation to Ellsworth Station (which used to be an American station before it was Argentinean). As a result, the Argentineans and one American were forced to spend a second winter there with minimal food.

If other icebreakers were going to come to our rescue, it probably would not be until spring—seven long, dreary, cold months away. And there was no guarantee we wouldn't be stuck for a second winter.

Or longer.

One of my early thoughts about wintering over, assuming we survived the experience, was *We have nothing to prove; Shackleton has already done it.* Although I did not want to be stuck there for the winter, part of me looked forward to the challenge, even though it would be more like being the tenth person to run a four-minute mile. Maybe spending the winter on an icebreaker in Antarctica would end up being a grand adventure, but it was not the kind I wanted. I had been looking forward to visiting great ports and seeing the world. I certainly wasn't going to see much of the world stuck in the ice.

Although I had concerns about our situation, I was not too worried. My natural bent is to look at things optimistically. *Of course we will survive this ordeal. It will be cold, desolate, and boring, but we will eventually get out of this mess. We're not in some wooden ship like Shackleton's. We're in a heavy-duty steel icebreaker—and we have a round bottom. We should be fine.*

But then I started to wonder.

What is it going to be like if we do get pushed out of the ice? And who is to say for sure we won't get crushed? The hull is torn and weakened. Maybe the ice will get caught in the tear in our hull and rip it apart.

I was certainly picking up on what Joe had noticed. If the big shots were telling us not to worry, why did they look so shaky themselves?

Obviously they knew a lot more than I did about the ship and the potential hazards we faced.

20

Survival

WHEN WE FIRST BECAME TRAPPED IN THE ICE PACK, THERE WERE MANY details about our situation which I did not know or fully comprehend. I have learned a good deal since. One thing I knew for sure was that it gets very cold in Antarctica during the winter, but exactly *how* cold? We were not anywhere near the South Pole. The coldest it had been prior to our becoming beset was 10 below zero. Growing up in Minnesota, I remembered one time when it was 30 below zero every day for an entire week. (Will Steger, the world-famous, world-class polar explorer, is a friend

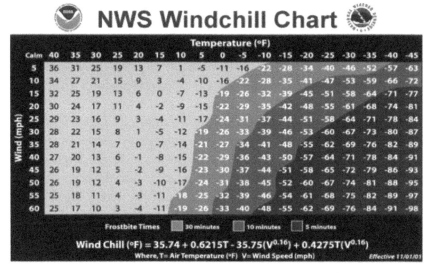

NWS Windchill Chart. (Courtesy of the National Weather Service)

and boyhood neighbor. Minnesota is good training ground for learning subzero survival techniques.)

As a kid, I had sledded, ice-skated, and skied in 10- to 20-below-zero weather without any major problems, so those kinds of temperatures did not worry me much. But I assumed it would sometimes get to 50 below zero in the Weddell Sea during the winter.

And then there was the wind factor. Antarctica is famous for frequent storms with hurricane-force winds—nothing like the comparatively mild winter winds I had experienced in Minnesota.

One of the things I was concerned about was frostbite. As you can see from the National Weather Service windchill chart, frostbite occurs in minutes if there is a 50-mile-per-hour wind, even if it is only 15 degrees below zero. This chart only covers up to 45 below zero. In a 50 mph wind and 50 degrees below zero, exposed skin essentially flash-freezes. During a typical Antarctic winter storm, which occur about once a week, wind velocities reach 90 to 100 miles per hour. The wind-chill effect would be horrific—and wind blasts of up to 200 mph have been recorded. Wind-blown snow will quickly fill up a small room if there is the tiniest crack or seam exposed to such intense velocities.

Frostbite occurs when ice crystals form in small capillaries. The affected skin looks like a thin layer of frost. The first time I saw it I was crossing a mountain ridge on skis with a group of friends. It was about 10 degrees above zero, but with a 30 mph wind. After about fifteen minutes, I began to notice patches of frostbite on the exposed cheeks of my ski buddies, proving that frostbite can occur even sooner and in milder conditions than the above chart indicates.

When frostbite occurs, the blood supply shuts off to adjacent tissues. If it is not quickly reversed, tissues can become permanently damaged or destroyed. Even more damage occurs if the frostbite is reversed by warming the affected tissues and then they refreeze. In either case, the only treatment for severe frostbite is removal of the dead tissue. If we were going to winter over in Antarctica, it was certain we'd be seeing cases of frostbite. I dreaded the thought of a case so severe it would require an amputation.

Although I knew it would be cold in Antarctica, I did not realize how quickly and severely the weather could change. One of the physicians

I worked with at Cape May, Dr. Tom Taylor, was also assigned to an icebreaker in Antarctica. He recalled the temperature once dropping *30 degrees in a single hour*. He also remembered the crew having to use base- ball bats to bust up ice which had accumulated on the upper decks. Too much ice accumulating on upper decks can actually cause a ship to roll over.

Some of the weather-related problems we would face were obvious, but I feared we could also face a host of other problems, including cri- sis situations that I could not easily anticipate. Astronaut Colonel Chris Hadfield touched on the nature of problematic situations in his book, *An Astronaut's Guide to Life on Earth*: "Expecting the best but preparing for the worst is . . . a seductively misleading concept." Instead, he wrote that we should understand that "there's never just one 'worst.' Almost always there's a whole spectrum of bad possibilities."

We had been assured that we would be fine in the ice pack because of our rounded bottom. The worst-case scenario, we were told, was that we would be pushed out of the ice pack, but not crushed. This seemed logical. At the time, I did not know that the rounded-hull concept had been well tested and proven during the previous century by Fridtjof Nansen and his ship, the *Fram* (see chapter 14).

Although the basic design of the *Glacier* was sound, I knew it was not foolproof. Within the 20-mile radius of where we were beset, there were over a hundred huge bergs. It did not take much imagination to realize that we would not fare well if we were forced against one of those bergs or, worse yet, caught between two of them.

Being forced out of the ice pack and spending the winter partially on our side did not seem so bad—compared to being crushed—but what would it be like? Imagine what life would be like with our ship lying at some awkward angle. What would happen to a round-bottomed ship, on top of an ice pack, exposed to hurricane-force winds? We could be tilted so much we would be walking on bulkheads more than decks.

Most of the equipment aboard the ship was heavily bolted and secured in place—things like stoves and refrigerators, beds and sinks, toilets and showers, storage cabinets and desks, as well as the only operating table. How would these things function at an odd angle? Would a toilet work at a 30-degree angle? Such extreme angles were not out of the question. In 1881 the USS *Jeannette*, a US Navy ship trapped in Arctic ice for two years, ended up at a 23-degree angle before it was crushed and sank. At that angle, the crew could not even stand unless they were hanging on to something bolted down.

Given our rounded bottom, which the USS *Jeannette* did not have, it seemed unlikely that we would be subjected to extreme angulation. The *Glacier* might be able to remain at a neutral angle some of the time, but with wind and ice pack pressure invariably coming more from one side, some degree of tilt was likely. In fact, that tilt could change back and forth as the ice pack and winds shifted. However, since the snow or ice would cover the outer decks much of the time, walking on even gently sloping ones could be treacherous.

One reassuring thing, which I did not know back then, was that even older wooden ships of conventional design, such as the *Belgica* in 1899, had survived a winter in the Antarctic ice pack. The way a ship like that could survive was by becoming frozen into a large field of ice, which maintained a relatively even pressure on the hull and buffered it from external pressures. Conversely, patches of open water surrounded by uneven ice floes could be very hazardous to ships of any design. However, evenly pressured ice pack does essentially nothing to divert the path of a large meandering iceberg.

Although an open patch of water can refreeze quickly in the Antarctic, the new ice is usually thin and weak. As a result, it provides almost no protection against heavy pieces of advancing ice. According to Antarctic expert Captain MacDonald, small chunks of heavy ice can "impinge upon, penetrate, and crush the ship through application of pressure upon small areas of the ship." Think what a woman in high heels can do to a softwood floor.

We were in an area with some open patches of water. But unlike the *Belgica*, we were in a significantly more hazardous area east of the Antarctic Peninsula. We were being driven toward the Peninsula, while the westerly *Belgica* had been carried away from it.

The pressure created by wind-driven ice is hard to comprehend. A small example of its force was seen in May of 2013 in Manitoba, Canada, as well as in Minnesota. A storm struck these two areas with winds of from 40 to 55 mph. Sections of lake ice broke up and were pushed ashore by the winds, creating small walls of ice that uprooted large trees and destroyed the foundations of some homes, including some made of concrete blocks and reinforced steel. Imagine what winds of from 90 to 100 mph could do, pushing much larger blocks of sea ice over a huge ocean surface. The larger pieces and tented ridges of ice, some 10 to 15 feet high, would create much more of a "sail" effect, on which the wind would act.

If the *Glacier* was forced partially or completely out of the ice, there was no guarantee the transition would be a smooth one, as we no longer had a uniformly smooth bottom. Ice could get caught in the indented and torn area of the hull, or if we were pushed into the side of a large iceberg, the top edge of the hull could catch. Pressure could build up and then suddenly release. How suddenly? Although unlikely, it could occur as suddenly as it did with the *Endurance*. The photographer on that ship, Frank Hurley, wrote:

> *We began to rise from the ice, much after the manner of a gigantic pip squeezed between the fingers. In the short space of seven seconds, we were shot from the floes and thrown over to port, with a list of 30 degrees . . . on deck, great was the chaos: dogs, candles, and sledges and emergency gear were thrown into an inextricable tangle.*

A sudden, violent thrust like that could certainly create chaos aboard the *Glacier*. Multiple major bodily injuries would likely occur, and I would be in charge of treating those injuries—assuming I was not too badly injured myself.

One of the major concerns we had was that the water-intake ports would clog up and freeze over. No water to cool the engines and generators would mean no heat, no electricity, no drinking water via our desalination units, no ability to maneuver, and so forth. In other words, a catastrophe. People can survive about three days without water. If we weren't able to evacuate the majority of the crew and all two hundred men remained aboard, and we were not able to distill freshwater, it wouldn't take long to drain our water tanks.

Given the ingenuity of our engineers, I imagined they could come up with some kind of a makeshift or jerry-rigged repair in order to get some kind of open piping far enough below the surface ice so that we would have free access to seawater. However, as we will later learn, even temporary freezing of intake ports can create a crisis.

Although we could make do with improvised pipes to feed our engines and our desalination units, the pipes probably wouldn't last long because of the constantly shifting pack ice. If we ran out of pipes, we would have to shut down the engines and resort to melting snow and ice for freshwater, which would involve a good deal of labor and more exposure to the elements.

Even if we had enough fuel and our rounded hull protected us from compressive forces, the top half of the ship remained vulnerable. Icebreakers have straight sides near the top of the hull, not to mention the straight sides of all the superstructures. Many of the icebergs or ice cliffs in Antarctica are over 100 feet tall. The combination of high-riding ice and drift-ice pressure could destroy our ship.

If the *Glacier* was crushed and we had to live on the ice pack, as was the case with Shackleton, we would be in serious trouble. We were not prepared for that kind of situation. One option considered by the senior officers was to set up a camp composed of twenty-five fifteen-man rubber lifeboats. These inflatable boats were fully enclosed with built-in canopies; however, there were no heating stoves, except for a few brought by scientific field parties. Moreover, we did not have enough suitable clothing if we weren't able to evacuate the nonessential crew, as there was only enough for about one-third of the men. And we had only five sets of snowshoes.

The lack of an adequate number of heating stoves would affect not only our ability to keep warm, but also to melt snow. Although snow would be easily obtainable, it normally takes approximately 10 gallons of snow to produce 1 gallon of water. Given the low moisture content of the dry talcum-powder-like snow in Antarctica, it could take 20 gallons of snow to create 1 gallon of water. Thus, it would be virtually impossible to produce sufficient water for a large crew.

In addition, this alternate plan did not take into account all reasonable contingencies. For example, the canopies on stationary lifeboats probably were not designed to withstand 100 mph winds. There was one good thing about using lifeboats, however. If the ice split beneath one of them, as had happened to two of Shackleton's men in a tent, at least they would not drown. (Shackleton's split-second rescue saved the pair.)

The thought of spending a winter on the ice pack in some flimsy shell was something I did not want to think about. I had been tent camping many times in Minnesota, but always during the summer when the main hardship was enduring attacks by our "state bird"—the ubiquitous king-sized mosquitoes. I had thought of doing some winter tent camping, but changed my mind after talking with friends, who managed only a few hours in their tents before the four of them decided to spend the rest of the night huddled together in a smelly outhouse.

If the *Glacier* remained intact but significantly tilted, our two helicopters would have to be removed from the shelter of their hangar and operated from the mostly flat surface of the ice pack. Fully exposed to the elements, they probably would not be able to function for long.

Unlike Shackleton, we had the option of getting additional clothing, equipment, and supplies via airdrops from fixed-wing planes, wind and weather permitting. But those windows of opportunity could be few and far between. Other problems, such as locating a white ship in a white sea, were virtually guaranteed.

As long as the ship was heated and we were able to stay aboard, we would not have to worry about frostbite. But there would be times when the men would have to leave the safety of the ship. For example, if we did an air evacuation from a continental ice plateau, we would need to helicopter about 160 crewmembers there. Such an undertaking would take a good deal of time. Long exposure to the elements could not be avoided. Many other things could go wrong during the ferrying process: a helicopter could go down, crewmembers could be stranded in a storm, or maybe a helicopter would not be able to fly at all.

Assuming we could transport the nonessential crew to the continent, which was critically important, then a fixed-wing plane theoreti-
cally could transport them. Airplanes routinely use large ice runways
in Antarctica, but those runways are groomed and flattened by heavy
equipment. The *Glacier*'s equipment did not include a bulldozer. Since
crevasses are common on glacial plateaus, our crew would have to find a
section of the continental ice shelf without any obvious crevasses—and
then hope there were no hidden ones that would collapse under a landing plane, or the weight of a person. In January of 2016, a helicopter
pilot safely landed on an Antarctic ice shelf but fell to his death when
he stepped out of his aircraft and plunged through a snow bridge into a
deep crevasse.

One can look to the 1933 expedition of Lincoln Ellsworth for examples of the problems fixed-wing planes face in Antarctica. Ellsworth was
a wealthy adventurer who wanted to be the first to fly across Antarctica.
His plan was to fly from the Bay of Whales on the Ross Sea to the Weddell Sea and then back—a total distance of approximately 3,400 miles.
His plane was parked on an ice shelf the morning the flight was supposed
to take place. Suddenly a series of "terrifying blastings and crashings"
occurred as a result of the ice breaking up. The next thing Ellsworth knew,
he was alone on an ice floe rocking in the ocean. The plane was nowhere
in sight. One of the mechanics was standing on a separate floe, which had
once been part of the runway. He and his men were rescued by his ship,
the *Wyatt Earp*.

The following year, Ellsworth attempted to take off from Deception
Island, but when one of his mechanics tried to start the engine, it would
not turn over. Apparently, a "block of frozen oil" in one of the cylinders
caused a connecting rod to break. Ten days later, after the engine was
repaired, they were ready to give it another try, but then the weather
turned bad. Ellsworth was about ready to return to United States when it
finally cleared. He and his pilot took off, but they had to return an hour
later because of storms.

Ellsworth tried again the third year with a different pilot. His first
attempt was aborted because of problems with a fuel gauge. On his
second attempt, he was forced to make three landings because of foul

weather. The first landing required a nineteen-hour layover, the second, a three-day layover, and the third, eight full days. The fourth leg of the trip ended in a forced landing because the plane ran out of fuel. They had to walk the rest of the way.

And all of these problems occurred during the Antarctic summer—the same season in 1979 when all 252 people aboard a DC-10 flight died after being caught in a "sector whiteout" condition and crashing into Mount Erebus.

Flying in Antarctica during the winter is almost impossible, even with modern aircraft. Flights to the South Pole normally stop in February. Even though February is technically considered the Antarctic summer, it gets down to 40 below zero at the pole by then. When temperatures are that low, planes begin to experience major problems; for example, "O-ring" seals start to fail and hydraulic fluid begins to freeze.

The first option for evacuating the bulk of the crew involved flying them out. If we chose this option, a Lockheed C-130 Hercules fixed-wing plane with skis attached and flown by US Navy pilots would be the aircraft coming to the rescue of the crew. The C-130 is a heavy-duty plane that can land and take off without any ground-support facilities. Navy fliers have developed a technique for creating their own snow runways. What they do is fly in just low enough so that their skis lightly touch the snow and ice. They skim along the surface, at just below takeoff speed, until they have created a runway of sorts. Then they take off and make another pass to create a second parallel runway, giving them not only a landing runway, but also one for taking off. However, these "runways" are never fully compacted, so there would always be the risk of a crevasse-spanning snow bridge collapsing beneath them.

The second option involved ferrying them longer distances to a ship safely located on the edge of the ice pack, north of our position. The problem with this was that open water at that time was 100 miles away, and the ice pack was beginning to grow at an exponential rate as winter approached. By the time another ship could be in place and the ferrying operation set up, the edge of the pack easily could be 150 miles away, meaning more exposure to the harsh and unpredictable elements for our two helicopters. Since only five to six men could be transported at a time, it would take twenty-four to thirty-six trips. Moreover, there was the danger of exceeding their 300-mile round-trip range,

Even if the majority of our crew were evacuated, it was likely that we would occasionally need to have supplies airdropped. I might need emergency medical supplies, or the ship might require replacement parts. The pilots would have to work hard to spot our white ship in the frozen white sea, given the amount of ice and snow. In any case, airdropped supplies rarely land with pinpoint accuracy, nor do they always survive a rough landing. In the past, a number of airdrops at the South Pole ended up only creating deep pits in the ice filled with destroyed material.

Assuming an airdrop did not land on our ship, someone was going to have to hike over the ice pack to retrieve it, facing the associated risks. For safety's sake, at least two men would have to make the trek. They would need to be roped together and travel with ice axes, in case one of them fell into a crevasse. Also, they could check each other for the beginning stages of frostbite, as a person so afflicted would not necessarily be aware. They would also have to wear appropriate goggles to avoid snow blindness, from which it can take up to ten days to recover.

A safe trekking route one hour might be extremely hazardous the next because of fissures and gaps in the ice. The ice is constantly shifting, and gaps covered with snow and loose ice can be undetectable. A cold snap quickly freezes over open leads in the ice. If the cold snap is followed by heavy snowfall, the snow has an insulating effect on the ice, so it won't freeze as quickly, or as well. Given this scenario, what seems like solid ice can easily break, leading to an icy and potentially fatal plunge into the sea.

We could survive with fewer airdrops if we decided to satisfy our craving for fresh food by eating the foods that were the mainstay of early Antarctic explorers—seal and penguin meat. One of these early explorers described the taste of penguin meat as follows: "The penguin, as an animal, seems to be made up of an equal portion of mammal, fish and fowl. If it is possible to imagine a piece of beef, an odoriferous codfish and a canvas-back duck, roasted in a pot, with blood and cod-liver oil for sauce, the illustration will be complete."

Although I have a healthy appetite and can eat just about anything, I do have my limits. I have never dared to taste lutefisk, a famous

Scandinavian dish made by taking dried fish, soaking it in a mixture of lye and water until it becomes gelatinous, and then cooking it. The "acquired taste" is so bad that I have seen bumper stickers which proclaim: "Lutefisk—Just Say No." (I would try lutefisk before I would eat penguin meat, however.)

We would also have to be concerned about problems associated with poor visibility, particularly whiteouts, which occur during storms that arise suddenly and unpredictably. Antarctica is famous for such storms. Whiteouts occur when sunlight is reflected back and forth between cloud layers and ice surfaces. Shadows are absent and the horizon disappears. One can no longer perceive topography or one's immediate surroundings. In such a situation, one could easily step into an open gap in the ice.

From my own experiences skiing in a whiteout, I know it can cause so much disorientation that it's difficult to tell up from down. At least when you're skiing you will eventually end up going downhill; gravity is still gravity.

A whiteout on a flat surface is quite a different thing. You could be 10 feet from the ship during a whiteout, get disoriented, and wander off to your death. That sort of thing has happened all too often in Antarctica. In one situation a man left his Antarctic base shelter to take a weather reading. He became disoriented during a subsequent whiteout and froze to death—within 80 feet of two buildings.

It was obvious we had far more to worry about than just being stranded.

21

The Polar Night

BASED ON WHAT I HAD LEARNED DURING MY PRE-DEPLOYMENT TRAIN-
ing, I could anticipate some of the psychological problems we might face
if we wintered over. People would likely become apathetic, listless, and
more or less depressed; at least, that seemed to be the pattern for people
who spent the winter in permanent shelters on land-based stations. However, my brief training did not teach me about what it would be like to
winter over aboard a ship. Clearly, it would be different from being on
terra firma. There also would be differences related to our situation aboard
the *Glacier*.

For starters, the forty people selected to winter over were basically
chosen for their technical abilities. As far as I knew, little, if any, con-
sideration had been given to which people would be most psychologi-
cally suited for coexisting in such difficult circumstances. I assume people
who were notoriously disruptive were excluded from the top forty, but I
couldn't be sure of that. After all, command had insisted on retaining a
sailor who became seasick within the breakwater of Long Beach Harbor,
despite my advice, because they were so focused on his technical skills.
Someone with very important technical expertise might have horrible
interpersonal skills. Even though I had some background in psychology
and psychiatry, I was not involved in the screening process.

When Shackleton chose his crew for the *Endurance*, he was acutely
aware of "the kind of chaps" he was selecting. In his book *The Heart of
the Antarctic*, he wrote: "The men selected must be qualified for the work,
and ... must be able to live together in harmony for a long period of
time."

When he screened candidates for his crew, Shackleton looked for people who were enthusiastic and likely good members of a team. He also looked for people who were adventurous, optimistic, and had a good sense of humor. One of the common questions Shackleton asked applicants was if they could sing. He clarified this question by saying, "Oh, I don't mean any Caruso stuff; but I suppose you can shout a bit with the boys?" He felt someone who was willing to sing, even if they did not have a talent for it, was the sort of person more likely to have good team spirit. In addition, he looked for people who were generally happy. He was quoted as saying, "Loyalty comes easier to a cheerful person than to one who carries a heavy countenance." Furthermore, he wanted people who were not afraid of hard work or menial tasks. At times, he expected everyone, including himself, to do things like scrubbing the deck.

Given the history of polar expeditions, it is quite clear that even one problematic person in this kind of confined environment can make life extremely difficult. When famed Australian explorer Douglas Mawson first wintered over in Antarctica, his life was made miserable by a truculent and paranoid crewmember. To make things worse, this crewmember was the only one who knew how to operate the radio. There was no way Mawson could force him to be cooperative. Consequently, their one link with the outside world was effectively severed.

—◦—

There are branches of the military services that have expertise in properly screening crewmembers based on psychological characteristics. That kind of psychological screening is not done for icebreaker crewmembers. In fact, some sailors are selected for icebreaker duty as a *punishment*. Such individuals would not likely be the kind of "cheerful person" Shackleton sought. I know of one case where a Coast Guardsman with a potentially significant medical problem—the last kind of person you would want deep in Antarctica—was scheduled for icebreaker duty as a form of disciplinary action. When I found out about this case, I was able to intervene before the assignment was carried out.

I also heard about a doctor being assigned to an Antarctic icebreaker because he had an intolerable personality. Apparently this doctor frequently irritated his fellow physicians, including one who was on good terms with the admiral's secretary. The latter allegedly asked the secretary, "Can you get rid of this guy?" The next thing this difficult doctor knew, he was assigned to an icebreaker going to Antarctica. As might be expected, this medical officer was none too happy about his reassignment. During the equator-crossing ceremony, he clearly expressed his unhappiness, saying, "No way am I going through that ceremony." His fellow officers gave him no assurance that a gang of sailors might not force him to participate. They told him, "You're on your own." So, rather than be "one of the guys," he barricaded himself in his room, reportedly threatening to shoot anyone who dared enter.

One can only imagine what kind of a jolly fellow he would be during a forced confinement in an icebound ship.

According to Ensign Frydenlund, there were many people in the Coast Guard during the time of our deployment who had been in trouble with the law. When they went before a judge, they were told, "Join the service or go to jail." Some of these lawbreakers ended up being assigned to the *Glacier*. For some reason, the enlisted men assigned to Ensign Frydenlund's section were castoffs of more than one other section. As he told me later, "There was a considerable leadership challenge in keeping the castoffs of the castoffs of the castoffs performing adequately."

I assumed that the Coast Guard did not feel it was necessary to do psychological screens on people assigned to icebreaker duty because prior to that time, an icebreaker had never been forced to winter over. If consulted, I would have advised some kind of psychological screening of crewmembers, if only for the reason that Antarctica deployments are so long, so distant, so risky, and so isolated.

In my professional opinion, the screening process for icebreakers should be more akin to that required of submariners, who have essentially no personal space, no escape from workplace conflicts, no sunlight for periods of time, disrupted sleep cycles, and so forth. In other words, they face many of the stresses sailors wintering over on a ship would face in a polar region. Submariners have to undergo a sophisticated battery of psychological tests known as the SUBSCREEN, which, according to Dr. Mark Bing, are aimed at identifying "atypical mental health and motivational problems that interfere with adapting to the submarine environment."

My cousin was on a nuclear submarine and claimed that the slightest sign of a significant emotional problem was enough to get someone permanently barred from submarine duty. I have no reason to doubt him. The unique and confined environment of a submarine or a wintering-over ship imprisoned in the ice pack is no place for someone with significant personality problems.

Of course, even with the best screening process, one can end up with inappropriate shipmates. I am sure that astronauts are well screened, yet I read about a Russian cosmonaut who suffered because of conflicts with a difficult crewmember. He was quoted as saying, "I wanted to hang myself, but I couldn't, because there was no gravity."

Even with the best crew, those overwintering on the *Glacier* would have to cope with inevitable nightmarish stresses. There would always be the risk, however slight, of the ship being crushed or torn apart. And everyone aboard our ship knew it.

We would not be able to avoid signs of pressure on the ship, such as the reverberating sounds of compressing ice. Having grown up in Minnesota, I had some idea of the kinds of sounds shifting ice make on a lake, but no idea of how horrendous those sounds could be in a polar situation. Based on my research, I learned that the sounds could be persistent or distinct, like "a distant clap of thunder." At times, the sounds and the pressure could be overwhelming. Alfred Lansing wrote in his book, *Endurance*: "There had been pressure in the past, but nothing like this. It moved through the pack like a sluggish shock wave . . . a chaos of churning, tumbling destruction."

Fridtjof Nansen's book *Farthest North* contains what is perhaps the most dramatic description of the awful sounds of ice under pressure:

For when the packing begins in earnest it seems as though there could be no spot on the earth's surface left unshaken. First you hear a sound like the thundering rumbling of an earthquake far away on the great waste; then you hear it in several places, always coming nearer and

*nearer . . . you feel the ice trembling, and hear it rumbling under your
feet; there is no peace anywhere.*

Such disturbances could go on for days at a time, interfering with
our sleep or just making people constantly edgy. Loss of sleep is far more
important than people realize, particularly if it is an ongoing problem.
Studies show that the vehicle accident rate increases by 18 percent the day
after daylight savings time begins. Losing even one hour of regular sleep
turns out to be significant. Those rare individuals who cannot sleep at all
do not survive. In between those extremes of lost sleep, there is a whole
constellation of significant emotional and physical symptoms.

In medical school, I learned that long periods of darkness are associated with depression and increased rates of suicide. In doing research for
this book, I learned that living in extended periods of darkness affects
such things as circadian rhythms—an essential component of sleep–wake
cycles. One study of miners in Svalbard, Norway, indicated that 88 percent of the men in this area of polar darkness developed sleep problems
lasting at least two weeks.

Studies have also shown that, among other things, thyroid function is
adversely affected by polar darkness. This effect is known as the "polar T3
syndrome" because of the changes in the T3 subtype of thyroid hormone.
Healthy young people notice "T3 moments [like] taking ten seconds to
realize 'S' comes before 'T.'"

I was particularly interested in writings I later discovered about an
early Antarctic explorer, Dr. Frederick Cook. He was not only someone
who wintered over on a ship trapped in Antarctic ice, but also a physician. He wrote *Through the First Antarctic Night* about his experiences
aboard the aforementioned Belgian research ship, the *Belgica*, a stoutly
built, wooden Norwegian steamship with an iron-reinforced bow. Originally built in 1884 as a whaling ship, she must have been a tough one. She
was still sailing in 1940 when the British scuttled her to keep her from
the Germans.

The *Belgica* got stuck in the ice pack on March 3, 1898, and remained
so until February 14, 1899. She was the first ship to winter over in Antarctica. She probably would have remained there for at least another winter

had the crew not opened a 1.5-mile-long channel the following summer by cutting through 5 feet of sea ice with handsaws.

Based on my ice-fishing experiences in Minnesota, cutting a small hole in 14-inch-thick ice requires a fair amount of work. I cannot imagine how much work would be involved in sawing through 5-foot-thick ice for such a long distance, but this example shows to what lengths a desperate crew will go to avoid spending a second winter in the ice pack.

Dr. Cook described the obvious stress of being stuck on a ship, drifting with the ice pack and fearing imminent destruction: "In this drift it is possible that the ship may be dragged over a submerged reef . . . a rocky shore, or against the formidable land-ice. In each case destruction of our vessel and a miserable death for all must be the inevitable result."

Similarly, nineteenth-century Arctic explorer Captain George De Long, drifting with the ice pack aboard the USS *Jeannette*, wrote: "We live in a weary suspense. . . . Living over a powder-mill waiting for the explosion would be a similar mode of existence."

Dr. Cook made many references to the effects of the polar night. As the darkness increased, Cook noted how the crew became indifferent and apathetic, finding it difficult to concentrate. "We are under the spell of the black Antarctic night," he wrote, "and, like the world which it darkens, we are cold, cheerless, and inactive."

About the only person who did not become a "chronic complainer" on Cook's ship was Captain Lecointe. Cook wrote, "The captain has had to do the most trying work, that of making nautical observations . . . in trying positions in the open blast for an hour at a time." In spite of frequent "frosted fingers, frozen ears, and stiffened feet," the captain remained in "characteristic good humor." Clearly, those who had important daily activities, like the weathermen in land-based stations, find it easier to cope with their situation.

For the most part, I anticipated that life aboard the *Glacier* while we were stuck would be boring. There would be very little for the crew to do with the ship frozen in place. The heating, generating, and water-distilling machinery would have to be kept running, but probably little else, as we would need to preserve fuel. Morale would suffer if crewmembers remained idle for long.

Shackleton was very aware of the negative effect of prolonged idleness. After his ship was trapped in the ice, he put a great deal of effort into keeping the men busy with productive work, like building doghouses on the ice pack for their sled dogs. Given the time the crew had, and their need to make life more interesting, they built doghouses out of snow and ice that looked more like castles than a humble doggie igloo. Unfortunately the doghouses didn't last long. They were all destroyed by the shifting ice.

Chief Toussaint was well aware of the importance of keeping the crew busy. Every morning before sick call, he had Joe Burke swab the decks in sick bay and then buff them to a shine. Then Joe had to do the same thing all over again in the afternoon. Chief Toussaint wanted to keep our quarters exceptionally clean, but he also wanted to keep the corpsmen busy, for their own good. Joe commented later that this kind of active routine was one of the things that helped him cope with the stresses of our deployment.

Shackleton also encouraged his men to play sports, such as soccer and hockey, wherever they could find stretches of smooth ice—usually where open leads of water had recently frozen over. I wished I had thought of bringing my hockey skates. (In Minnesota, it's one of the few outdoor activities one can enjoy six months a year.)

Shackleton worked hard to maintain morale, in part because he clearly cared about his men. One of the reasons he was such an effective leader was because he put his men first. He went out of his way to establish a personal and amiable relationship with each of his crewmembers. When someone became sick, he was the one to personally nurse them back to health. He would even give up his bed and sleep on a bench in order for a sick man to be more comfortable.

When major decisions had to be made, Shackleton consulted with everyone before making the final call. His men did not necessarily agree with all of his decisions—and some were ill advised, like one to forgo stockpiling readily available game—but they abided by them. They greatly respected him as their leader. The fact that Shackleton could also be "one of the guys" made his leadership style particularly effective for men in a stressful and confined situation.

When we became icebound, I was unfamiliar with Shackleton's leadership style or the styles of other famous Antarctic expedition leaders. Historians generally agree that the famed British explorer Captain Robert Falcon Scott was a difficult leader. Scott believed in military hierarchy. Shackleton was under Scott's leadership during the first attempt to reach the South Pole. He grew to detest Scott and vowed to be a very different kind of leader. Sir Raymond Priestley, British geologist and early Antarctic explorer, famously wrote: "For scientific discovery give me Scott; for speed and efficiency of travel, give me Amundsen; but when disaster strikes and all hope is gone, get down on your knees and pray for Shackleton."

Based on what I knew about Captain McCrory, his leadership style was closer to Scott's than Shackleton's. There certainly was a hierarchal structure aboard the *Glacier*. I thought that significant changes in his leadership style were unlikely, even if we were down to a crew of forty. When I later learned about the kinds of things Shackleton did, such as scrubbing the deck, initiating a song, or giving up his bed for the comfort of a sick person, I could not imagine our CO acting in the same manner. Nor did I believe he would be consulting with each of the wintering-over crewmembers before he made any major decision. It just did not seem to be in his DNA.

Another cause for concern while wintering over was the food we would have to eat. I knew the morale of the men could be significantly affected by our diet. I was certain that our meals would become boring and monotonous. We would have little, if any, chance to replenish our supplies. For those of you who have never gone weeks without tasting fresh food, it is hard to imagine how much you miss it. I had never been much of a salad eater before the trip, but halfway through the trip, I would dream about the taste of a juicy fresh tomato or the satisfying crunch of chilled crisp lettuce.

Historically, polar explorers on long treks seem to have done quite well with simple menus, like pemmican (a mixture of dried beef and lard), hard biscuits, and tea. But this food-tolerance phenomenon, according to Vilhjalmur Stefansson, who wrote *The Friendly Arctic*, works only for men who were, as he put it, "working hard and for a purpose. Those at winter

The *Glacier*, prior to removal of the 5-inch guns in 1968. (NavSource Online)

quarters who have nothing to do except prepare equipment for the work of others and keep the ship and camp in condition, are as difficult to please as clerks and bookkeepers at a city boardinghouse."

About the only strenuous physical work we would be routinely doing aboard the *Glacier* would be chipping ice from the vessel, which would be tedious, unpleasant, and dangerous. For the most part, we would just be sitting around, waiting for the sea ice to break up in the spring. It would be hard to avoid becoming listless and apathetic.

As for myself, other than handling emergencies, there would not be much for me to do. Much of the work I had been doing was related to things that would happen when the men were in port—things like stitching people up after a drunken brawl or treating new cases of venereal disease or a cold virus. Also, I would not have to tend to the injuries commonly occurring in rough-and-tumble seas. On the other hand, if we wintered over, my staff and I would be treating minor "frost burns" caused by warm flesh sticking to cold metal. And there was a good chance we would be treating psychological maladies often associated with a wintering-over situation. I had to hope that I would be in a good-enough mental state myself to be an effective counselor.

Studies have shown that some of those who cope best with confinement in harsh conditions are those who are good at entertaining themselves. Apparently, someone who is less needful of social interaction with others, and functions well independently, is more likely to do well. However, even extroverts need privacy from time to time, and this is difficult to find in a confined environment.

Even though Captain McCrory had informed the crew that we were going to be beset for the winter, he did not tell command back in United States that we were stuck. As one of the junior officers put it, "That would have been like calling out the [rescue] dogs." Reportedly, he was just telling command that we were resting in one place in order to carry out stationary research activities. I couldn't tell why he was withholding this information from the outside world. I guessed that he was acutely embarrassed about our predicament and dreaded telling his superiors about the mess we were in. This lack of full disclosure did not sit well with the men. Feelings of distrust grew. No one was going to try to rescue us—if indeed that was even possible—if they didn't know we needed rescuing.

22

Movement

WE WERE STUCK ONLY 8 MILES FROM THE EASTERN PORTION OF THE
Filchner Ice Shelf, close to where it abuts against Coats Land. Viewed
from the *Glacier*, the face of the shelf was about 150 feet high. The shelf
gradually extended southward to a height of approximately 2,000 feet,

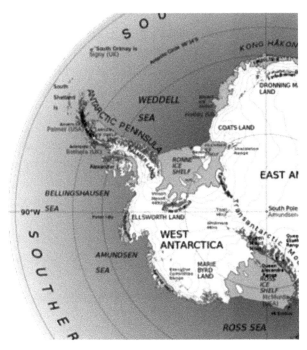

(Courtesy of Wikimedia Commons)

and it was within easy reach of our helicopters. I could imagine the bulk of our crew being airlifted from that shelf.

What I could not imagine was how I would feel about being left behind.

This shelf was named after Wilhelm Filchner, the leader of the German Antarctic Expedition, which reached this portion of the Weddell Sea aboard the *Deutschland* in early 1912. Like Shackleton, Filchner hoped to traverse the continent from the Weddell Sea to the Ross Sea. At the time, no one knew if Antarctica was a single landmass or merely a collection of islands connected by ice.

If I had known about all of the problems Filchner experienced, particularly the emotional stresses associated with his expedition, I would have been even more uncomfortable about our situation aboard *Glacier*. Reportedly, one of the officers on the *Deutschland* committed suicide even before Filchner reached the ice pack. If I had known this, I would have asked myself, *If polar expeditions were causing some people so much stress before they even got trapped in the ice, how much worse would it be afterward?*

Once the *Deutschland* reached the ice shelf, Filchner could not get its captain, Richard Vahsel, to agree to set up their base on the inland portion of the continental ice shelf; instead, Filchner was forced to set up his base on a floating portion of the ice shelf. Vahsel falsely and knowingly assured Filchner that the huge glacial tongue was firmly grounded on the ocean bottom.

After eight days of intensive work, Filchner's base was almost set up on the ice shelf, but then it broke loose and started drifting out to sea—along with an 18-mile-long piece of the shelf, which threatened to crush their ship. They had to back the ship up and use their longboats to recover as much of their floating base as they could.

Like the *Deutschland*, we would also have to worry about a large section of the ice shelf breaking off and drifting into us. Another danger was the possibility of being caught in a tsunami-like wave if a large section of the adjacent ice shelf suddenly broke loose. One of the explorers who preceded Shackleton, Carsten Borchgrevink, almost drowned in waves caused by the calving of a section of the Ross Ice Shelf.

If a very large piece of the ice shelf suddenly broke off, not only would we have to worry about it crushing us, but we would also have to worry about it creating a massive wave that could swamp us. The largest recorded wave in modern history was over 1,720 feet high. It occurred on July 9, 1958, in Lituya Bay, Alaska, when an earthquake sheared off a large chunk of a glacier and hillside into a narrow bay.

The *Deutschland* became beset on March 6, 1912, and remained so until September of that year, when it finally escaped. Morale during the six-month wintering-over period was horrible, with Filchner and his scientific crew enduring open conflicts, insults, and abuse from Vahsel and the ship's crew. It was so bad that Filchner had to carry a sidearm with him because he feared for his life.

The bad news for us on the *Glacier* about Filchner's experience was that it showed how seriously behavior and morale could deteriorate during a Weddell Sea winter. The good news was that the *Deutschland* survived the winter, even though it was beset. However, unlike the German ship, we were drifting with the ice pack, meaning we had to worry about being pushed into the denser and more-dangerous ice along the eastern side of the Antarctic Peninsula.

All of us on the *Glacier* selected to winter over seemed resigned to our fate. We were going to be traveling wherever the ice pack took us, and since our early drift pattern was the same as Shackleton's, we assumed we would fare no better. Following in his path, we were headed for denser ice, and the chances of being crushed against an ice shelf or towering iceberg were all too real.

Between February 20 and February 23, our position barely changed, other than a slight drift toward the continent. Although we still had a small area in which to maneuver, I assumed the ice would squeeze in around us to the point where we could not move at all. It was only a matter of time.

Beyond our narrow strip of broken ice, the ice pack was a solid mass, accentuated by buckled ice ridges 10 to 15 feet high, extending to a frozen horizon. The elevated ridges were an obvious sign of the relentless pressure compressing the ice. I had the ominous feeling that the ice would soon be battering the sides of our ship.

The distant view toward the south, along the path we had broken, had fewer pressure ridges, but that expanse of ice, along with the *Glacier*, was drifting toward the massive continental ice shelf.

On February 26 we experienced a miracle. A freak storm hit us, with atypical westerly by southwesterly winds. It was exactly what we needed to push the ice pack back toward the northeast. We finally had some leads to follow—narrow, but far better than none.

Our helicopters kept searching for more as we started slowly moving toward the east, but I wasn't breathing a sigh of relief yet. We were still 100 miles from open waters.

We began to cautiously zigzag through the ice pack. In heavy ice concentrations, it is almost impossible to travel in a straight line. In general,

Following a lead. (Courtesy of US Coast Guard Archives)

the quickest way between two points in the ice pack is the longer way. In polar regions the ice is rarely made up of a single solid sheet. Instead, it is made up of separate pieces that are always on the move because of winds and currents. If there are no obvious leads, the trick is to find the seams, and hope they don't end in an impasse.

Heavy ice is much less of a problem if one can find adjacent areas of open water in which to push it. The problem we had was that most of the stretches of open water we saw were narrower than our ship. Even when we found leads, or seams leading to one, we had to be extraordinarily careful in how we approached them. Since we had a damaged hull—and we still didn't know the full extent of the damage—we had to make sure that we approached denser areas of ice with our intact port side, so it would take the brunt of the blows. It was like off-road driving through a desert filled with giant boulders in a car that steered safely in one direction, but less so in the other.

The sailor at the helm was under strict orders regarding exactly when he had to notify the CO before approaching thicker ice pack. It was like we were picking our way through a minefield. Our helicopters operated almost continually, looking for navigable leads. All too often, the news the pilots brought back was bad: Either they saw no leads, or only minuscule ones. The leads had to be adequate, as the last thing we needed was to get stuck in some impenetrable cul-de-sac.

Joe, who had ancillary duties as part of the flight crew, spent time up on deck in the early hours of the morning. As long as there was light—almost twenty-two hours per day—the helicopters kept flying. It was blustery and frigid. Joe could have used a heavy-duty parka, but had to get by with his medium-weight jacket. Much of the time there was little for him to do. He said, "I thought they were using me for a windbreak."

As soon as the helicopters landed, Joe and the other members of the flight crew surrounded the helicopters and asked, "What did you see?" The usual response was more bad news.

We were fortunate when we first started making some headway because none of the prevalent storms coming from the north or the east struck us. But our progress was uneven. Although we followed the leads available, we could not consistently head in the desired direction. It was as if we were trapped in a maze.

On March 1, after only two days of uneven progress, the winds shifted and started blowing from the north. The ice packed in around us. Wind-driven snow and overcast skies restricted visibility. Helicopter flights had to be canceled. We were stuck again.

I was feeling anything but optimistic. The gloomy weather matched my mood. When I would go up on deck, all I could see were thick uneven fields of ice punctuated by pressure ridges—ice thrust out of the ocean and piling on top of itself. I imagined the ice pack I could not see was even more impenetrable.

The following day, the winds relented. For part of the day, we made good headway in a northeasterly direction, but we soon ground to a halt. The bitter disappointment of being trapped again was tough to take. Beer and pizza were served in a feeble attempt at boosting our morale.

Joe noted that we were "stuck in some heavy slush which is next to impossible to move."

It was one thing to be blocked by dense pressure ridges, but quite another for the mighty *Glacier*—the largest icebreaker in the free world—to be blocked by heavy slush. Even small ice particles could halt our progress if there were enough of them and they were under heavy pressure. It was like trying to push through a mountain of sand. And if we stayed there much longer, this slurry would only become thicker and turn into solid ice.

The repeated setbacks weighed heavily on the crew. Winter was fast approaching, with every day getting shorter. We desperately needed to find areas of open water.

The crew seemed serious and somber. There was no joking, wisecracking, or lighthearted banter. For the most part, the crew kept their thoughts to themselves.

I spent more time in my room. I tried to pass the time by reading or playing my guitar, but it was hard to concentrate. I lost all interest in jumping rope or trying to get exercise. Only rarely did I walk up to the bridge. My camera sat on my desk. There was little to see except a monotonous white expanse.

After a day stuck in heavy slush, the winds surprisingly shifted in our favor. Leads started opening up with the help of light winds coming from the south. We were getting closer to open ocean, yet we knew another bad storm, coming from the prevailing direction, could seal our fate and leave us icebound for the dreaded Antarctic winter.

Amazingly, southerly winds continued to blow. The ice pack thinned out, and the pressure eased. On March 2 we started sailing south toward the Caird Coast. Even though we were traveling back toward the continent, the hope was that we would reach the typically more-open seas along the edge of the continent. The idea was to reach our originally planned escape route along the Caird Coast. We zigged and zagged and smashed our way in that general direction for two days. Our ship often shuddered and lurched like we were in an earthquake. The noise of ice grinding and cracking against our hull was almost constant.

There was another ship caught in the Weddell Sea at the same time, the *General San Martín*. This Argentinean icebreaker was also beset, but much closer to open water. On March 4, its helicopter landed on our flight deck. One of the Argentineans gave us more-detailed information about their situation. It was clear that we could extricate them from their predicament—if we could reach them. Our icebreaker was much more powerful, and they were in an area of thinner ice. (In 1960, the *Glacier* had come to their rescue in a similar situation.)

On March 5, Joe was on the flight deck when one of our reconnaissance helicopters landed. The deck crew rushed to the helicopter to hear what the pilot had to say. There was a good lead going south all the way to the Caird Coast. Joe was thrilled. He said, "It was like hearing that the Cubs had finally won the pennant." (Following a 108-year hiatus, the Cubs won the pennant in 2016.) The *Glacier* wasted no time heading in that direction.

After seven days of zigzagging within a 30-mile radius—as if we had been led by a drunken sailor—we finally slammed through the edge of the ice pack and reached the relatively ice-free waters along the continental ice shelf. It was like we had just busted out of jail.

Altogether it had taken us eleven days to escape our icy prison, during that time we'd felt like we were scheduled for the electric chair, with no reason to expect a pardon from the governor.

Free at last!

Once we were in open waters, we started sailing in a northeasterly direction. We were able to reach the *General San Martín* later that same day. Its crew was playing music and dancing with joy when we arrived. We had rescued them before, and they knew we could do it again.

The *General San Martín* had tried everything, including using explosive charges, in their attempt to create a channel in the ice. The major effect of the explosive charge was to blow out some of the windows on their bridge. It did nothing to help them break free. Since Ensign Frydenlund could speak a little Spanish, he was transferred to the Argentinean ship to coordinate operations for the duration, mostly communicating with them by drawing diagrams on their windows.

In order to set the *General San Martín* free, we had to break a channel of open ice into and completely around their ship so that they had room to maneuver. It took us three days, but we did it, allowing the *General San Martín* to sail into open waters.

The icebound *General San Martín*. (Courtesy of Joe Burke)

Barring another catastrophic storm from the northeast, we were going to leave behind the dismal prospect of the darkness and perils of an Antarctic winter. It was time to celebrate! We had a big party on the *General San Martín*. Unlike our ship, they had an ample supply of good wine and it flowed freely. Joe described "gallons and gallons of champagne. . . . It was a great party. They were very fine people and very thankful. . . . It was one of the best days of the trip."

The Argentineans had some delicious food for us. I particularly remember eating a tasty salad with an ingredient I had never seen or tasted before, hearts of palm. Ever since, whenever I eat hearts of palm, I am almost invariably transported back to that celebratory occasion on the edge of the Weddell Sea ice pack.

After our "coming-out party," it seemed that we had survived the worst we could expect to encounter during our voyage. The trip was more than half over. We had hit an iceberg and survived. We had penetrated deep into the Weddell Sea, in spite of our damaged hull. We had escaped the trap that had ensnared Shackleton. Maybe the rest of our deployment would be smooth sailing.

After all, what more could possibly go wrong?

23

Confrontation

After rescuing the Argentineans, we continued eastward to Halley Bay (77° 31' S, 26° 36' W), located along the northeastern edge of the Weddell Sea. We exchanged a brief visit with the members of the British station. I was not part of that visit, but didn't care; I was just glad we were no longer icebound.

Around this time we heard about another ship in distress, the *Fuji*. Reportedly, this Japanese ship was stuck east of us, in ice 25 to 30 feet thick. If we went to her rescue, it would change our deployment plan. Instead of visiting Valparaiso, Chile—our scheduled "rest and recreation" (R&R) port—we might be going to Cape Town or Rio. Whichever port we hit, it was going to be one of the highlights of our trip. Any stop would be better than another in Punta Arenas.

The rumors about going to rescue the *Fuji* didn't last long. We learned that its crew was somehow able to extricate themselves, which meant we were back to our mission, as planned, still looking forward to our liberty in Valparaiso.

Perhaps disappointment over missing a good liberty port contributed to one of the sailors becoming surly and noncompliant. As a result, the captain threw him into the brig and restricted him to a diet of bread and water. It was a short-term punishment, which apparently worked, as he behaved for the rest of the trip.

Except for this one sailor, most of the crew, including myself, was in a good mood. We had escaped the ice pack, rescued the Argentineans, and were looking forward to five days in Valparaiso—the "Valley of Paradise"—during the homeward leg of our voyage.

Those good feelings didn't last long.

On March 20, Joe Burke penned: "A rotten day news-wise. They told us we are going to skip our R&R liberty call in Valparaiso, Chile, so we could get home early. As far as most of the crew, including yours truly, this is a big screw. We haven't had any good liberty to speak of on this trip, and now this." The following day Burke wrote, "This trip has been one disappointment after another."

Good liberty ports were extremely important for the morale of the crew, the vast majority of whom were single guys. Even for guys like Joe, who was borderline homesick almost the entire trip, getting home a few days sooner in no way made up for the loss of that good liberty port.

When I later spoke with Captain Coste, the *Glacier* CO between 1980 and 1982, I asked him how he felt about liberty ports. He said, "I tried to hit as many as I could." Captain Coste also told me there might have been another reason why a number of crewmembers were upset about not stopping in Valparaiso. Apparently, unbeknownst to me, certain crewmembers had a preexisting arrangement in Valpo—a standing reservation with a certain brothel exclusively available to the men of the *Glacier*. It would have been a nice perk for the guys who liked that kind of risky behavior.

One of the other former Coast Guard icebreaker captains with whom I consulted, Captain James Fournier, summarized his view of leadership this way: "You take care of the crew and they take care of everything else." According to Captain Coste, Fournier was very popular with his crew, even though he was a stricter disciplinarian than some. I got the distinct impression that neither of these captains would have bypassed an important liberty port.

Skipping Valparaiso was not, in my opinion, taking care of the crew. Certainly, the majority of the officers and crew were not consulted before the CO made this decision. Shackleton, I am quite certain, would have done things differently.

My disappointment about skipping Valparaiso was probably worse than what most of the crewmembers were feeling. I certainly felt I had been the victim of a "big screw." I was furious. The main reason why I had volunteered for this deployment was because of all the glorious liberty ports we were supposed to hit. Even though I'd been disappointed to learn that Valpo was the only port we were going to hit on the way home, I'd planned to make the best of our time there.

I had heard there was terrific surfing near Valparaiso. While I was an enthusiastic surfer, I wasn't very good. I had backed off many a wave so that I would not collide with a better surfer catching a wave just ahead of me. Most good surfing spots in America were too crowded for my level of skill, but an isolated beach with waves all to myself—as I imagined they would be off the coast of Chile—well, that would be a dream come true. Maybe I could even find time to catch some glacier skiing in the Andes. I was sure I could find fun things to do in either Valpo or Santiago.

So much for my plans. Along with everyone else's, they were down the drain.

Since we were not going to stop in Valparaiso, we were not going to refuel. Apparently the CO figured we could continue our deployment and make it all the way back to Long Beach if we conserved fuel and skipped our scheduled liberty. One way to conserve fuel was to shut off the air-conditioning units when we crossed the equator. This wasn't going to be a big problem for Captain McCrory, whose top-deck quarters would be cooled by ocean breezes, but most everyone else would have to endure temperatures of 110–120 degrees below the main deck.

The combination of skipping our best liberty port and arbitrarily having to conserve fuel struck me as a terrible decision.

Since it had just been made, I thought there was a chance I could get the captain to change his mind. I decided to have a one-on-one discussion with him, even if it involved taking a risk. *What is he going to do to me if I confront him?* I thought. *Throw me in the brig?* My answer to that question seemed evident: *He's not going to throw me in the brig. I'm the only doctor on this ship.* So I scheduled a meeting with Captain McCrory.

I vividly remember waiting in the passage outside his stateroom. I began to have doubts. I was so nervous I was almost shaking. I couldn't stand still, pacing back and forth in an area about three paces wide. My mouth was dry, my thoughts, racing. *He could still throw me in the brig.* A captain on a ship at sea can do just about anything he wants. He is almost like a god—even more so in an isolated situation like deep in Antarctica.

Mark Twain, who worked on and piloted boats on the Mississippi, once wrote: "All men—kings and serfs alike—are slaves to other men and to circumstance—save alone, the pilot (or captain)—who comes at no man's beck and call, obeys no man's orders and scorns all men's suggestions."

My fears about standing before someone with Godlike powers did not stop me. As I entered his stateroom, I remember thinking how big it was compared to my own. It was richly furnished, and conveyed at least one message: Rank has its privileges. The CO's manner was neither friendly nor hostile; it was sort of matter-of-fact, mixed with a bit of curiosity. After all, it was the first time I had ever approached him about anything of apparent significance. He was at ease. I was not. I was in his domain.

I can still vividly recall the essentials of our conversation. It went like this:

"What did you want to see me about?" he said.

"Your decision to skip liberty call and refueling in Valparaiso."

"What about it?"

"I don't think it's a good idea."

He just looked at me.

I continued. "The crew has been through a lot. It would really be a boost to their morale if they had a good liberty port to look forward to."

"Some guys would just as soon get home early."

"I'm sure that is true for some, but I don't think it's true for the majority."

"Not everybody gets what they want."

"I understand that," I said, trying to control mounting feelings of anger. "But I'm also concerned about the effects of cutting back on using fuel. It could cause problems. For example, guys tell me we won't have air-conditioning when we cross the equator."

"They'll survive. It's been done before."

"Maybe, but I think it's taking an unnecessary risk."

"It's not your call."

"It's my job to be concerned with the health of the crew."

"You're not the captain," he said, with an edge to his voice.

"It sounds like your mind is made up," I said, my volume rising.

"It is," he said emphatically.

By this time, I was visibly upset. Personally, I was angry about skipping Valparaiso, and I knew I was acting as a spokesperson for the majority of the sailors who were not in any realistic position to confront the CO. I knew my primary responsibility wasn't making sure any of us got good liberty—as important as that was. My primary responsibility was for the health and safety of the crew. That was my line in the sand, and from my perspective, he was crossing it. I didn't think he was taking this seriously enough. I suspected his decision was based primarily on self-serving motives. Some crewmembers had told me that he had a plush desk job in DC, and he was anxious to get back to it. That may have just been scuttlebutt, but whether it was or not didn't matter to me in that moment.

"Look," I said angrily, "if anyone gets hurt on this cruise because of your decisions, I don't know what I can do, but I'll do whatever I have to, to get your ass in a sling."

At this point I half expected him to say, "You're being insubordinate to a superior officer. I'm throwing you into the brig." Instead, he looked at me incredulously. And then with a sneering, arrogant laugh, he threw out his chest, raised his head, and bellowed, "You can't touch me." He looked at me with an air of contempt and absolute superiority. Like what I was saying was so absurd that it didn't require another word. It was clear that nothing I could say would make a difference, so I just walked out.

I was totally taken aback by his arrogance. And it hurt to be so summarily dismissed. It was like he had not given one iota of credit to anything I had said. He acted as if he was a giant and I was a bug.

That may have been so, but perhaps I could do something that would really sting. I had no idea what that might be, and I was grinding my teeth in frustration. Nonetheless, I was determined to think of something to make him suffer the consequences of his poor judgment, particularly if anyone was injured due to his actions.

That was the last discussion of any substance I ever had with Captain McCrory. For the rest of the cruise, I avoided him as much as possible. Maybe I shouldn't have lost my temper with him, but I wasn't sorry about it. I didn't swear at him. I didn't call him names. I had delivered the message I wanted to deliver. At least I had the satisfaction of not pulling any punches.

We had to go back to Palmer Station to pick up the Seabees. I don't know how they would've made it back to the United States if we had not escaped the Weddell Sea. That would have been one unhappy bunch of sailors if they'd had to winter over at Palmer Station.

As we were heading back around the Antarctic Peninsula, we were once again hit by rough seas. The ship was pitching wildly back and forth. Joe almost got seasick. Many of the crew did get sick, including Danny O'Keefe, and a few others were injured due to the rolling seas. Without Danny's help, Joe, Chief Toussaint, and I were busier than ever.

After being battered by heaving seas for three days, things quieted down. In spite of the loss of our good liberty port, we could still enjoy the beauty of the area. On March 23, Joe wrote, "A full moon at sea is really fascinating and pretty. We've had plenty of nice scenery on this trip, but that is all."

We reached Palmer Station on March 26, but didn't stay long. We picked up the Seabees to take them back to Punta Arenas.

The following day we headed back toward Drake Passage. And more bad weather.

On March 27, Joe wrote: "Today has been so super out of this world rough that at times it feels like the ship is going to tip over . . . things are breaking off the walls."

After one day of liberty in Punta Arenas, we boarded the ship and headed back to Palmer Station. We could have refueled while we were there, but did not, apparently because it would have taken another day or two to do so, and the CO seemed confident we had enough fuel to make it back to Long Beach, as long as we instituted conservation measures.

Conservation measures that would prove to be costly.

24

Life or Death

THE FOLLOWING DAY, APRIL FOOL'S DAY, WAS NOTHING TO JOKE ABOUT. There was an explosion, which occurred when a muffler device called a "silencer" ruptured inside the ship's huge smokestack. The silencer contained diesel fumes and unspent fuel. When those pressurized fumes hit the relatively oxygen-rich air within the stack, there was a "blowback"—an explosion in the opposite direction of the one intended. The insides of the stack were coated with old diesel fuel and carbon deposits, which caught fire. The intense heat affected essentially all the compartments adjacent to the smokestack. A storage room containing linen burst into flames. Fires broke out on multiple levels and raged out of control.

The "general quarters" alarm sounded when the fire began, and I immediately went to sick bay, my assigned station. I was joined by my corpsman Danny O'Keefe and four litter bearers.

Shortly after the fire began, one of the crewmembers was brought to sick bay suffering from smoke inhalation. It was the same Black sailor who had nervously expressed his concerns about my being able to care for him before we'd left Long Beach. For the sake of patient confidentiality, I will call him Fred.

Fred was walking, with assistance, when he came into sick bay. He was coughing, looked weak, and had a pained expression, but he did not appear to be in a crisis. I told Danny to give him oxygen, which was easiest to do if he was lying on the surgical table.

After Fred was settled and on oxygen, I suddenly noticed smoke coming in under the door off the surgical suite. I opened the door and

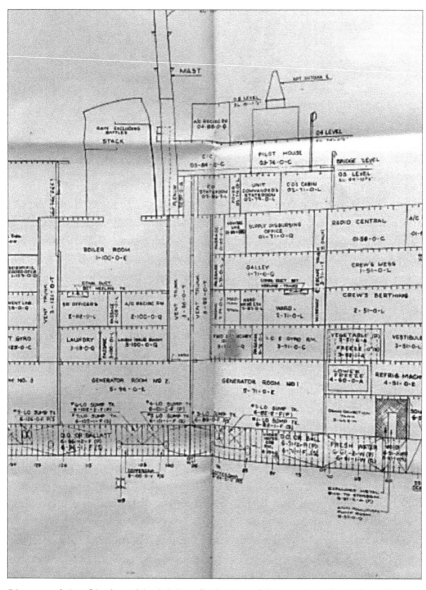

Diagram of the *Glacier*, with sick bay (in bottom right quadrant just above the generator room, marked by a triangle), adjacent to smokestack. (Courtesy of US Coast Guard Archives)

saw open flames and smoke coming from a storeroom several feet away. The storeroom was adjacent to the smokestack.

I quickly closed the door and went to the front room of our three-room suite. Smoke continued to pour in. It looked like we would have to evacuate our station. I called the bridge, told the officer of the day about our situation, and asked for permission to vacate our general quarters station, which he immediately granted.

As I was hanging up the phone, Danny rushed into the room with a panicked look on his face. "Our patient—he stopped breathing," he said.

I didn't know what to think.

I rushed into the surgical room, which was by then half-filled with a thin haze of smoke. Fred was lying there, motionless. I was hoping that his lapse in breathing had been temporary. It wasn't. His heart was beating, but he was definitely not breathing.

I grabbed an "ambu bag"—a squeeze-bag type of appliance used for forcing air into a patient's nose and mouth—and started ventilating him. I could feel the heat radiating through the adjacent wall. Smoke kept billowing in through the seam of the adjacent door. I knew we couldn't stay there much longer.

We moved Fred into the next room and laid him on the deck, where the smoke and heat were less intense. I continued to ventilate him with the ambu bag. It was getting harder to see as more smoke spilled in.

I soon started having problems with the ambu bag. Air seemed to be leaking out around the mouthpiece. I couldn't tell if the problem was with the bag or with Fred's lungs. I thought he was possibly experiencing spasms in his bronchi, the main airways leading into his lungs.

Whatever the cause, he wasn't breathing, and the ambu bag wasn't working. If I was not able to get air into his lungs, he was going to die. I did not have a respirator or any other equipment used for artificial respiration. There was only one other choice—mouth-to-mouth resuscitation.

I had never done mouth-to-mouth resuscitation before. It felt weird doing it, particularly on a man, but I didn't hesitate for a second. I was going to do whatever I had to do to revive this sailor. My main concern was that mouth-to-mouth breathing wouldn't work either. I knew I had strong lungs. I also had extra energy from the adrenaline surging through my body, and I damn well was going to use every ounce of my strength to breathe for him.

When I started the mouth-to-mouth, I could feel the resistance in Fred's lungs. Thankfully, the force of my breath was stronger, and I could feel air going into his lungs. Although I felt an immediate sense of relief when I saw his chest start to rise, the air I was forcing into his lungs was becoming smokier by the minute. We needed to get out of there.

There was a major problem, though. The hatches had been sealed as part of the general quarters drill. The only way through the sealed hatches was via a scuttle, something like a large horizontal porthole that could be sealed tight. The situation was this: I had to be able to move Fred quickly. If I stopped breathing for him for more than a minute or two, he could suffer brain damage. There was no way I could stop giving him mouth-to-mouth resuscitation, help haul him up the ladder, squeeze him through that narrow scuttle, crawl through the scuttle myself, put him back on the deck, and restart resuscitation in the amount of time necessary to prevent long-term damage.

I told the litter bearers standing next to me, "You have to open the hatches. We can't move him until you do." Two of them ran off to open the hatches. The other two stood there while I continued breathing for Fred.

The smoke kept getting thicker and the temperature was starting to rise. I remember looking up at the two remaining litter bearers. The smoke was so dense that I couldn't see them clearly, but I could tell they were sweating and looked nervous. There was nothing they could do until I gave the order to evacuate. I was scared stiff. It wasn't the fire that was so scary, although it certainly was; it was the thought that my patient might die. This sailor, who I had promised to take care of in any emergency, who had come into sick bay alive, might leave it dead.

I had seen many patients during my brief medical career, and several had died, but all of them either had been very old, fatally injured, or had been suffering from incurable illness. And they were in a hospital, where I was part of a team of doctors. They were patients I hardly knew.

Although I did not know Fred all that well, he was a shipmate. He was young and healthy. I was his one and only doctor. If he died, I would forever blame myself, merited or not.

I had never seen a case of smoke inhalation before. I didn't know the natural course of this malady. Maybe there was something about it that was irreversible, like some severe cases of heatstroke, but I couldn't allow myself to think that way. All I knew was that I absolutely had to save him.

My eyes started to water. The acrid smell of the smoke was getting worse. I felt like coughing, but I was able to suppress the urge. I kept breathing for Fred, and his chest continued to expand with each breath. I was worried about pushing more smoke into his lungs, but there was nothing I could do about it except get him out of sick bay as soon as possible.

After what seemed like forever, we got the word that the hatches were open. We moved quickly. It took less than a minute to get Fred up to the next level. That level was also smoky, but much less so than in sick bay. We laid him out on the deck where I continued to give him mouth-to-mouth resuscitation. Once I felt he was well oxygenated again, which took another five minutes, we moved him up another level, where the smoke was barely detectable. I continued to breathe for him.

By this time, I was starting to feel exhausted and light-headed. I suppose I could have asked Danny to take over for me, but I wanted the immediate tactile feedback I got from doing the breathing myself. As I continued breathing for Fred, I could feel that the resistance in his lungs was decreasing. I could also feel that I had used up most of my adrenaline. I decided to try using the ambu bag again. Thankfully, it worked.

Sometime during this interval, the ship's photographer came by and snapped shots of my giving mouth-to-mouth resuscitation and another of my using the ambu bag. (I only recently ran across these shots while doing research for this book. I hadn't known that these photos existed.) I was totally oblivious to his presence or to the other onlookers. I think a line of chorus girls could have been dancing next to me and I wouldn't have noticed.

Given that the ambu bag was working, I felt more optimistic about Fred's surviving, but then I started worrying about brain damage. A person can go three minutes without oxygen before brain damage begins to occur. I didn't think he had gone that long, but I wasn't sure. The idea of him surviving, but being severely impaired, flooded my thoughts. Another

Contact sheet of *Glacier* fire; mouth-to-mouth resuscitation, upper-left-hand corner. (Courtesy of US Coast Guard Archives)

five minutes passed before he regained consciousness. I knew he was going to live. I anxiously waited to see if he could speak. It was only about ten seconds—I remember holding my breath—and then Fred opened his eyes and looked from side to side. There was a bewildered expression on his face. Then he focused on my face.

"What's happened, Doc?" he said distinctly, but with a raspy quality to his voice.

Those were some of the best words I'd ever heard. It was as if he had just awoken from a long nap. He was going to be fine.

A huge sense of relief passed over me. "You passed out," I said. "You weren't breathing, so we had to breathe for you for a while."

"Oh," he said, almost nonchalantly.

It seemed Fred was taking the whole incident in stride. I guess I had expected him to be freaked out, given how nervous he had seemed prior to leaving port. But he had obviously become a lot tougher during the deployment.

I was greatly relieved that I'd been able to keep the promise I'd made to him before the trip, one based partly on a hope and a prayer.

With assistance, Fred was able to stand up and was soon walking on his own. He had no symptoms other than a nagging cough. Based on subsequent research, I found out that he was incredibly lucky to have survived. Along with smoke inhalation, it's likely he also suffered carbon monoxide poisoning. I later learned that Fred suffered from claustrophobia. When he was forced to fight a fire in a small smoky compartment, he probably was also feeling panicky. Most likely, he was hyperventilating, which meant he had sucked in even more smoke and carbon monoxide.

Carbon monoxide binds with hemoglobin, the oxygen carrying protein in red blood cells. It binds to hemoglobin 230 times stronger than oxygen. Consequently, it is much more difficult for oxygen to displace carbon monoxide and reach the tissues, making this type of poisoning particularly tenacious and dangerous. Fred most likely had been in a borderline state of oxygen deprivation the entire time I was trying to resuscitate him. Some of the oxygen we had given him had been absorbed in his plasma, which was transported to his tissues, even though his hemoglobin was mostly saturated with carbon monoxide. The extra oxygen he got from my mouth-to-mouth resuscitation was barely enough. His life had likely been hanging in the balance. It was a very close call.

Fred returned to his full duties without any residual problems, except for one. For the rest of the trip, he had to endure his new nickname, "Smoky."

From what I gathered at that time, stack fires were not all that uncommon aboard icebreakers. We had actually had a very small one the night before, which was quickly brought under control. What was most unusual about the stack fire that almost cost Fred his life was its severity. Most shipboard fires—of any type—are extinguished in a matter of minutes. This particular fire lasted almost three hours before it was completely under control.

Ensign Frydenlund thought this fire was the most dangerous event of our entire deployment. Since the fire was so severe and affected essentially every level of the ship, it could have knocked out the ship's control systems, meaning we wouldn't have been able to steer or maneuver, and we quickly would have broached. In this sideways-to-the-waves, dead-in-the-water position, we would have been in great danger of capsizing.

The fire was scary for everyone. Joe was stationed on the flight deck, where he could see pitch-black smoke pouring out of the smokestack. All he knew was that the fire was out of control. And that the deck below him contained tanks of aviation fuel. According to one of the crewmembers belowdecks, the fire did come close to the JP-5 fuel tanks.

So why was this fire so bad? According to a junior engineering officer that I interviewed in 2012, it was partially, if not substantially, related to the CO's decision to conserve fuel for our nonstop voyage home. He told me that Captain McCrory's fuel-conservation measures, which he described as being "overly zealous," resulted in half the engines being shut down. The rest of the engines had to work more, and thus ran hotter. It was his opinion, as I understood it, that this change in engine heat is what led to the explosion that precipitated the stack fire.

One of the yeomen (sailors who do administrative and clerical work) told Joe Burke that the fire was caused by a change in the fuel-feed setting, which delivered a "too lean" fuel mixture to the engines. Ensign Frydenlund recalled that there was some change made to the engines one hour before the explosion. Another senior officer that I interviewed in 2014 seriously doubted that Captain McCrory's fuel-conservation measures had anything to do with the conflagration, but he was not on the *Glacier* during our deployment.

From the information available to me, it seems logical that something was done to the engines that contributed to a fire of such extreme proportions. The other possibility is that the entire episode was merely a coincidental event, unrelated to any error, which occurred at a time when the *Glacier* was using only half her engines.

I didn't think the fire was merely a coincidence. In retrospect, I'm glad I wasn't told anything, whether true or not, that would have led me to believe that the CO had a role in that huge stack fire. If I had felt he was in any way to blame for a near fatality, any confrontation with him would have made our first quarrel seem like a mild difference of opinion in comparison. I could have ended up being thrown in the brig. Or, if it had been two hundred years ago, my fate could have been much worse, like being marooned on an iceberg, being keel-hauled (dragged across the bottom of a barnacle-encrusted hull), or being hanged from the highest yardarm.

━ ⬩ ━

About two weeks after the major fire, we were again called to general quarters. Another fire. After the big fire, everyone was more than a bit traumatized. I know I was. There are few things scarier than a poorly controlled fire aboard a ship. I was afraid we would have another fire like the last one, only this time, I feared the fire could be even worse.

I remember sitting at my desk in sick bay waiting for the smoke to come pouring in. The preliminary report we heard was that the fire was in the engine room, because smoke was pouring out of the voice tube on the bridge. The voice tube was a means of shouting commands to the engine room, in case the intercom system was not working. A primitive device, but effective. We knew a fire in the engine room could be very serious and could lead to an explosion.

It didn't take long to determine the source of the fire. Someone realized that the voice tube had been sealed off—just like the toilet drainpipe in sick bay had been—when the ship had been refitted. Apparently, people had been using the voice tube as a trash receptacle. All it took was someone discarding their smoldering cigar butt down the tube to start a fire, with smoke subsequently pouring out of that tube.

It was the most innocuous fire one could imagine. A glass of water put it out. We laughed when we found out about it—laughter combined with an enormous sense of relief.

25

Mountainous Seas

On April 4, 1970, we landed at Palmer Station. We off-loaded gear in the morning and headed home in the afternoon, a long, nonstop trip of 7,400 miles. No stopping in Valparaiso. No refueling. For most of us, a bad way to end our trip.

It was Danny O'Keefe's twenty-first birthday, and we celebrated with a wine party. We made a mess of sick bay, but everyone had a good time. I don't remember where we got the wine. Most likely one of the crew had done some trading with the crew of the *San Martín*. Copies of *Playboy* magazine were the probable currency.

The seas became heavy as we headed into Drake Passage for the sixth time. Extremely heavy. And then it got worse. The waves were not only tall—they were massive. They seemed more like broad mountains than steep cliffs.

The navy has official terms for seas of a certain height. Waves averaging between 5 to 8 feet in height are described as "rough," 12- to 20-foot seas are "high," and 20- to 40-foot seas are "very high." Waves above 40 feet are described as "mountainous." The navy does not have a term to describe the kinds of seas confronting us that day. The Berkshires, Urals, and Adirondacks are all mountains. The behemoths we faced were more like the Alps.

The power of a wave is proportional to the distance between the crests. With small waves, the crests are quite close. On a good surfing day, the distance between crests might be something like 50 yards—just enough time to paddle hard to avoid being caught in the breaking wave. Those kinds of waves are about 8 feet high when they hit the slope of the beach or a submerged reef. They have many tons of power. The actual swell, though, is closer to 4 or 5 feet. It is only when the swell hits the slope of the beach or a reef that the waves wall up.

In the open ocean, you do not expect the swells to get too high because they generally are not hitting anything to force them upward. Consequently, something like a 25- to 35-foot swell in the open ocean is huge. It takes a lot of wind and a long distance, or "reach," for that much water to pile up on top of itself.

The reach around the Antarctic continent is essentially infinite. The waves can build and build forever if the wind is strong and constant enough. But winds can only blow so hard and last for so long, so waves never reach their theoretical maximum.

We were not dealing with theoretical waves in this case. We were dealing with the real thing.

I vividly remember standing on the bridge, which was 60 to 70 feet above the surface of the water. The air was cold and misty, with a moderate gusty wind. It was not as if we were in some raging hurricane, with chaotic waves and a lashing wind. It was more like a distant storm had produced an extraordinarily steady and powerful swell. The crests of the waves we were sailing toward were at eye level when we were standing on the bridge. The legendary "graybeards." Foaming relentless monsters, rolling along the horizon of a foreboding sky.

To me, the waves seemed otherworldly. It was as if I were watching a movie scene from another planet—someplace with different proportions, a different atmosphere, a different law of gravity. I had been at sea for over four months, and after traveling more than 10,000 nautical miles, I had seen very rough seas. I had crossed Drake Passage five times. I had seen every kind of weather imaginable—but still, the sight of those waves was unreal.

It was not just the height of the waves that was so incredible. It was also the distance between the crests. The distance was at least a quarter of a mile. The large trough between the waves was flat. In the midpoint between the crests, it felt like we were in some deep valley, which would have felt almost safe, except for the fact that we were on a collision course with an oncoming mass. It felt like we were going the wrong way on a narrow one-way street, on a motor scooter, with a cement truck heading straight for us.

The initial slope of the oncoming wave was almost gentle, but then it became progressively steeper. I remember thinking, *We have to get up that slope as far as we can or it will bury us.*

I was thinking of the times when I had been pounded by big oncoming waves while surfing—times when I felt I was in the middle of a giant washing machine before the wave would finally spit me out just long enough to take a breath before the next wave pounded me. The trick with surfing is to paddle like hell and try to at least reach the frothy peak of the wave, where you hope your momentum is enough to punch through it.

I had the same hope for our ship as it strained to climb up the long and massive slopes. The farther up we climbed, the better I felt, just like when I was surfing. I kept thinking, *We need to reach that punch-through point.* I dreaded the thought of our ship falling just short of that point. I imagined the ship flipping over backward, landing upside down, and then being crushed by the breaking wave. This was a washing machine of cosmic proportions.

The few times I was on the bridge during the storm, we always managed to climb at least three-quarters of the way up those churning giants, but sometimes the last quarter of the wave was too steep. Our bow would be buried by the thundering onslaught and sheets of water would smash into the windows on the bridge. Luckily, our momentum was always enough to break through the crest, after which I would breathe a sigh of relief.

And so it continued—hour after hour, for almost two days—all while in waters where there were scattered icebergs. At times, it was so bad that the bridge took on "green water" (water on a deck from massive waves). One of the junior officers on the bridge estimated that the rolls the *Glacier* was taking were sometimes 60 degrees in each direction, but never as much as 65. The ship would roll in one direction and then suddenly get hit by a wave striking from the opposite side. At times, the men on the bridge were knocked off their feet. A couple of sailors suffered head lacerations. They had to lock their elbows around railings in order to maintain their footing.

In 1985 a Coast Guard sailor aboard the *Polar Star* icebreaker would die from head injuries he suffered after a rogue wave caused him to lose his balance. He fell to the deck, which was tilting at a 35-degree angle. He rocketed along the deck about 40 feet, from one end of the bridge to the other, where his head crashed into the helm console.

Above our bridge on the *Glacier* was a steel canister containing signaling flags. Some of the waves were so high that they crushed the canister, meaning some were over 80 feet tall.

Caught in a sea where some of the waves were as tall as an eight-story building, the best the *Glacier* could do was plow ahead at 3 to 5 knots, about one-third its normal cruising speed. Sailing any faster would have increased the chances of the ship being damaged from the impact of the waves.

Joe recalled being belowdecks, amidships, when he felt the ship stagger and the deck start to buckle beneath his feet. In other words, there was some danger of the ship breaking in half.

And things were breaking throughout the ship. A steel cabinet bolted to the bulkhead sick bay came crashing down. Some of the other things that broke loose included large cylinders of compressed gases, like acetylene. If the neck had snapped off one of those cylinders, it could have shot ahead like a rocket-propelled torpedo and exploded through the side of our hull or exploded within the ship. The damage could have been massive.

The outside temperatures were above freezing, which was critical. If it had been below freezing, the wind-blown spray would have started to form "glaze ice," which has a high density and easily sticks to metal surfaces. Ice forms most readily high up on a ship. Topside ice adds to the roll angle of the ship, which was the last thing we needed.

There were barely enough able-bodied men to adequately control the situation. Only about 15 to 20 percent of the sailors at that time were fully functional. Most were debilitated by severe seasickness. I didn't know how many from that afflicted group were assigned to critical functions. According to one of the operations officers with whom I spoke, we needed a minimum of four people on the bridge and eight in the engine room in order to adequately control the ship—and that was assuming "nothing went wrong."

I am one of those fortunate individuals who never gets seasick, but the second day of the storm was more than I could take. I had to lie down for about an hour before the nausea subsided. I was still functional, but I wasn't doing the ship any good.

It seemed like the torturous storm would never stop. The ship was constantly pitching and rolling—often, I was told, through 103 degrees of arc. I was also told that at 105 degrees of arc, the ship would roll over. I thought the 105 degrees was an absolute limit, but apparently, it was not. I didn't know that at the time. We evidently had some rolls that were even worse, but I didn't experience any like that when I was on the bridge.

If we had capsized, there would not have been time to lower the lifeboats. We all would have been killed. Those of us who did not drown immediately would have died from exposure. About ten to fifteen minutes in those icy waters would have done it. As far as I knew, there were no rescue vessels in our area. Even if there were, rescue operations would have been almost impossible in such a raging sea. The worst thing for me was I knew how close we were to capsizing. I kept thinking things like, *Another 2 degrees of roll and we've had it.*

The nights were the worst. It was impossible to sleep. Our bathtub-bottomed ship was constantly rolling. Huge rolls—maybe death rolls. The oscillations had a certain rhythm. The end of each tilting arc lasted only a few seconds or less before reversing direction. But sometimes the roll would be bigger and the ship would seem to lie on its side. For five long seconds or so the ship would remain motionless. Those were the times when it felt like the ship was going to turn over completely—likely, the times we exceeded 105 degrees. One more good wave or a blast of wind during one of those extreme rolls would have finished us.

I thought we were all going to die. And this brink-of-disaster moment kept happening over and over. It was a nightmare. It felt like someone was holding a six-gun to my head and playing Russian roulette. He'd pull the trigger and the hammer would fall on one of the five empty chambers. Then he'd grab a new gun and repeat the whole process.

I was afraid—but not terrified. If the *Glacier* did capsize, death probably wouldn't have been all that painful. If I didn't drown immediately, I would pass out from hypothermia, and then drown, or my core body temperature would drop to the point where my heart would simply stop beating. There were, I thought, worse ways to die. If it was going to happen, it would happen.

I was being fatalistic, which was better than being scared to death. Also, I was fortunate in that I was not married and had no children. It would have been scarier and more depressing if I thought I was going to leave behind not just loved ones, but family who needed and depended on me.

In a weird way, I thought there would be one good thing about my dying at that time. One of the reasons why I hadn't wanted to go to Vietnam was because I was afraid of dying there. I would consider that to be a normal fear, but I knew some people would have considered me a coward if I'd expressed it. That fear in itself would not have stopped me from going to Vietnam. While I knew that about myself, there was no way to prove my courage. If I died aboard the *Glacier*, I thought people would at least say, "He died serving his country."

The storm finally started to subside by the third night—at least to the point where I was confident we would not capsize. I was exhausted from constantly fighting the pitching and rolling. I was irritated and frustrated.

My frustrations reached a peak that third night. I could not sleep and I was hungry. I went into the kitchen in the officers' mess and opened up the refrigerator, looking for a snack. All of a sudden, the ship lurched. Things started flying out of the refrigerator. I tried to hold back the onslaught of food with my hands, arms, and body. It was hopeless. I was in a one-way food fight and losing badly. Covered in tomato sauce, mustard, and egg yolks, my shirt looked like a cheap and odiferous copy of a Jackson Pollock painting.

I wanted to scream! Not wishing to wake anybody fortunate enough to be sleeping, I choked out a string of barely audible expletives as I chased after the bottles and containers tumbling at my feet. Then I spent the next half-hour cleaning up the slippery, rocking mess.

⸻

By the afternoon of April 10, the weather was much warmer, and the seas were relatively calm. Joe noted, "The air was super fresh and intoxicating. It was the kind of day that makes you feel that it is good to be alive."

Although Joe didn't mention it, I suspect one of the reasons he felt so good was because we were, in fact, alive. We had survived a horrific storm and lived to tell the tale.

26

The Last Straw

It was oppressively hot as we sailed through the tropics. Most of the crew was miserable from the heat, particularly those with living quarters below the main deck. It wasn't too bad in my stateroom, which was on the main deck, even though I didn't have a porthole for ventilation. I assumed Captain McCrory's well-ventilated stateroom a couple of levels above the main deck was relatively pleasant.

In contrast, the temperature in the junior officers' quarters was often 110 degrees, and it was even hotter in the enlisted men's berthing area. The heat in the engine-room compartments must have been at least 120 degrees. Those extreme temperatures were hot enough to kill a sailor who was not well hydrated. Many of the men ended up sleeping outside on the hard steel of the open deck. One of the junior officers described it as "a survival technique."

Even a sailing ship, one without our massive diesel engines, would have fared poorly in that kind of heat. For example, when the *Gauss*, sailing to Antarctica in 1901, reached the tropics, the heat was so bad that it melted the pitch waterproofing seams on the main deck. The melted pitch dripped through the wooden planks, plugged the ventilators, and generally made a mess. Reportedly, tar pitch begins to soften at 149 degrees Fahrenheit. I don't think it ever got that hot on our ship, but it likely was close to 130 degrees at times.

We could have avoided this intolerable heat if the CO had allowed us to use the ship's air-conditioning system. Although we had four generators, he allowed the use of only one. He also removed half the lightbulbs on the ship. If we had refueled in Valparaiso, and recharged our emotional "batteries," none of these drastic measures would have been necessary.

I later learned that supposedly there were extenuating circumstances related to these fuel-conservation measures. When the Coast Guard brass learned that we had a damaged ship that would have to go into dry dock, the CO was told to bring the ship into port low on fuel.

Some of the Coast Guard officers I later interviewed, who did not have an opportunity to closely study the facts, suggested that Captain McCrory chose the nonstop route because he needed to burn off excess fuel, thus complying with the advice he had been given. At first I thought that argument made some sense, but still didn't think it justified creating a situation that impacted the health, safety, and morale of the crew. When I considered the matter further, I realized there was *no justification* for the nonstop route. If we had gone to Valparaiso, we would have traveled farther, thus giving us a chance to burn off *more* fuel, not less.

During this period of intense heat, one member of the crew suffered a significant injury. He admitted to me later that he had not been sleeping well because of the intolerable heat, and as a consequence, he was not fully alert during the day. He was assigned the task of working with an unfamiliar piece of equipment, the purpose of which was to separate fuel from water. Since we were low on fuel, it was necessary to try to extract every ounce of fuel from a flooded fuel tank.

While working with this unfamiliar equipment one day, this sailor lost control of it. The heavy top portion of the apparatus slammed down on his middle finger, amputating approximately one-quarter of it. It was not a clean amputation. A shattered, V-shaped, jagged portion of bone extended about one-third of an inch beyond the damaged soft tissue. If you have ever snapped a chicken wishbone, you have an idea of what a splintered bone looks like, but that kind of injury looks much worse when surrounded by the crushed and bleeding tissue of someone's finger. It was immediately apparent that he was going to need a partial amputation followed by a tissue graft to cover the exposed bone.

It was the kind of injury best treated by a skilled hand surgeon, which was a reasonable alternative, given that we were relatively close to our home port. My goal was to preserve as much tissue as possible. I saw him every day thereafter to treat the wound. Fortunately, I was able to keep the viable tissues healthy and the wound free from infection during the last part of our trip, ensuring a good outcome with his eventual surgery.

From my perspective, this hand injury was the last straw. I felt there was a direct correlation between this man's injury and the CO's ill-advised decision to skip a refueling and liberty stop. Lack of sleep secondary to the heat was likely a contributing factor to the injury, as well as his working on an unfamiliar piece of equipment designed to separate fuel from water.

I had told the CO that if anyone were injured as a consequence of his decisions, I would hold him accountable. Had that injury not occurred—if it was just a matter of missing a good liberty port—I would have let everything go, but the threat I had made was not an idle one. I was furious, but I was also frustrated. Captain McCrory had said, "You can't touch me." He was probably right. Short of punching him in the nose or cussing him out, what could I do? Thankfully, I had a cagey and clever ally in Chief Toussaint.

"You know there's one thing you can do," he said.

"What's that?" I said.

"Doctors have to write a summary trip report. That report has to go up through the chain of command. Everyone has to read and sign off on it before it's sent to the next level."

"So the CO will have to read this report and pass it on without changing it?"

"That's right."

"And you're not going to be held accountable for anything I put in this report?" I did not want Toussaint, who had his career to think of, to get into any trouble on my account.

He did not say anything. His mischievous smile was all the response I needed.

"Thanks," I said. "That's exactly what I'm going to do."

On April 19 Joe wrote, "It was a very sunny and hot day but they have the air-conditioning on within the ship, so it isn't impossible to live." Unfortunately, we had already endured six days of extreme heat. It was nice to finally have some air-conditioning, but for the poor sailor who lost the tip of his finger, it was too little, too late.

We were getting close to Long Beach and I had several sailors who were very worried, and with good reason. They had contracted a rare type of venereal disease called chancroid. It left them with open ulcers on a favorite part of their anatomy. I treated all of them with the recommended antibiotic, but it didn't work. I was also concerned about their getting a secondary infection, so I had them come to sick bay each day so we could soak their open wounds in hot soapy water. All of these chancroid-afflicted patients had girlfriends and/or wives waiting for them when they got home. I am sure at this point they wished they had heeded the warnings Toussaint and I had given them, but I was not about to sermonize. I needed to cure these sailors, and fast. Fortunately for all of them, the second antibiotic I chose worked. There are not a lot of "total cures" in medicine. This was one of them, and it was greatly appreciated.

The most common medical problem we had as we sailed back toward Long Beach was sprained ankles. In order to beat the heat, we primarily lived on deck. One of our favorite ways of passing the time was playing volleyball on the flight deck. The volleyball was attached to a cable tether, so we didn't have to worry about it going overboard. However, the deck we played on had ridges and tie-down holes, almost unavoidable hazards. In addition, playing volleyball on a rolling deck added to the challenge. Fortunately I had learned all about taping up sprained ankles during my first few months of my shore assignment at Cape May, New Jersey, and none of the sprains were severe.

The last entry in Joe's diary is dated April 25, 1970: "Tomorrow is the big day. . . . I can hardly wait to step ashore and live like a human being again. This trip has been a real experience and I'm happy and thankful for all I

Final day of deployment. From left to right: myself, Joe Burke, Danny O'Keefe, Chris Short, William "Sal" Salvatorre, and Chief Warren Toussaint. (Photo Courtesy of Joe Burke)

have learned. I will sure be glad to get home, though. I don't think I really care to leave the States again."

The following day we pulled into Long Beach. The entire crew was up on deck wearing our dress blues. A throng of cheering and smiling people lined the pier. There were a few mothers holding babies in their arms who had been born during our deployment, and there were many "West PAC Widows" anxious to be reunited with their husbands. The chiefs had a betting pool about who was going to be the first to make love with his wife. I won't say who won that bet, but I will say it was a certain Frenchman I knew well—a very proud Frenchman.

As we approached the pier, I was standing next to Commander Dirschel. He looked at me and said, "Who are those funny-looking men with bumps on their chests?" I laughed. It seemed like we had been away that long.

It was good to be home.

When the *Glacier* arrived in Long Beach Harbor, one of the sailors shouted out to a buddy waiting for him on the pier: "We're so low on fuel, they'll have to tow us to dry dock." The dry dock was only a few miles away, so I suspected some exaggeration on his part, but my later research suggested he may not have been off by much.

Deployment statistics on the *Glacier* show that between 1955 and 1987 it traveled 944,050 miles, the equivalent of more than forty-three times around the world at the equator. One of those times was during our deployment, when we traveled 25,000 nautical miles. During those thirty-two years, it burned 38,526,906 gallons of diesel fuel. Based on those statistics, the *Glacier* averaged about 40 gallons per mile. If those figures are accurate, then our huge ship was down to roughly 100 gallons or less when we arrived at our home port.

According to Ensign Frydenlund, there was no fuel left in the main tanks, only in the "day tanks," which held at most enough fuel for twenty-four to forty-eight hours of sailing. If we were that low on fuel, we were lucky we hadn't been delayed by a huge storm toward the end of our trip. If we had been, we very well could have run out of fuel, lost power, and ended up in serious trouble.

Apart from the health and safety considerations, the decision to skip our one good liberty port clearly had a negative effect on crew morale, suggesting that the latter was not a high priority for the CO. In the "Morale and Recreation" section of the ODF70 report, the only things discussed were the equipment, supplies, and activities provided for this purpose. The report does not contain a single word about the crew's actual morale during any part of the deployment, as if barbells and bingo cards were more important than hearts and minds.

27

Trip Report

PRIOR TO LEAVING THE *GLACIER*, I COMPLETED WHAT WAS ESSENTIALLY a "Deployment Summary Report"—the one I had learned about from Chief Toussaint. (Unfortunately, I lost my copy of the report and other important documents when my home burned in a California wildfire in 1993.) It was a factual, chronological narrative of our trip from my perspective as the ship's medical officer.

The tone of the report was strictly professional. In it I expressed my opinions about ill-advised or hazardous medical situations we had faced, including some I thought could have been reasonably avoided, such as the lack of an anesthesia machine, the air-conditioning hiatus, the partial finger amputation, the decision to skip Valparaiso. I also wrote of the stresses associated with being trapped in the ice and facing the possibility of having to winter over. I did not say it was Captain McCrory's fault that we became trapped in the ice, but I did criticize his decision to skip refueling in Valparaiso, not only because of its effect on morale, but also because I felt it was unnecessary, potentially dangerous, and a proximate cause of a finger amputation.

I had Chief Toussaint proofread my report before I turned it in. He read it with raised eyebrows but had no dispute with anything I had written. In fact, he approved it with a veritable wink and a nod. If the CO had some explaining to do, it was not his problem. He was simply the messenger.

The other thing I had written during our last mail stop in Punta Arenas was a letter to the Coast Guard asking to be reassigned to the boot camp in Alameda. In it, I stated that since I was again on the West Coast, and traveling with essentially all of my possessions, I could save them shipping and travel expenses if they approved my request. I was going to San Francisco anyway to visit my girlfriend.

My request was turned down. I would be heading back to Cape May, New Jersey. The Coast Guard would cover all my travel expenses.

One of the last photos I took of my trip was an exterior shot of the hull of the *Glacier*. It was a striking mess—all stained, scraped, and dented, as well as charred from the fire. Later shots taken by Chief Toussaint while the ship was in dry dock reportedly showed below-the-waterline hull damage that was as bad as we had imagined. (Unfortunately, those photos are not available.)

The arrival of the *Glacier* was sufficiently newsworthy that it merited an article in the Long Beach newspaper. It included an interview with Captain McCrory, in which he described our deployment as essentially routine, with only minor problems. The article included a photo of him hugging his young daughter, who apparently was quite impressed with the bushy beard he had grown during our deployment. It was a sweet photo. Also, it showed a different side to the CO than the one I had come to know.

The *Glacier* had survived our deployment, but it was never quite the same—at least not according to Captain Clarence Gillett, commanding officer of the *Glacier* between 1974 and 1976. When he first took command, he noticed a flattened area on the starboard side of the hull. Apparently the Coast Guard did not have the money to completely repair the damage suffered during our deployment. According to him, that area remained vulnerable and was easily damaged on subsequent deployments.

The *Glacier* remained in active service until June of 1987, when it was decommissioned. Her nearly 1,000,000 nautical miles of voyaging included twenty-nine Antarctica deployments. She was widely recognized as one of the best icebreakers in American history.

In October of 2000, President Bill Clinton transferred the *Glacier* to the "*Glacier* Society," who hoped to rehabilitate the icebreaker and use it for future humanitarian and scientific efforts in polar regions. In spite of the society's best efforts, it was not able to raise sufficient funds. That noble ship never sailed again.

As CO of the *Glacier*, Captain McCrory completed my "Commissioned Officer's Efficiency and Progress Report" at the end of our deployment, but I did not see it until I began doing research for this book. This document was an official critique of my work and personality. For the most part, I felt his criticisms were fair. For example, he indicated that I had a better-than-average ability to act independently, communicate, express myself, and supervise others. He indicated he was generally satisfied with my work as a medical officer, writing, "He has handled each case competently."

Under the "Remarks" portion of the form, McCrory wrote: "Makes judgments outside the field of his professional competence and is emotionally expressive on the justice of his opinions. This has been discussed with him." Again, I would consider that a fair criticism.

In the subsection headed, "Ability to get along with others," I would have given myself a better-than-average grade. I think most everyone on the ship would have agreed. Instead, he gave me a slightly less-than-average rating, marking the box labeled, "Occasionally causes unpleasant situations." I had to laugh when I read that. I thought it was an understatement to describe the kind of confrontation I'd had with him as being "unpleasant." It was gut-wrenching for me. And I guess it was none too pleasant for him either. Although he had boasted that I could not begin to touch him, apparently I had.

I returned to Cape May, along with all of my gear, and Uncle Sam picked up the tab.

A week after I'd resumed my duties as a general medical officer, all of the dental and medical officers had a chance to meet with Admiral Fishburne, the commander of all US Public Health Service doctors assigned to the Coast Guard. He was an impressive and likable person. He gave us a short talk and then asked us if we had any questions or comments.

I quickly raised my hand and said, "Yes, Admiral. Is there any chance I could be reassigned to the boot camp in Alameda?"

He replied in all sincerity, "We'd love to, Doctor, but we couldn't afford the shipping expenses."

My jaw dropped. I had thought the chances of a transfer were unlikely, but being denied because of shipping expenses? I was very tempted to throw up my hands or argue the point, but I bit my tongue. I was not about to make a scene, largely because of my respect for Admiral Fishburne. Also, I realized it was another one of those "You're in the army now" kind of military moments. You've probably heard of the word *snafu*—a military acronym for "Situation normal, all f——d up."

About three weeks after I got back to Cape May, I received a letter from Admiral Fishburne. It was about my trip report. Apparently, it had taken a while for my report to go through the chain of command. The letter was an Official Letter of Commendation. After reading the letter, it was clear to me that he had carefully read and considered my report. He indicated that he was going to take action on most of my recommendations. And in this official letter, he was almost effusive in his praise, writing, "This was the finest trip report I have ever read."

I was not expecting any praise—certainly not from an admiral. It was some of the nicest and most satisfying praise I had ever received. An esteemed leader had given me a sincere, thoughtful, and totally unexpected compliment. It left me with a sense that Admiral Fishburne, like Shackleton, truly cared for his men.

A week later, I received an entirely different kind of letter. It was from Captain McCrory. The tone of his letter was one of seething rage. He condemned my writing a report that reflected badly on some of his decisions. In essence, he said that I, as a doctor, had no right to criticize the judgment of a captain.

The letter bothered me a bit, but I didn't dwell on it. I did not fully understand what he felt he could accomplish by writing such a letter. After all, I was no longer under his chain of command, nor would I ever be again. I reasoned that he just needed to blow off steam. He must have been sitting on his anger for some time. Since my trip report had gone up through the chain of command, he had obviously read it before Admiral Fishburne. In any case, it was not a letter to which I was going to respond.

About a week after I received Captain McCrory's scathing letter, I heard that Admiral Fishburne had somehow found out about it. I don't know how; I certainly didn't tell him, nor did I tell anyone close to him.

It seems unlikely that the CO would have sent Admiral Fishburne a copy of the letter he sent me, but it could have happened, either because he was feeling a need to defend himself, or because he felt so self-righteous. Or perhaps because he wanted a critical letter in my personnel file, in case I planned to become a career officer.

In any case, Admiral Fishburne reportedly was furious when he found out about Captain McCrory's letter. The scuttlebutt I heard was that Admiral Fishburne was so incensed that he charged down to Coast Guard headquarters and told the Coast Guard brass, "I want this man frozen in rank. He does not deserve to ever become an admiral."

Admiral Fishburne's reaction is certainly plausible, if for no other reason than the way branches of the service work. Say, for example, that an army general has just awarded a soldier a medal for bravery or some other meritorious act, and this award is shortly followed by a navy admiral officially condemning the soldier for this very same act. The general might have taken it personally.

At the very least, Captain McCrory should have thought twice before he jumped all over someone in another branch of the service and no longer under his command. Moreover, if his purpose in writing the letter was to adversely affect my career, then it was a waste of his time and energy. I never intended to pursue a career in government service, and I'd made no secret of that fact. The CO made some bad decisions. His vitriolic letter to me was certainly one of them.

If Captain McCrory had been feeling good about our deployment, and clearly satisfied with his performance, I think he would have been much more inclined to ignore my report. Conversely, the emotional intensity of his letter suggests to me that he may have felt dissatisfied, defensive, and emotionally vulnerable. It may have been that he still had a slim hope of becoming an admiral and viewed my report as negatively impacting his chances.

At the end of my deployment, my view of Captain McCrory was decidedly negative. In retrospect, I realized that my view partly had to do with my own shortcomings and hang-ups. Relationships are always a two-way street. For my part, I certainly did not go out of my way to develop rapport with him; in fact, I'd mostly avoided him. Also, when it came to authority figures, I did not cut them much slack unless I greatly respected them.

In doing research for this book, I learned much more about Captain McCrory and his positive aspects. A junior officer who ran the ship's store during one deployment under Captain McCrory was full of praise. The CO was so impressed with the officer's moneymaking skills that he recommended the Coast Guard pay for him to receive a master's degree in business administration, which the Coast Guard agreed to do. This junior officer later became a successful businessperson. A good part of his success, he felt, was because of Captain McCrory.

Another junior officer with whom I spoke, who ended up having a career in the Coast Guard, approved of Captain McCrory's aggressive attempt to reach the oceanographic buoys. He thought the CO was a "gung ho" kind of person, and he liked that. He admitted that he had some reservations about McCrory, but they were minor ones. He estimated that about half the officers liked the CO and the other half did not. One of the enlisted men I communicated with thought Captain McCrory was a good CO, and he had spent two years under him. If I had contacted more people, I'm sure I would have found others with complimentary views.

Captain McCrory succeeded on many fronts. He clearly had excellent seamanship skills, as evidenced by such things as our eventual escape from the Weddell Sea, as well as our surviving the last crossing of Drake Passage. I would be the first to admit that it took one hell of a sailor to get us safely through that experience. He must have had a good record of accomplishment or else he never would have become a captain. He was ambitious, which I think was both a blessing and a curse. His efforts were officially recognized. Our unit was given a Meritorious Unit Commendation by the Navy for our Operation Deep Freeze work in 1970, which was not surprising, given all of the work we did for the navy and Operation Deep Freeze, in spite of having a torn hull. Furthermore, Captain McCrory was honored by having a mountain named after him in Antarctica—Mount McCrory. That's a big feather in anyone's cap.

Following his retirement, Captain McCrory never took on another job, but he did meaningful work for charitable organizations. He was no Shackleton, but that would not be a fair comparison. That would be almost like saying the average professional basketball player is no Michael Jordan. In many respects, he did a good and competent job.

Like many captains, Captain McCrory had a big ego, but he certainly controlled it better than some. After all, Magellan died because he thought he could get people to change their religion, simply because he'd ordered it. Captain Cook died because he thought he could trade a small boat for a king. These famous men died because of a combination of bad decisions and huge egos. Captain McCrory never got to savor the glory of rescuing those buoys, which certainly would have been a major accomplishment. And maybe I bruised his ego with my trip report. But the important thing—as was the case with Shackleton—we all survived.

28

Answers

OF ALL THE MAJOR DANGERS WE SURVIVED—HITTING AN ICEBERG, THE
stack fire, huge seas in Drake Passage, and getting trapped deep in the
Weddell Sea—I think the latter was both the most significant and the
most avoidable. Furthermore, it represents the kind of unique peril any
ship traveling in a polar region might face.

One of the big questions I had prior to writing this book was why
did we end up facing a Shackleton-like situation when and where we did?
Was it just bad luck? Was it solely Mother Nature's fault? Was it human
error? Or was it some combination of all of these factors?

The answers to these questions were mostly contained in the "Operation Deep Freeze 1970 Report" (ODF70). After leaving the buoy site and
reaching the relatively open waters along the coast—and before becoming
trapped in the ice pack—Captain McCrory indicated that his plan was
"to proceed to the Filchner Ice Shelf shore lead to conduct USARP [US
Antarctic Research Program] events . . . along the ice shelf to a position
westward of the Argentine Base General Belgrano." He continued: "The
cutter planned a later return to the vicinity of the S-62 current meter
site [the buoy site] pending more favorable conditions based on NAVO-
CEANO ESSA satellite ice data."

In other words, research along the continental ice shelf, which we
could do almost anywhere, was something he intended to do only until
weather changes allowed him to return to the buoy site. Retrieving the
buoys remained Captain McCrory's primary goal.

This goal hardly seemed realistic to me, given the time of year and
the previous impenetrable conditions at the site. It was as if those buoys

obsessed him—like Captain Ahab with Moby-Dick. However, I cannot say with certainty that Captain McCrory had that kind of motivation. His sole impetus may have been to complete a mission to which he had been assigned. As a military person, particularly one coming out of World War II, the idea of completing a mission, regardless of the costs, likely was something rigidly ingrained in his psyche.

According to Ensign Frydenlund, the main reason we were in the Weddell Sea at all was to retrieve the buoys. He suspected that Captain McCrory was motivated more by a fear of failure than by an obsession or a pursuit of glory, because the combination of tearing a hole in the hull and not retrieving the buoys could have been interpreted by his command as a "failed mission."

Whatever his motivation, the CO knew that the area in which the buoys were situated was covered with large floes and multiyear ice compressed into pressure ridges. He knew that what little open water was left in the area was forming new ice. He knew it was getting late in the season. Despite all of these factors, and knowing the risks we faced, he continued to plan a return to the site. It seems he was hoping for a miracle, with the odds decidedly stacked against him—and us.

The storm that struck us and trapped the *Glacier* was not an anomaly. During that time of year, storms coming from the east or the north are the rule and not the exception. The ODF70 report noted that during the last two weeks of February, 67.3 percent of the storms that hit us came from that direction, all of which increased our chances of being pushed toward the impassable ice along the eastern edge of the Antarctic Peninsula and our becoming trapped.

The big storm coming from the northeast began on February 20 and continued until February 24. Captain McCrory either knew or should have known about that storm and its likely consequences. Although Thor Kvinge and one of the junior officers aboard the *Glacier* were particularly knowledgeable about weather and ice conditions in Antarctica, according to Ensign Frydenlund, the CO did not consult with either of them.

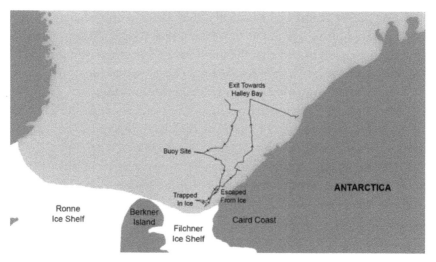

Path of *Glacier* before, during, and after being trapped in ice pack. Map from ODF70. (Graphic by Sage Design)

We reached the coast on February 21. If safety was the primary concern, we logically should have started heading east. Although we would have been heading into the storm, we also would have been heading toward our planned escape route and more-open waters. If we had sailed east, we might not have been trapped at all. If we had been, at least we would have been closer to the edge of the ice pack, which would have made a later escape much easier. Instead, when we reached the Caird Coast, and our intended northeasterly escape route, the CO turned west, and we continued traveling west for two days.

This graphic illustration of the official map from ODF70 shows our two westward penetrations into the Weddell Sea. The first western deviation was to the "Buoy Site." After leaving that area we traveled in an arc to the coast and then made our second deviation to the west, to the "Trapped in Ice" site south of the buoys.

When I looked at the map and noted where we got stuck relative to the buoys, it left little doubt in my mind as to why we ended up trapped where we did, and when. But my assumptions could be wrong. I will leave it up to the reader to make their own decisions.

It is possible that if we had reached the coast and immediately turned east, or stayed in the general area, we would have fared no better. However, the map above shows that the point where we turned west intersects the area where we *eventually* reached the clearer waters along the coast, the area that had always been our intended escape route.

After finally breaking free from our ice prison, I assumed the CO had totally given up on the idea of retrieving the buoys. *Why would anyone risk getting trapped again just to retrieve some nonessential objects?*

But the records suggest otherwise. When we visited the British station at Halley Bay, we still were in heavy ice and hundreds of miles east of the buoy site. Here is what Captain McCrory wrote in ODF70 about his intentions when we departed there in March:

GLACIER departed Halley Bay ice dock at 100400Z and proceeded northward to investigate the ice conditions in the vicinity of the S-62 current meter site [the buoy site] last observed on 19 February 1970.

Despite all that we had been through, early on March 10 the CO was *still* expressing a plan to return and pick up those damn buoys. At that point, we remained in about six to eight oktas of ice and winter was fast approaching. When I first read that sentence, I thought, *Was he crazy?*

The next line answered that question. He was not.

In the following text, he reversed what he had just written:

Retrieval of the S-62 current meter was abandoned on 10 March 1970 due to unfavorable ice conditions observed . . . and expected refreezing throughout the entire area south of 72-000S [the buoys were at 74° South] forecasted by NAVOCEANO 6 March 1970.

In this second section he states that he was going to abandon further efforts to retrieve the buoys because they were about 150 miles south of an expected area of refreezing. When Captain McCrory wrote the first section, above, I assume he knew what he was going to write in the second; and furthermore, he must have known how bad the ice conditions were outside Halley Bay. This begs the question, *Why write the first section at all?*

Perhaps he wanted to show his supervisors that he was a tough, diehard, mission-oriented captain just doing his job. Or maybe he was seeking glory and wanted to show that he was the kind of captain with the right stuff to become an admiral. Or maybe it was something else. I will let the reader decide.

Ten days after writing these contrasting statements, Captain McCrory announced that we would be traveling nonstop from Antarctica to Long Beach. Although a mission orientation argument could be made for the CO's persistent buoy-retrieval efforts, essentially the opposite was true for his decision to skip Valparaiso. Stopping in this liberty port was not only part of our original plan, but also the reasonable thing to do for crew morale. Moreover, it was the logical thing to do to better calibrate how much fuel to take on for a safe voyage back to Long Beach—without having an excess amount of fuel aboard when the ship went into dry dock. Why would a mission-oriented captain make an illogical decision contrary to the original mission? I don't know the answer to that question. Maybe the thing that Captain McCrory needed most for his own morale toward the end of our deployment was just to go home.

Several years after our deployment, one of our Coast Guard icebreakers successfully and safely retrieved all of the oceanographic buoys. They did it with a dragging operation. Using this more-conservative approach with hooks and lines, they were able to retrieve the buoys with all the data intact. I don't know the exact circumstances of this successful retrieval, but I do know it couldn't have been done without Mother Nature's cooperation. If the Weddell Sea's natural forces aligned to create an extreme barrier, the efforts of even a score of icebreakers would have been futile.

The other big question I had when I started doing research for this book was how much danger were we actually in when the *Glacier* was trapped in the ice? Why did the officers who told us not to worry about our predicament look so worried themselves? What did they know that I did not? What were the chances that our ship would be crushed? What were the chances we would end up in a Shackleton-like situation—needing to survive on the ice pack—or worse?

When Captain McCrory first announced that we would be spending the winter in the Weddell Sea, he appeared grim and solemn, but not nervous. At that time, no modern-day Coast Guard icebreaker had ever been destroyed by ice-pack pressure. He could have assumed the odds were in our favor. But were the odds that good? Were the odds worth the risk?

Historical records give us a clue.

In February of 1960, the *General San Martín* almost succumbed to pressure from the ice pack. It was caught in a storm off the west coast of the Antarctic Peninsula—as opposed to the more-dangerous east coast. Pack ice driven by 100-knot winds forced the ship against fixed ice along the shore. It tilted onto its side, with a 25-degree list. The pressure caved in thirty frames along the starboard side and knocked off one blade of its starboard propeller. The crew had to jettison 500 tons of cargo to prevent the vessel from sinking.

In 1975, the *Glacier* was on one of its many deployments to Antarctica when it again became icebound in the Weddell Sea, this time off the tip of the Antarctic Peninsula. It had again gone to the rescue of the *General San Martín*. (One would almost think the Argentinean ship was accident-prone, but it was just underpowered for severe conditions, and in this particular case it had developed engine problems.) During the rescue attempt, working in 25-foot-thick ice, the *Glacier* sheared off two of its three prop blades on one shaft. The blades weighed 6 tons each. Fortunately, the blades on its other shaft were not damaged, but due to its drastically reduced mobility, the *Glacier* also became trapped.

Although the *Glacier* rested only 2 miles from an open lead in the ice, it could not maneuver enough to reach it. Wintering over seemed to be its only option. With winter fast approaching, the public affairs officer for Operation Deep Freeze (ODF) in New Zealand, Bill Neal, said attempting to break through a total freeze would be "like trying to cut through steel."

I was very impressed by the instructions the captain, Clarence Gillett, CO of the *Glacier* between 1974 and 1976, received when beset—instructions we never received when we were in a similar situation. In my opinion, the instructions he received from his superiors focused on one of the most critical elements of a wintering-over situation: crew selection. The official communication read:

The prospect of inclusion of a scientific party in the wintering-in group must be carefully evaluated. Oceanographic [research] on a ship beset is not practical. Any people assigned should be carefully screened. Compatibility under existing conditions is far more important than technical competence.

Captain Gillett started evacuating nonessential personnel. The ship was close to an Argentinean air base easily reachable by its helicopters. After completing a partial evacuation, the ship was able to make some headway, in spite of its damaged prop. After struggling for nine days, the *Glacier* eventually reached open water. It was a close call, but it escaped.

Using this example, one could say, 25-foot-thick ice, only one good prop, and yet *Glacier* escaped. That ship was built to handle tough conditions. And I would mostly agree with that point of view. However, 2 miles from open water and near the northern tip of the Antarctic Peninsula is one kind of problem; stuck deep in the Weddell Sea 100 miles from open water is another.

In my view, the best example of the vulnerability of a Coast Guard icebreaker in the Antarctic is the USCGC *Westwind*. The *Westwind* was the fourth of seven Wind-class icebreakers. It was launched in March 1943 and commissioned in September 1944. Her hull, according to one technical report, was of "unprecedented strength and structural integrity." It was incredibly powerful, particularly in relation to its relatively short length. Moreover, in 1974 it underwent an extensive refit to strengthen the bow. At the same time, its engines and propeller shafts were replaced. When all the work was done, it seemingly was ready for anything.

In 1984, the *Westwind* was cruising in the Weddell Sea in light, loose, brash ice when it was struck by a major storm. During the storm, the ice quickly congregated into heavy brash ice, which the *Westwind* could not overpower. The crew helplessly watched as the ship was blown into the edge of the massive Larsen Ice Shelf. Furthermore, the strong current undercutting the ice shelf sucked the ship against it. Then, *the intake ports iced up*—which very likely would have happened if the *Glacier* had remained in the ice pack for the winter.

Because of the blocked intake ports, there was no circulating water to cool *Westwind's* engines. The engines had to be shut down. The powerless ship was dragged and scraped along the towering ice cliff. It then struck a protrusion, which started to tear open the port side of the hull 6 feet above the waterline.

The *Westwind* captain sent the following message to *Glacier, Polar Star,* and COMNAVSUPPORTFORANTARCTICA:

Situation: Extreme Emergency . . . vessel against 100-foot sheer ice shelf cliff . . . Flooding in forward rec deck . . . Shell and deck plate buckled . . . List 8.5 degrees; 30-foot gash 6 feet above waterline . . . Gash continues.

The relentless pressure of the ice pack kept forcing the port side of the crippled *Westwind* into the massive ice shelf. The port side kept coming apart at the seams. A 2- to 3-foot-tall and 140-foot-long tear opened up. Fortunately for the *Westwind*, the rupture remained 6 feet above the waterline. At the time, the situation looked hopeless. It was so dire, the captain was on the verge of issuing orders to abandon ship.

Before the situation turned into a total catastrophe, the crew injected enough steam into the intake ports to partially unplug them. They were then able to get sufficient water circulating to cool the engines and restart them. With the engines running, they made enough headway to start moving toward open water.

The ship limped to nearby King George Island, where it safely anchored. For the next nine days, the crew worked nonstop to complete a temporary repair, after the Coast Guard had airlifted them 20 tons of equipment and supplies, including 9 tons of steel plating and 6 tons of neoprene gaskets. Once the temporary repair was completed, the ship continued on to Buenos Aires for more repairs.

What was it like for crewmembers of the *Westwind* during this near catastrophe? Two quotes from the Military.com website (names withheld for privacy) give us a good idea.

The USCGC *Westwind* against Larsen Ice Shelf. (Courtesy of US Coast Guard Archives)

I was a SN [Seaman] on board Westwind *when we were stuck in the ice shelf in 1984. . . . I will never forget the sound of the frames exploding apart from the pressure and the stress. They actually piped "Now all hands make preparations to abandon ship." They were firing up to help to put crew onto the shelf, where a group of Adélie penguins were watching us.*

The second quote was not as well written, but it certainly conveys the feeling of what this experience was like.

I was EM [electrician's mate] . . . while making my rounds in the rudder room I noticed that rudder was jam being puch [sic] passed its limit. Then all I heard next was the sound of GQ, when I went up to the deck all I could see was this wall of ice, light blue in color the ship was listing I even reach out and touch it, it was that close. To this day I still tell the story of how close I was to death. I thank God for saving me and my shipmates.

The *Westwind* finally made it back to the United States. It was lucky. If the gash had been at or below the waterline, the ship would not have survived. Although it did survive, it never reentered full service. Apparently, the damage was too expensive to fix. The ship was decommissioned in 1988, and eventually sold for scrap.

When I spoke with a former *Glacier* CO, Captain Coste, about *Westwind's* near catastrophe, it was his opinion that this incident could have been avoided. He felt the ship should not have been traveling near a massive ice shelf in stormy conditions. Once it was clear a storm was coming, the captain should have headed into the storm and away from the ice shelf.

In essence, Captain Coste's opinions about the *Westwind* would equally apply to the situation we faced on the *Glacier*. Once Captain McCrory knew the big storm was coming in from the northeast, he should have started heading into it—and away from the denser ice in the western Weddell Sea.

Considering the lessons of history, I believe that the same thing that happened to Shackleton and his crew could very well have happened to the *Glacier*. If a ship drifts with the ice pack in the Weddell Sea long enough, the odds are good that it will eventually collide with, or rest against, some immovable object like an ice shelf, a huge berg, a shallow reef, or the pointed edge of a small berg in solid ice pack. Then all it takes is either the force of the collision, the movement of the ice pack, or a big storm to destroy a section of the hull—which could be enough to sink the ship.

Ships in Antarctica, including our best icebreakers, are banged up and damaged all the time. Busted props, crunched bows, punctured hulls, you name it, all can and do easily occur. It is unavoidable. It comes with the territory. As an old-salt sailor friend of mine said, "Antarctica is one fucking dangerous place."

That's just the way it is in Antarctica. One way or another sailing in Antarctica always comes down to a risk–reward scenario. It's a very dynamic and immensely powerful environment. Sailing there requires an abundance of caution and a constant awareness of potential dangers. We cannot bend the powers there to our will. Quite simply, the awesome natural forces in Antarctica will never be tamed.

Looking back on our voyage, I would have readily accepted becoming trapped in the ice if we had been trying to rescue another ship or attempting a lifesaving operation or working to provide vital supplies to a base. Then, the risks would have been worth it. An unofficial Coast Guard motto is, "You have to go out [on a rescue mission], but you don't have to come back." But to take major risks, with a damaged hull, to retrieve some nonurgent, nonessential hardware and data? I don't think so. However, my cultural orientation as a doctor begins with the Hippocratic Oath, which is "First, do no harm." A hard-core military man has a different perspective when it comes to completing a mission. And I am sure readers will have their own opinions.

We made one good try at attempting to recover the buoys. I was fine with that. A more easterly route into the Weddell Sea would have been less punishing on the ship, but we made it to the buoy site anyway. It was one of our missions. However, it did not work. The conditions were just too difficult. I think Captain McCrory should have just accepted that fact—as hard as it may have been for him—and headed for safer waters.

A primary duty of a captain is the safety of his ship and crew. Although Captain McCrory was an experienced and competent captain, he made some bad decisions in my opinion and took some unnecessary risks—risks that exceeded the potential rewards, underestimated Antarctica's massive powers, and were based on questionable motivations. We were lucky we did not end up like the *Westwind*—or suffer a fate like some modern-day *Endurance*.

Captain McCrory retired from the Coast Guard as a captain in 1975. According to his second wife, Sally Anne McCrory, whom he married several years after retiring, he claimed the reason he did not make admiral was because "he did not have a good mentor." Whether or not Captain McCrory could have made admiral, he must have been proud to have served his country for so many years.

I greatly appreciated that the US Public Health Service gave me the opportunity to proudly serve my country. And I was particularly glad to have been associated with such an excellent and honorable service as the US Coast Guard.

My deployment with the *Glacier* began with a set of false assumptions. I assumed the work would be easy. After all, I thought I would be dealing with a relatively small group of healthy men, particularly in comparison with the vast population of civilians and military patients I had been taking care of at Cape May. Also, I was going to get to see all these exotic and beautiful ports. It was going to be like a government-paid travel vacation. The downside, I thought, was that Antarctica was going to be little more than a faraway, dull, boring place.

In fact, everything I anticipated was almost the opposite of what I experienced. The work wasn't easy. At times, it was incredibly stressful. It was an enormous responsibility—much more so than I'd ever expected. And Antarctica was not the dull, boring place I'd imagined. I was blown away by its beauty, its ruggedness, its wildlife, the magical spell it cast over me. Although I missed all those exotic ports, the incredible adventures I lived through ended up being far more interesting, important, and enriching. My time aboard the *Glacier* gave me the opportunity to experience life—to venture into the unknown and surmount challenges beyond my wildest expectations. It was not the trip I had initially hoped for. In many ways, it was much, much more.

Epilogue

WHAT ABOUT THE TWO MODERN-DAY ICEBREAKERS MENTIONED IN THE introduction—the *Snow Dragon* and the *Akademik Shokalskiy*? As you may recall, the latter Russian ship was trapped in the ice in December of 2013 during a storm off the coast of Antarctica, near Commonwealth Bay. Initially, it was stuck only 2 miles from open water. The *Snow Dragon*, twice as large, also became icebound during the subsequent rescue attempt. An Australian icebreaker, *Aurora Australis*, initially deemed capable, did not attempt a rescue. The ice pack had become too thick. The nearest help was more than a week away.

Were these trapped ships in much danger? Far more than seemed obvious. They were both under pressure from the ice pack. Although most of it was composed of surface sea ice, it also undoubtedly contained iceberg chunks, which are rock-hard. One of these, particularly one with a sharply angled shape, could have pressed into a hull with enough force to have ruptured it. Or the ice pack could have pushed the ships into, or over, some immovable object, like a rocky reef. The results in either case could have been catastrophic.

Was this dangerous situation the fault of the Russian captain? I don't think there is a clear-cut answer to that question. Both the captain and the mostly Australian passengers knew they were in heavy ice the day before they were beset—and they knew a blizzard was coming. The day the ice trapped them, the Russian captain strongly advised those leaving the ship, the tourists and scientists, to return quickly. He knew they had to head for open waters as soon as possible.

They did not heed his warning. They lost time because of problems with an amphibious ATV (all-terrain vehicle). And they dawdled. The captain could not leave without them. By the time they returned to the ship, it was too late.

Expedition leader Chris Turney claimed to be "surprised" about their predicament. He should not have been surprised at all. He knew, or should have known, they were in a risky situation, and should have explicitly followed their captain's advice. I believe Turney and other leaders of the expedition were quite aware of the dangers they ended up facing, but did not want to unnecessarily alarm all those concerned about their situation. Some people in the media ended up referring to the group as the "Ship of Fools."

Regardless of who was to blame for the Russian ship getting trapped, and later, the Chinese ship, something had to be done. Who or what was going to come to their rescue? In that particular situation, it was either going to be Mother Nature or the US Coast Guard. Knowing the unpredictability of the weather in Antarctica, I would have pinned my hopes on the latter.

There was only one heavy-duty Coast Guard icebreaker in service at the time, the *Polar Star*. It was nine days away when it was called upon for the rescue, yet the ship and its crew rushed to answer the call.

Commenting on the rescue, the Coast Guard Pacific Area Commander, Vice Admiral Paul Zukunft, said, "Our highest priority is safety of life at sea, which is why we are assisting in breaking a navigational path for both of these vessels."

That is the Coast Guard I know and love—taking the risks necessary to save human life—and making safety of life at sea their highest priority. The *Polar Star* was capable of breaking 6-foot sea ice while traveling at 3 knots. With backing and ramming, it could break ice up to 21 feet thick. The ice around the two trapped icebreakers was at most 10 feet thick. There was no question that the *Polar Star*, with twenty-five times more horsepower than the Russian vessel, had the ability to free the two ships, but it had to carefully approach the situation.

A former captain of the *Polar Star*, Captain Jason Hamilton, noted how satellite data and surface ridges could provide only an estimate of ice conditions. He noted that the Coast Guard ship would have to be careful, saying, "You break the ice in a manner so you can back out," so as to avoid ending up "in extremis." Wise words.

Just as the *Polar Star* arrived on the scene, Mother Nature did an about-face. The winds shifted significantly, and a wide crack opened in the ice. The crews of the two ships were glad to have backup support from the US Coast Guard, but they were able to escape on their own power. A dramatic rescue by the US Coast Guard was not necessary.

All of this was headline news. What did not make the news was the heroic effort the *Polar Star* made and the hardships they endured just to get there—50-knot winds, 20-foot seas, and 40-degree rolls. Its crew was beaten up answering the call, but they made it. It is what they do.

Vice Admiral Zukunft released a subsequent statement. He said, "We are extremely pleased to learn that both the *Xue Long* (aka, Snow Dragon) and the *Akademik Shokalskiy* freed themselves from the ice. This case underscores the dynamic and harsh operating environment and the necessity for Polar Class Icebreakers in the Antarctic."

Although there are dangers associated with traveling to Antarctica, it is a spectacularly beautiful place. In my opinion, the risks faced by the normal tourist wishing to go there are well worth it. My wife, Gail, went on a trip to Antarctica several years ago. I did not go with her. It was an expensive trip, and I prefer to go to places I've never been before. But I really wanted her to go. She is one of those fortunate people who has seen a great deal of the world. For example, she has been to Africa five times. She loves wildlife and beautiful scenery. I was quite certain she would enjoy Antarctica. She loved it. In fact, she said it was the best trip of her life.

Gail's only real concern about the trip was how well she would tolerate the crossing of Drake Passage. She is prone to seasickness, and knew from my tales how rough such a crossing could be. During her trip, Drake Passage was incredibly calm, both coming and going. It was as if she were crossing a large, tranquil lake. Sometimes you get lucky.

I should have joined her on the trip. She saw and experienced some things that I never did, such as making shore landings from Zodiac boats,

Icebreaker graveyards by Christopher Michel. (2.0 Generic License and Wikimedia)

listening to lectures from naturalists, and spending more time walking on the continent.

Although I am sure I would have enjoyed the trip, I also would have found the experience unsettling. So much of the land ice has melted. Gail learned that temperatures in Antarctica are rising faster than any other place in the world. Over the past fifty years, the average temperature in Antarctica has risen between 4 to 5 degrees. The most significant warming has been on the Antarctic Peninsula, where it has risen 5.4 degrees. There are many reasons why these changes have occurred. Scientists almost unanimously agree that human factors like the burning of fossil fuels, deforestation, and the release of methane gases are primary factors causing climate change. What most people don't realize is that almost 90 percent of the freshwater on the Earth's surface is held in Antarctic's massive ice sheets. If it all melted, ocean levels would rise by 60 to 70 meters. The risks we face are real. We all must strive to do our part to combat global warming.

The areas where typical tour ships travel today are much safer, but no less spectacular than many of the areas I was privileged to see aboard the *Glacier*. However, I would not recommend that average tourists travel deep into the Weddell Sea.

If you ever get a chance to take a voyage to Antarctica, do your research. Make sure you are sailing on a good ship with an experienced captain and crew. Follow their directions. Avoid unnecessary risks. Be prepared for difficult weather and rough seas. And then I would have just one word of advice.

Go.

ACKNOWLEDGMENTS

When I started this project, I knew I would be searching for help and information resources—much more than I ever realized. Although I vividly remembered the key events in this book, I by no means remembered exact sequences or all the important details. I was most fortunate to locate Joe Burke, one of the two junior corpsmen assigned to the *Glacier*, whom I had not seen or spoken to since 1970. Not only did Joe have his own rich memories, he had also kept a daily diary during our deployment that he allowed me to use as I saw fit. His information, photos, and supportive friendship have been invaluable.

I also benefited tremendously from information and feedback I received from Coast Guard officers who had either been assigned to the *Glacier* at some point in their career or to one of the Wind-class icebreakers. Commander David Frydenlund heads that list, followed in no particular order by Commander Richard Goward, Lieutenant Howard Waters, Captain Robert Hammond, and Captain James Fournier.

Other Coast Guard members who made a contribution (and I failed to get their ranks) include Louie LaRiccia, Dick Morris, and Fred Santesteban, as well as some Coast Guard members who made significant contributions but preferred to remain anonymous.

Although health problems prevented me from speaking with Captain McCrory prior to his death, I received considerable help from his second wife, Sally McCrory. She provided me with a copy of the *Glacier*'s Official Deployment Summary for 1969–1970 that ended up being my single most important research document. The National Archives and the Coast Guard archives in Washington, DC, also provided a number of important documents. Thanks to the staff of both of these organizations.

Books, magazines, and Internet resources, as listed in my bibliography, were the sources for another veritable mountain of interesting and useful information.

When it came to editorial assistance, Roger Labrie's input and sage counsel made a huge difference. In addition, I had the major help of a former editor, my wife, but mostly I have to thank her for her loving support during the entire process.

Thanks to a recommendation by my friend, Michael Edelstein, MD, I joined the San Fernando Valley Writers' Club, which led to my becoming part of a critique group, composed of four all-stars: Doug Douglas, Kay Henden, Lori Hamilton, and Bob Okowitz. Their patient and thorough reviewing of my work, as well as their encouragement and friendly tutelage, were all tremendously important.

Numerous people have read and commented on earlier drafts of this book, beginning with my wife, Gail Bunes, my daughter, Kelly Creith, and my close friend Dr. John Ehrhart. Subsequent readers included Bob Rogers, Karen Rogers, Scott Creith, Chris Creith, and Chuck Dekyser. Chuck also kept me abreast of the current state of the Coast Guard's polar icebreakers.

Lastly, I need to thank my agent, Eric Meyers; my publisher, Rick Rinehart; and my final editors, Melissa Hayes and Janice Braunstein. It has been a pleasure to work with such outstanding professionals.

Bibliography

My goal in writing this book was to scribe an interesting, educational, and accurate work of nonfiction rather than a scholarly work. Consequently, I did not specifically note reference sources. Below is a listing of the primary sources I used in creating this book.

Books

Barrel, John F. *Quest for Antarctica: A Journey of Wonder and Discovery*. Bloomington, IN: iUniverse, Inc., 2011.

Behrendt, John C. *Innocents on the Ice: A Memoir of Antarctic Exploration, 1957*. Niwot: University Press of Colorado, 1998.

Bergreen, Laurence. *Over the Edge of the World: Magellan's Terrifying Circumnavigation of the Globe*. New York: Harper Perennial, 2004.

Hadfield, Colonel Chris. *An Astronaut's Guide to Life on Earth*. New York: Little, Brown and Company, 2013.

Hurley, Frank. *South with Endurance*. New York: BCL Press, 2001.

Landis, Marilyn J. *Antarctica: Exploring the Extreme*. Chicago, IL: Chicago Review Press, 2001.

Lansing, Alfred. *Endurance: Shackleton's Incredible Voyage*. New York: Carroll & Graf Publishers, 1999.

MacDonald, Edwin A. *Polar Operations*. Annapolis, MD: US Naval Institute, 1969.

Morrell, Margot, and Stephanie Capparell. *Shackleton's Way*. New York: Viking, 2001.

Murphy, David Thomas. *German Exploration of the Polar World*. Lincoln: University of Nebraska Press, 2002.

Nansen, Fridtjof. *Farthest North: The Epic Adventure of a Visionary Explorer*. New York: Skyhorse Publishing, 2008.

Neider, Charles. *Antarctica: Firsthand Accounts of Exploration and Endurance*. New York: Cooper Square Press, 2000.

Nick, Charles. *Sir Francis Drake: Slave Trader and Pirate*. New York: Scholastic, Inc., 2009.

Plimpton, George. *Ernest Shackleton*. New York: DK Publishing, 2003.

Pyne, Stephen J. *The Ice: A Journey to Antarctica*. New York: Ballantine/Natural History, 1988.

Reader's Digest. Antarctica: Great Stories from the Frozen Continent. Surry Hills, NSW, Australia: Reader's Digest Services, 1985.

Sides, Hampton. *In the Kingdom of Ice: The Grand and Terrible Polar Voyage of the USS Jeannette.* New York: Doubleday, 2014.

CURATED VIDEOS

Copy and paste the web page addresses, if reasonably available, into the URL (Uniform Resource Locator) space. The URL is usually at the top of the screen in the address bar of your Internet browser. These are videos by other individuals or organizations and may include short ads. You can also do an Internet search via Google or some other search engine by typing in the exact title of the article or the specific descriptive phrase. In some cases, this latter approach is the preferable and/or the only method that works.

"Amazing Whale Video from Quarks Antarctic Peninsula Voyage," 2:34, April 15, 2014, https://www.youtube.com/watch?v=5xS_68S5zrg. Breaching, diving, and close-up views of whales and killer whales. (Google title in quotes.)

Antarctica: A Year on Ice, by Anthony B. Powell. Netflix, 1 hour, 32 minutes. An unforgettable film of the sights, sounds, and emotions experienced by those who spend a year in Antarctica.

"Antarctica Condition 1 Weather," by Anthony Powell, August 23, 2006, 1:03, https://www.youtube.com/watch?v=qz2SeEzxMuE. (Google title in quotes.)

Continent 7: Antarctica, TV miniseries (2016). Seven one-hour-long documentary programs produced by *National Geographic* that include dramatic footage of scientists working in harsh conditions and the USCGC *Polar Star* confronting problems breaking a channel into McMurdo Station.

Cool Hand Luke (1967) movie trailer. A good-quality video is available on YouTube, April 6, 2013, by 43shen, 2:50. (Google "Cool Hand Luke 43shen.")

"Drone Shots of Antarctica: Views of the Antarctic Peninsula taken by Kalle Ljung," Kalle Ljung, 8:17, https://vimeo.com/124858722, December 2014.

"Emperor Penguins: The Greatest Wildlife Show on Earth," BBC, December 11, 2009, 4:14, www.youtube.com/watch?v=MfstYSUscBc. Features baby penguins, penguin colonies, and penguins tobogganing.

"Emperor Penguins Speed Launch Out of the Water," by Paul Nicklen and *National Geographic*, 2:51 HD (high density), October 26, 2016, www.youtube.com/watch?v=A9mbCNs47FI.

"Iceberg Tsunami Gone Wild," by barbecueengineer, July 19, 2012, 2:28, www.youtube.com/watch?v=HB3K5HY5RnE. Illustrates danger of being too close to a calving iceberg.

"Killer Whales 'Gang Up' to Capture Seal," by Lindblad Expeditions, *National Geographic*, August 30, 2011, 3:11. (Google title in quotes.)

"Marine Ship Icebreaking Antarctica," January 25, 2009, 2:45, www.youtube.com/watch?v=qx-XckwVSyg. View from bow of breaking loosely packed sea ice.

"More Trouble for Cruise Ship Stuck in Antarctica, Rescue Impeded," ABC News, 1:49, December 28, 2013, https://www.youtube.com/watch?v=cdab82IYp-U (or Google quoted title.)

The Pursuit of Endurance*: On the Shoulders of Shackleton*, by Luc Hardy, 52 minutes, https://vimeo.com/ondemand/pursuitofendurancemovve. Nine adventurers sail from Elephant Island to South Georgia Island and then attempt Shackleton's epic crossing of it.

"Up Close with Humpback Whales in Antarctica," by Lindblad Expeditions, *National Geographic*, January 9, 2014, 1:50 HD (high definition), https://www.youtube.com/watch?v=OLDyoNg2xR4. YouTube close-up shots from Zodiacs with reactions from tourists. (Google title in quotes.)

"World's Deadliest: Seal vs. Penguin," *National Geographic Wild*, July 23, 2012, 2:24, https://www.youtube.com/watch?v=nuD58l1aD4c. Shows leopard seals swimming, stalking, and killing a penguin.

"World's Greatest Icebreaker," by Patrick Kelly, October 7, 2009, 3:57, www.youtube.com/watch?v=a8h-pArWZyY. Aerial view of US Coast Guard Cutter *Healy* in the Arctic (it's not big enough to break ice in Antarctica).

Index